Palgrave Studies in Workplace Spirituality and Fulfillment

Satinder Dhiman, *Editor-in-Chief*
Gary Roberts and Joanna Crossman, *Associate Editors*

By way of primary go-to-platform, this Series precisely maps the terrain of the twin fields of *Workplace Spirituality and Fulfillment* in the disciplines of business, psychology, health care, education, and various other allied fields. It reclaims the sacredness of work—work that is mind-enriching, heart-fulfilling, soul-satisfying and financially-rewarding. It fills the gap in scholarship in the allied disciplines of Workplace Spirituality and Flourishing. Using a comprehensive schema, it invites contributions from foremost scholars and practitioners that reflect insightful research, practices, and latest trends on the theme of workplace spirituality and fulfillment. The uniqueness of this *Series* lies in its anchorage in the moral and spiritual dimension of various positive forms of leadership—such as Authentic Leadership, Servant Leadership, Transformational Leadership, and Values-Based Leadership.

We welcome research monographs and multi-authored edited volumes representing myriad thought-positions on topics such as: Past, Present and Future Directions in Workplace Spirituality; Workplace Spirituality and World Wisdom/Spiritual Traditions; Culture Studies and Workplace Spirituality; Spiritual, Social and Emotional intelligence; Nature of Work; Mindfulness at Work; Personal Fulfillment and Workplace Flourishing; Workplace Spirituality and Organizational Performance; Inner Identity, Interconnectedness, Community and Transcendence; Managing Spiritual and Religious Diversity at Work; Spirituality and World Peace Imperative; Sustainability and Spirituality; Spirituality and Creativity; and Applied Workplace Spirituality in Health Care, Education, Faith-based Organizations, et al.

Anil K. Maheshwari
Editor

AI and Consciousness in Organizations and Society

A Diversity of Perspectives

palgrave
macmillan

Editor
Anil K. Maheshwari
Maharishi International University
Fairfield, IA, USA

ISSN 2662-3668 ISSN 2662-3676 (electronic)
Palgrave Studies in Workplace Spirituality and Fulfillment
ISBN 978-3-031-91469-0 ISBN 978-3-031-91470-6 (eBook)
https://doi.org/10.1007/978-3-031-91470-6

This Palgrave Macmillan imprint is published by the registered company Springer Nature Switzerland AG
The registered company address is: Gewerbestrasse 11, 6330 Cham, Switzerland

Dedicated to all my teachers and students, and to my colleagues in the Management, Spirituality and Religion (MSR) Division of the Academy of Management

Preface to the AI and Consciousness Book

I have been planning to write about Artificial Intelligence for many years. However, this field changes so rapidly that new developments and applications seem to develop almost overnight. Nevertheless, it was fun presenting Artificial Intelligence in the context of Higher Consciousness, my other area of passion.

I organized a colloquium on this theme for the Management, Spirituality and Religion Division of the Academy of Management. This book flows out of the many excellent presentations and conversations at that event. I am grateful to all of my friends and colleagues for contributing to this book.

My colleagues encouraged and supported me in writing this book. I am also thankful to Nupur Maheshwari for excellent editing of the final version of the whole manuscript. Finally, thanks to Maharishi Mahesh Yogi for providing a wonderful environment of consciousness-based education that provided the inspiration for writing this book from wholeness.

I also wish you, the reader, a happy and healthy life. May you be able to take advantage of AI from a higher consciousness and flourish.

Fairfield, IA, USA
December 2024

Dr. Anil K. Maheshwari

Contents

Part I

1 **The Interplay of AI and Consciousness: Implications for Organizations and Society** 3
Anil K. Maheshwari

2 **V-Theory of Transcendence for Achieving Peace in the Age of Artificial Intelligence (AI)** 19
Anil K. Maheshwari

3 **Dharma Matrix: An Open Architecture for Ethical Decision-Making in the Age of AI** 39
Anil K. Maheshwari, Sharda S. Nandram, and Payal Kumar

4 **AI and Consciousness: Adding Spiritual to Scientific Perspectives** 63
Tom Culham, Jyoti Bachani, and Chris Laszlo

Part II

5 **Transforming Consciousness-Based Education in the Age of AI** 83
Anil K. Maheshwari

6 **Human and Artificial Intelligences: Different Yet Complementary** 113
Mohan Raj Gurubatham and Deeppa Ravindran

7 **Creativity, Consciousness, and AI in Organizations** 135
Anil K. Maheshwari, K Davina Frick, Ira Greenberg, and Danielle King Colby

8 **AI and Well-Being: Utopia or Dystopia** 155
Anil K. Maheshwari

Part III

9 **Consciousness and AI for Sustainable Development: A Case Study of Plastics** 181
Anil K. Maheshwari and Sriman Banerjee

10 **Systems Thinking Mindset in the Age of AI** 205
Larry Ebert and Alfonso Montero

11 **From Innovating Conventional AI to Conscious AI Technology** 229
R. Ray Gehani and G. Tom Gehani

Index 251

Notes on Contributors

Dr. Jyoti Bachani is a Full Professor of Strategy and Innovation at Saint Mary's College of California. She is a former Fulbright Senior Research Scholar, with degrees from London Business School, UK, Stanford University, USA, and Delhi University, India. She is the co-founder of the US and India chapters of the International Humanistic Management Association. Her research focus is practice-oriented ways to humanize organizing and pedagogy in the digital era, leading with arts-based methods of visual arts, improv, and poetry.

Sriman Banerjee is a distinguished expert in packaging, medical devices, environmental sustainability, artificial intelligence (AI), and machine learning, with 25+ years of experience at Takeda, GlaxoSmithKline, and other global organizations. He serves as adjunct faculty at multiple universities and holds a bachelor's in mechanical engineering, with postgraduate studies in packaging, plastics, and management. Currently pursuing a PhD in Sustainability Management at MIU, he champions innovation, sustainability, and AI-driven healthcare advancements.

Danielle King Colby is an artist, collector, writer, and curator. She studied studio art and art history at Harvard University. Her recent work utilizes AI technology to explore alternative art histories and timelines and to investigate capitalist and art historical ideals of beauty and femininity. She is currently the CFO & COO of ClubNFT and Right Click Save.

Larry Ebert is an instructor at the University of San Francisco and Golden Gate University, a leadership and innovation consultant, systems thinker, writer, and researcher. He is currently researching the impact of AI on critical thinking and creative thinking for individuals, organizations, and society, and is developing a framework for assessing human-AI collaboration that embodies systems thinking and consciousness perspectives. Larry is also a professional musician exploring spiritual dimensions of work and play.

K Davina Frick is a Professor at Johns Hopkins University, Baltimore, USA. He teaches economics for decision-making, business leadership and human values, frameworks for analyzing health care markets, and a course on how the U.S. health care system in the past, present, and future facilitates innovation.

Dr. R. Ray Gehani is the Founding Director of the **Institute of Innovations for Transformation** based in Kent/Akron, Ohio to innovate transformative technologies. Dr. Gehani has been active in the Management, Spirituality & Religion Division of the Academy of Management wherein he organized multiple workshops on consciousness and spirituality of Mahatma Gandhi, Ram in his exile journey, and Krishna giving the Sermon on the Battlefield in the Bhagavad Gita. John Wiley & Sons published Dr. Gehani's ***Management of Technology & Operations*** in 1998 and has been marketing it worldwide for the past 25 years. Dr. Gehani has engineering degrees from I.I.T., Kanpur, I.I.T. Delhi, and Tokyo Institute of Technology (on a Japanese National Fellowship). He also has MBA from **International Management Institute** and another PhD from the **City University of New York**. He loves poetry, cooking healing dishes, and a persuasive pursuit of World Peace.

Dr. Tom Culham, formerly a senior business leader, obtained a PhD in Education late in his career. He currently lectures and conducts ethics education research at Simon Fraser University's Beedie School of Business. Tom proposes that education and management can benefit by drawing on: neuroscience, psychology, virtue ethics, Daoist contemplative practices, and emotional intelligence.

G. Tom Gehani helped retail giant **Target** innovate roll out diverse potato lines nationwide. He was an early collaborator with mega-entrepreneur **Jack DORSEY** developing Square point-of-sales digital payment device for artists and trainers, crafts - people and consultants. With an economics degree from the **University of Michigan, Ann Arbor**, he is deeply engaged with robotics and A.I. for transformative innovations, while teaching snowboarding to Minneapolis kids during the winter weekends.

Ira Greenberg is a Professor and Director of Painting, Drawing and Creative Computation, at Southern Methodist University, USA. With an eclectic background combining studio arts and computer science, Ira Greenberg has been a painter, 2D and 3D animator, print designer, web and interactive designer/developer, programmer, art director, creative director, managing director, art and computer science professor, and author.

Mohan Raj Gurubatham, B.Sc.; Psychology (Bolton UK), M.A. Media (Leicester UK), MBA Maharishi International (Iowa), and PhD; (University of Iowa). He is an adjunct at MIU, Iowa, and a faculty member at HELP University, Malaysia. With extensive global consulting experience and internationally published. He was a TC3 member of IFIP within UNESCO, focusing on technology and education best practices. Research interests are in psychology, learning, transcendence, and organizational transformations. His cognitive model was well-received at the World Summit of the Information Society in Geneva. He is a full member of the APA, AOM, and CIM in the UK.

Dr. Payal Kumar is an accomplished author and editor, who has contributed extensively to leadership and mentoring literature, emphasizing diversity and inclusion. Her global experience enriches her academic and professional endeavors. She is an elected officer of the MSR division of AOM.

Chris Laszlo is a Professor of Organizational Behavior at the Weatherhead School of Management in Case Western Reserve University, USA. As one of the originators of the concept of sustainable value, he reframes sustainability as a business opportunity, turning environmental and social risks into drivers of innovation, greater employee engagement, and a new, inimitable source of competitive advantage.

Dr. Anil K. Maheshwari is a professor of Management at Maharishi International University. A prolific author and researcher, he integrates consciousness, leadership, and technology. He has published 16 books and over 50 papers, and actively leads scholarly initiatives at the Academy of Management, advancing holistic, values-based education for global well-being.

Alfonso Montero, EdD, is a leadership educator, global speaker, and systems thinker whose work explores posthumanism, consciousness, and organizational transformation. He teaches in graduate leadership programs and co-leads a coaching and consulting practice focused on adaptive leadership and embodied systems change. His scholarship engages spiritually informed approaches to AI and systems thinking, inviting deeper reflection on leaders' becoming and relational intelligence within increasingly machine-woven realities.

Deeppa Ravindran is currently a Pilates Teacher who has more than 2500 hours of teaching experience and has outreached to about 10,000 students in Malaysia. Deeppa was formerly a programme coordinator at PAN Asia Pacific and has completed her MBA in HELP University, Malaysia.

Prof. Dr. Sharda S. Nandram is a Full Professor on Business and Spirituality at Nyenrode Business Universiteit and a Full Professor of Hindu Spirituality and Society at Vrije Universiteit (VU) Amsterdam. She is also the Chief Diversity Officer at VU. Her curiosity in connecting disciplines (trained as psychologist and economist and in spirituality) led her to complete an MBA course in managing AI and Cyber Security (in 2023).

List of Figures

Fig. 2.1	Four major states of consciousness	22
Fig. 2.2	V-Theory: A 2-step model of Transcendence. *Source* Maheshwari (2023)	28
Fig. 2.3	Lebanon Peace Project	32
Fig. 2.4	Washington Peace Project	33
Fig. 2.5	Super-radiance effect: coherent collective consciousness improves Quality of Life	34
Fig. 5.1	Paradigms of education (Adapted from Llewellyn & Pearson, 2011)	90
Fig. 5.2	V-theory: a 2-step model of transcendence	92

List of Tables

Table 2.1	Seven states of consciousness	23
Table 2.2	8 limbs of Yoga Sutras	24
Table 2.3	5 yamas of Yoga Sutras	25
Table 2.4	5 niyamas of Yoga Sutras	26
Table 3.1	Comparing the concept of Dharma across Dharmasastra, Mahabharata, Upanishads, and Ramayana	46
Table 3.2	Dharma matrix	48
Table 3.3	Comparing Eastern *Dharma* traditions with Western ethics and virtues frameworks	52
Table 4.1	Hindu levels of consciousness and knowledge	72
Table 5.1	States of consciousness	92
Table 5.2	Benefits and challenges of merging AI-based and consciousness-based education	103
Table 8.1	Highlights beneficial and maladaptive impacts of AI across many aspects of human life	165
Table 9.1	Relationship between DC and SD	183
Table 9.2	A framework of interplay between AI and SD	187
Table 10.1	Spirituality embodies principles of systems thinking	217

Part I

CHAPTER 1

The Interplay of AI and Consciousness: Implications for Organizations and Society

Anil K. Maheshwari

Introduction

The twenty-first century presents a paradox: on the one hand, the rise of artificial intelligence (AI) offers unprecedented technological advancement, and on the other, there is a growing recognition of the need for the development of consciousness (DC) in individuals and organizations to frame and navigate the complexities of a rapidly changing world. AI and DC represent two powerful, yet distinct forces, each with the potential to shape the future of business and society. While AI drives innovation, efficiency, and scalability, DC fosters ethical decision-making, emotional intelligence, and holistic well-being. In the interplay of these two powerful concepts lies the opportunity to create a flourishing, business-driven world for all.

Consciousness is the fundamental basis of all existence. Higher Consciousness is the basis for morality and ethics, and creativity and

A. K. Maheshwari (✉)
Maharishi International University, Fairfield, IA, USA
e-mail: akmaheshwari@miu.edu

A. K. Maheshwari (ed.), *AI and Consciousness in Organizations and Society*, Palgrave Studies in Workplace Spirituality and Fulfillment,
https://doi.org/10.1007/978-3-031-91470-6_1

innovation, among other human capabilities. AI is a product of human consciousness and innovation. AI refers to the simulation of human intelligence in machines that are programmed to think, learn, and solve problems autonomously. AI includes various technologies such as machine learning, natural language processing, computer vision, and robotics, and is already transforming business operations across industries by improving efficiency, automating routine tasks, and providing data-driven insights for decision-making.

However Capable AI Becomes, It Will Never Become Conscious

AI can simulate aspects of human cognition, even as it remains fundamentally different from human consciousness (Searle, 1980; Tegmark, 2018). While generative AI can describe itself, create text and graphics and videos, and can even ask intelligent questions, it is yet to reach a level of general intelligence where it may mimic overall human thinking. It will not know what it means to BE. This book explores how higher consciousness can assert its primacy in managing AI while reflexively leveraging AI to deepen human consciousness itself. We discuss this interplay from various angles. In this chapter, we discuss it in the context of decision-making, education, and organizational leadership. We examine AI's role through a consciousness-centered approach that respects the distinctiveness of human experience and seeks to integrate ancient Vedic knowledge wisdom into management practices (Kak, 2021; Maheshwari & Biberman, 2024).

Consciousness and Machine Intelligence

The question of whether machines can attain consciousness has sparked a debate among AI researchers, neuroscientists, and philosophers (Chalmers, 1995). A few years ago, Defence Advanced Projects Agency (DARPA) in the United States managed a large-scale project through Stanford Research International (SRI). This project brought together AI researchers, computer scientists, philosophers, and science managers for workshops in the United States and in the UK. The primary task given to this gathering was to explore whether computers of the future would become conscious. While they weren't necessarily looking at the near future, they were asked to consider the possibility a few decades from now. During the deliberations, they conducted a poll. The results were fascinating—there was a near-even split. About 50% of the participants believed that computers would become conscious at some point in the future, while the other half thought this would never happen.

Those who believed computers would become conscious were mostly from the field of algorithm development. Their argument was grounded in the idea that the brain is a machine, and once we understand how it works—how it processes information and executes algorithms—we will eventually be able to replicate these processes in computers. The assumption here is that at some point, the complexity of a machine will match that of the human brain, and the computer will become conscious.

Opponents, often informed by quantum mechanics and philosophy, argued that consciousness is not an emergent property of computational processes but a unique, indivisible phenomenon that transcends physicality (Kak, 2021). Their argument is based on the interpretation of quantum mechanics, particularly the Copenhagen interpretation. Quantum mechanics is arguably the deepest framework in science. According to its Copenhagen interpretation, there is a fundamental divide between the physical world and the conscious observer. Consciousness and physicality are separate and cannot be reduced to one another. From this perspective, consciousness does not emerge from any kind of operation or machine (Laszlo et al., 2021).

There's another argument that strengthens this position. It is that the embodied world, or the physical universe, operates according to laws. If consciousness could emerge simply from the complexity of a system, one could theoretically have a conscious entity embedded within a larger, more complex system. However, one cannot have a conscious agent existing within another conscious agent. This supports the idea that consciousness is a unity.

Erwin Schrödinger, one of the founders of quantum mechanics, famously embraced the idea that consciousness is singular, while minds are many. Minds are simply vessels through which the unified light of consciousness shines. Consciousness is the primary reality, and the brain, despite being a machine, cannot generate it. What we perceive as the contents of our mind is illuminated by consciousness, and this light cannot be replicated by a machine. That said, despite this division in opinion at the DARPA/SRI workshops, everyone agreed that AI would continue to grow in influence. AI and machines will become increasingly pervasive, especially in decision-making across various fields. We can already see that human beings are willing to cede significant decision-making power to machines, particularly in contexts like autonomous driving and decision systems.

The Ethical and Economic Implications of AI on Society

AI's growth will undoubtedly influence various economic sectors, from transportation to education (Brynjolfsson & McAfee, 2014; Autor et al., 2020). For example, self-driving cars are being tested and implemented in various parts of the world. While this may seem like a small technological advance, the societal consequences are profound. These autonomous vehicles promise increased efficiency but could also displace millions of workers globally, particularly in the transportation industry. In the United States, about half the jobs are tied to the transportation sector. In addition, the disruption caused by automation will not be limited to the transportation industry; it will affect numerous sectors, including academia. Universities and colleges will need to undergo a major transformation to adapt to this new reality. Many universities, particularly in the United States, are already struggling with the rising cost of education and declining demand for traditional degrees. To survive, educational institutions will need to radically change their approach to teaching and learning, moving away from rote memorization and prescriptive learning toward fostering creativity and innovation. There may not even be a need for as many professors in the future. AI-driven teaching platforms, such as Khanamigo, could allow a few top teachers to record lectures that could be distributed worldwide, with AI tutors providing personalized support to students.

This shift would be hugely disruptive, and one of the significant disruptions could be a further collapse in fertility rates. As people lose their jobs and face economic instability, fertility rates, which are already declining in countries like South Korea, China, and Japan, will likely continue to drop. In the most populous country India, the fertility rate has declined to just above the replacement rate of 2.1 children per woman. These changes—shrinking populations and economic contraction—will force societies to reorganize themselves, leading to unforeseen social and organizational consequences. While much of the current global conversation focuses on climate change, the decline in populations will lead to re-examining many of the issues currently associated with overpopulation. Declining unemployment and fertility rates will have profound social and economic consequences (Acemoglu & Restrepo, 2018; Frey & Osborne, 2017).

AI can radically improve efficiency and accuracy in decision-making. However, it lacks the ability to consider the ethical, emotional, and long-term consequences of business choices. This is where the development of higher consciousness becomes critical. Without conscious leadership and ethical oversight, AI-driven decisions could lead to unintended negative consequences, such as environmental degradation, economic inequality, and the erosion of human well-being.

Decision-Making with Consciousness and AI

Decision-making is one of the prime functions of management and leadership. One of the most significant benefits of AI in business is its ability to enhance decision-making. AI systems can process and analyze vast amounts of data in real-time, providing business leaders with actionable insights. For example, predictive analytics tools can help companies forecast demand, optimize pricing strategies, and allocate resources more effectively. Data-driven decision-making helps reduce human biases and errors in the analysis of complex datasets. However, human consciousness is not something that arises from physicality—it is primary, and it exists outside the physical system. It suggests that all living beings are interconnected and that we are not separate from animals or other life forms. This interconnectedness fosters compassion and encourages us to view the web of life as a unified whole.

A shift in self-understanding from higher consciousness will bring about significant changes at both the individual and societal levels. However, transitioning to this new understanding will be difficult. The disruptions that are coming—whether they are driven by technology, economics, or population decline—will create immense challenges for societies around the world. Conflicts over resources and worldviews will intensify, and as more people lose their jobs, mass migrations and social upheaval are likely to occur. While we believe that these disruptions will be severe in the short term, we are hopeful that a consciousness-based approach to society and management will help us navigate these challenges more effectively. We believe that by focusing on the development of higher consciousness, we can build more resilient, compassionate societies.

Our approach is grounded in the concept of *dharma*—of ethical living and decision-making (Maheshwari et al. Dharma chapter, this volume). When we educate future leaders, we aim to instill the values of ethics, authenticity, joy, and systemic thinking. By bringing these principles into management, we can develop organizations that are not only efficient but also compassionate and wise. When it comes to AI, the system could eventually reach a crisis where something new must emerge, but that may not be accomplished by another machine. That is where human consciousness comes in, with its infinite creativity (Gurubatham chapter, this book). AI will evolve in its own ways, but there will be points where humans will need to intervene to make the right decisions to break logjams and move the process forward. The recent COVID years are a good example: decisions made by machines or even a combination of humans and machines are now being reexamined, and people realize some of them were not the best decisions.

Consciousness-based decision-making contrasts with algorithmic decision-making by integrating awareness, empathy, and moral judgment, which are currently beyond AI's capabilities (Maheshwari, 2023). AI operates within a defined system of rules and data, whereas consciousness embodies a dynamic interplay of subjective experience and transcendent insight (Mullainathan & Spiess, 2017). Notably, leaders grounded in a consciousness-centered approach are better equipped to navigate complexities that AI, governed by binary logic, cannot fully grasp (Bostrom, 2014; Floridi, 2018).

Yuval Noah Harari, a prominent historian and author, has extensively explored the implications of artificial intelligence (AI) on human consciousness and society. In his book *Homo Deus: A Brief History of Tomorrow*, Harari discusses the potential for AI to surpass human capabilities, leading to a future where intelligent algorithms could outperform humans in various domains. He raises concerns about the possible obsolescence of Homo sapiens in an era dominated by data-centric paradigms. Harari emphasizes the distinction between intelligence and consciousness, noting that while AI can process vast amounts of data and solve complex problems, it lacks subjective experiences and self-awareness. He warns that as AI becomes more integrated into societal structures, it could manipulate human culture by generating human-like language, thereby undermining foundational cultural artifacts such as laws and institutions. In his recent work, *Nexus: A Brief History of Information Networks From the Stone Age to AI*, Harari examines the evolution of information networks and their impact on human societies. He cautions that AI, as an "alien intelligence," possesses the potential to operate autonomously, challenging existing societal mechanisms and posing existential threats if mismanaged. Harari underscores the necessity for a nuanced understanding of AI's capabilities and limitations, advocating for robust ethical frameworks to ensure that technological advancements serve to enhance human well-being rather than diminish it.

Consciousness and AI in Creativity and Innovation

Human creativity, an expression of consciousness, allows for transcending established frameworks, which remains challenging for AI (Maheshwari et al., creativity chapter, this volume). AI produces results that can sometimes seem creative. However, as a formal system, AI is a logical system with axioms and rules. The system produces output based on these rules, and that is how a computer-based system works. It cannot go outside of the framework of its axioms. While it can explore various combinations, creativity requires stepping outside the framework. The universe and society are constantly changing, and formal systems do not cover all possibilities. Gödel's incompleteness theorem illustrates this—i.e., within a formal system, certain truths cannot be proven.

There is also a question about what it would mean for machines to be conscious. Imagine a robot that behaves like a human in every way. One could hold a conversation like an AI chatbot does, and we might not be able to distinguish it from a human initially. But with enough probing, we would perhaps find its limitations. Perhaps humans don't have these limitations. It is important to remember though that many people also live within very constrained frameworks, not much richer than that of an AI machine.

For example, the story of Elias Howe, the inventor of the sewing machine illustrates this point. He was struggling with the design of a machine that would reduce the amount of manual labor required for sewing. One day, while in a trance-like state, Howe had a vision of indigenous people with spears that had holes in the tip. When he woke up, he realized that this was the design he needed for his sewing machine needle. Many scientists and inventors have had similar experiences, where the solution to a problem appears spontaneously, seemingly from outside the mind.

Roger Penrose, who won the Nobel Prize in Physics a few years ago, provides a modern example of this phenomenon. Penrose had been working on the problem of irregular tiling, a problem that mathematicians had been struggling with for years. One day, while crossing the street, Penrose had a sudden insight. He rushed back to his office, and the solution came to him in a flash. This kind of spontaneous, out-of-the-box thinking is characteristic of consciousness-driven creativity.

Historical examples, such as Elias Howe's intuitive breakthrough for the sewing machine and Roger Penrose's insights into tiling, illustrate creativity as a process not replicable by algorithmic means (Kak, 2021). This implies a future where creativity-centered roles will gain prominence, and educational models will need to adapt to cultivate skills uniquely suited to human creativity (Runco, 2014).

Indian Knowledge Systems and AI

Ancient Indian wisdom has long explored the relationship between consciousness and intelligence. Indic wisdom traditions such as Hinduism, Buddhism, and Jainism offer valuable perspectives on consciousness. Ancient texts like the *Vedas, Bhagavad Gita, Upanishads, Mahabharata,* and *Ramayana* provide holistic frameworks for understanding life. These texts emphasize unbounded non-dual consciousness and interconnectedness of all life. By embracing humility and creativity, leaders can tap into deeper levels of connection and motivation for selfless service. *Yoga Sutras* offer the eight-limbed path called the *Ashtanga Yoga*, which provides tools for deepening self-awareness helping individuals cultivate a state of being that is open to creativity, empathy, and intuition (Maheshwari, V-theory chapter, this volume). One can integrate teachings from the *Bhagavad Gita, the Upanishads, and the Yoga Sutras,* into modern management models. Tao provides similarly rich holistic knowledge and principles for engaging with the world (Xiu, this volume). The goal is to develop conscious, wise leadership that can navigate the complexities of today's world. By combining AI with ancient wisdom traditions, it may be possible to foster holistic, sustainable growth in organizations (Culham et al. this volume).

Concepts such as consciousness-based leadership and *dharma* (ethical living) align closely with sustainable management practices that prioritize inner development alongside organizational goals (Maheshwari, 2021, 2023). In the Vedic tradition, there are deities like *Vishwakarma* that are associated with machines, and there are rituals for machines. When everything is conscious, machines too could have infinitesimal amount of consciousness (Nader, 2015). From consciousness comes ether, then air, light, water, and finally matter. During the dissolution of the universe, the process reversed. This means that consciousness pervades the entire physical universe, including machines. However, the Indian knowledge system also says that the minds of humans and animals work like machines. This is the idea behind the *karmic* chain: that we are governed by our past *karmas* (experiences) and instincts. We are free only when we are one with pure consciousness. In the Vedic tradition, there is a prominent phrase—*Shivoham*—meaning "I am Shiva," or "I am consciousness." This recognizes the ultimate freedom from all constraints of the body, mind, and past experiences and instincts. There is also the concept of *Sanatana Dharma*, which refers to the eternal and ever-relevant teachings of Indic traditions, to bring fresh interpretations of spiritual insights to management education (Maheshwari et al., Dharma chapter, this volume). This approach helps us modernize spiritual traditions like Hinduism, Jainism, and Buddhism, making them relevant to contemporary teaching and learning environments, particularly as AI becomes increasingly pervasive.

We examine next how AI impacts us, how we differentiate various types of intelligence, and how these compare to consciousness itself. We also contrast the idea of becoming (which represents change) with being (which represents the centered and quiet essence of consciousness). From the perspective of Lord Shiva, the cosmic force responsible for destruction and rebirth, these two powerful forces—AI and Consciousness—mirror the eternal dance of Shiva and Shakti, creation and destruction, intellect and wisdom. If wielded without balance, AI could lead to societal and environmental destruction. If AI, however, is integrated with the development of consciousness, it could pave the way for a flourishing, business-driven world, one that is not only prosperous but also sustainable, ethical, and aligned with the well-being of all stakeholders.

The ABCDs of Intelligence and Consciousness

While AI is revolutionizing education and management, many people still confuse intelligence with consciousness (Maheshwari, CBE chapter this volume). Let us define the ABCDs of intelligence:

- Artificial Intelligence (AI): This is the simulation of human intelligence through machines, enabling them to perform tasks that typically require human cognition, such as decision-making and problem-solving.
- Biological Intelligence: This encompasses the intelligence of all living things, including humans, animals, plants, and ecosystems. It involves both conscious and unconscious processes, and there are multiple levels of cognitive functions across different species. Unlike AI, which operates on a binary (on/off) system, biological intelligence is layered and dynamic, involving a mix of conscious, subconscious, and unconscious processes.
- Creative Intelligence: This refers to the ability to access inner unbounded consciousness and master circumstances, act with awareness, and make decisions that reflect a higher level of understanding (Maheshwari, V-theory chapter this volume). Creative intelligence has been widely explored in scientific research through its technique of Transcendental Meditation (TM). It holds great potential for advancing our understanding of human behavior and decision-making.
- Digital Intelligence: This involves using digital tools to gather, analyze, and interpret data, enhancing productivity and decision-making. Digital intelligence is essential for integrating human and AI capabilities, expanding the boundaries of what is possible in management and research.

This framework underscores that while AI enhances efficiency, it cannot replicate the holistic, empathetic, and contextualized judgment intrinsic to conscious intelligence. A well-known example is Gary Kasparov's experience with IBM's Deep Blue (Gehani & Gehani, this volume). Initially, Kasparov lost to the AI-driven chess system, but when given access to the same wealth of knowledge and data that the AI had, Kasparov could beat the AI. The lesson here is clear: while AI can handle vast amounts of data and make decisions based on patterns, it lacks the creativity, intuition, and ingenuity that human consciousness brings to the table. When humans and AI collaborate, the combination can lead to better outcomes, leveraging AI's efficiency and human creativity.

The Limits of Machine Consciousness

Kak (2021) examines this question from both the perspectives of computer science and quantum mechanics. He concludes that machines, no matter how advanced, will never achieve consciousness. For those who argue that machines will become conscious, one of the more unsettling implications is that these conscious machines might eventually decide that humans are unnecessary. After all, if machines become conscious and can perform all of the tasks that humans do, why would they keep us around? Fortunately, our position is that we don't have to worry about this because machines will never achieve consciousness.

However, machines will increasingly take over jobs that have traditionally been performed by humans. The success of recent AI chatbots has made it clear that much of what humans do is simply algorithmic. Many of the tasks we perform at work are prescriptive—they follow a set of rules or procedures. From a psychological perspective, human behavior can be understood at three levels: cognitive (thinking), affective (feeling), and behavioral (acting). Computing systems can mimic thinking and behavior, but they struggle with emotions. Will AI ever be able to genuinely simulate human emotions? Human beings will likely perform creative tasks and those requiring higher level soft skills such as emotional intelligence (Gurbatham, this volume).

While AI can process vast amounts of information and make incremental improvements, true creativity requires thinking outside the box, ad infinitum. This kind of creativity is spontaneous and cannot be reduced to a set of rules or algorithms. There are numerous examples in history where breakthroughs occurred when individuals weren't actively thinking about the problem at hand. This suggests that consciousness is something transcendent that interacts with the mind and allows us to access creative ideas (Maheshwari, V-theory chapter).

In the *Vedic* tradition, the mind is said to have three layers: the lower layer consists of memories and associations; the middle layer is the intellect, where logical connections are made between memories; and the uppermost layer is the ego, which is associated with bliss and transformation. Above these layers is the light of consciousness, which illuminates the mind and allows for creativity. Through training and discipline, one can bring this light of consciousness closer to the mind, which enables access to truly original ideas (Maheshwari, V-theory chapter this volume).

This process often happens spontaneously, sometimes during dreams or moments of relaxation.

The challenge for us is to make this capacity for creativity more accessible to young people (Maheshwari et al. Creativity chapter, this volume). In the future, as populations decline and traditional jobs disappear, the demand for creative work will increase. Jobs in the arts, sciences, and design—fields that require original thinking—will be in high demand. How do we structure education to foster creativity? How do we prepare young people to access their creative potential in a world where AI is increasingly taking over prescriptive tasks?

Some argue that what we mean by emotion might be a positive or negative value attached to a memory or association and could be programmed into AI. For example, an AI could classify certain inputs as "positive" or "negative" and respond accordingly. However, this doesn't take us to the realm of freedom or creativity. A great mystery, from a scientific perspective, is the mystery of freedom. On the one hand, science tells us that everything is governed by laws, but we also like to believe that we are free. We are only free when we realize that we are pure consciousness. By integrating consciousness into our understanding of society, management, and education, we can build a future where creativity and compassion are at the center of human endeavor. We believe that this shift will have a positive influence on all aspects of life, from personal well-being to the well-being of our organizations and communities (Maheshwari & Biberman, this volume).

Benjamin Libet's famous experiment showed that decisions we think we make consciously are actually preceded by brain activity. Quantum mechanics offers some insights into this. For example, the quantum Zeno effect shows that an observer can influence a physical process simply by observing it. This aligns with the Vedic idea that a deity creates reality through observation. In Vedic tradition, the idea of *moksha* (liberation) or *nirvana* is not just about being freed in the next life. It's about finding that place of freedom within. This is where creativity comes in—when you discover that inner freedom, new possibilities open up and creative ideas emerge.

AI resides within the box, attempting to broaden the scope of the box as it moves from the known into the unknown. In the *Vedic* tradition, there's manifest reality (with many truths) and unmanifest reality (with one truth). AI is limited by its inability to integrate multiple truths, in most current AI systems. AI will attempt to integrate additional elements, and adaptive AI systems will keep evolving. We believe that there will always be a role for humans. If machines did everything, humans would become unnecessary, and we would question the meaning of the universe itself.

A Vision for a Flourishing World

The dance between AI and consciousness opens up a golden age of business. Just as Lord Shiva's *tandava* dance balances creation and destruction, AI and consciousness together can bring about a world where businesses contribute not only to economic prosperity but also to the well-being of the earth and its inhabitants. In this vision, AI is an agent of service, not domination. AI will help businesses operate more efficiently and innovate faster, but it will do so in a way that respects human dignity and planetary boundaries. Consciousness, meanwhile, acts as the guiding force, ensuring that AI is used ethically, with compassion, and in alignment with the principles of *dharma*—the cosmic law of righteousness. Businesses in this world are driven by a sense of higher purpose, and not just profit. They recognize their role as stewards of the earth and as agents of positive change. They hope to use AI to address global challenges like poverty, inequality, and climate change, all while creating value for their stakeholders.

There are other, more critical, perspectives that directly challenge this hopeful narrative, and demand the consideration of the impact of AI on ignored non-dominant communities in non-dominant countries that may live from different codes of conduct that are intrinsically more in harmony with nature. Higher consciousness should include the impact of unnecessary burdens of an AI-driven world on such communities and their desires to be left to their own ways. Perhaps AI could progressively be trained on the practices and knowledge based of these communities.

To summarize, the interplay between AI and consciousness highlights the fundamental limitations of machines in replicating the essential depth and scope of human awareness. By incorporating consciousness into management practices, society can shape a future where AI complements rather than replaces human potential. The Vedic tradition offers a profound guide for understanding consciousness, while AI serves as a tool for enhancing, rather than replacing, human wisdom. The rest of the book tries to illuminate many perspectives on this.

Synopsis of the Rest of the Book

In the rest of section "Introduction", Maheshwari presents V-theory of transcendence and how it helps experience pure consciousness and flourish in the age of AI. In the following chapter, Maheshwari, Nandram, and Kumar discuss the Vedic notion of *dharma*, which upholds the universe. They present a *dharma matrix* as a way of practically living with assistance from AI. In the next chapter, Culham, Bachani, and Laszlo survey western and eastern notions of spirituality and their interplay with AI for improving management practices. That completes section "Introduction".

In section "However Capable AI Becomes, It Will Never Become Conscious", we relate thinking and well-being with AI. First, Maheshwari expounds on the unique paradigm of consciousness-based education, and how AI can support it and take it to the next level. Next, Gurubatham and Raveendran discuss the future skills required for work in the age of AI, and how emotional intelligence and other softer skills may be the more important skills after all. Then Maheshwari and colleagues share a rich and fascinating conversation among themselves and show the immense diversity in their approaches to how AI may help and hurt the creative world. Finally, Maheshwari discusses how AI and development of consciousness can help create well-being.

In section "Consciousness and Machine Intelligence", we cover more macro situations. Maheshwari & Banerjee discuss how AI and Consciousness impact the sustainability of the planet and life on it. They particularly examine the case study of plastics which has been a tremendous boon for industry, and now a major driver of environment challenges. In the next chapter, Ebert and Montero present five principles for the development of a Systems Thinking Mindset to deal with the enormous complexity of AI and consciousness. Finally, Gehani and Gehani present the historical narrative of how AI emerged and how it may be developed and rolled out from an innovation diffusion perspective.

References

Acemoglu, D., & Restrepo, P. (2018). Artificial intelligence, automation, and work. *Journal of Economic Perspectives, 33*(2), 3–30.

Autor, D., Mindell, D., & Reynolds, E. (2020). *The work of the future: Building better jobs in an age of intelligent machines*. MIT Press.

Bostrom, N. (2014). *Superintelligence: Paths, dangers*. Oxford University Press.

Brynjolfsson, E., & McAfee, A. (2014). *The second machine age: Work, progress, and prosperity in a time of brilliant technologies*. Norton.

Chalmers, D. J. (1995). Facing up to the problem of consciousness. *Journal of Consciousness Studies, 2*(3), 200–219.

Culham, T., Bachani, J., & Laszlo, C. (this volume). AI and consciousness: Adding spiritual to scientific perspectives.

Ebert, L., & Montero, A. (this volume). Systems thinking mindset in an age of AI.

Floridi, L. (2018). *The fourth revolution: How the infosphere is reshaping human reality*. Oxford University Press.

Frey, C. B., & Osborne, M. A. (2017). The future of employment: How susceptible are jobs to computerisation? *Technological Forecasting and Social Change, 114*, 254–280.

Gehani, R., & Gehani, T. (this volume). From innovating conventional AI to conscious AI technology.

Gurubatham, M., & Raveendran, D. (this volume). Human and artificial intelligences: Different yet complementary.

Kak, S. (2021). The limits of machine consciousness. *Journal of Artificial Intelligence and Consciousness, 8*(1), 15–28.

Laszlo, C., Waddock, S., Maheshwari, A., Nigri, G., & Storberg-Walker, J. (2021). Quantum worldviews: How science and spirituality are converging to transform consciousness for meaningful solutions to wicked problems. *Humanistic Management Journal, 6*, 293–311.

Maheshwari, A. K. (2021). Higher consciousness management: Transcendence for spontaneous right action. *Journal of Management, Spirituality & Religion, 18*(6), 77–91.

Maheshwari, A. K. (Ed.). (2023). *Consciousness-based leadership and management, volume 1: Vedic and other philosophical approaches to oneness and flourishing*. Springer.

Maheshwari, A. K. (this volume). Transforming consciousness-based education in the age of AI.

Maheshwari, A. K. (this volume). Artificial intelligence and well-being.

Maheshwari, A. K. (this volume). V-theory in the age of artificial intelligence.

Maheshwari, A. K., & Banerjee, S. (this volume). Consciousness and AI for sustainable development.

Maheshwari, A. K., & Biberman, J. (2024). Artificial oneness: Bridging the human machine divide. *Journal of Management, Spirituality & Religion.*

Maheshwari, A. K., Frick, K., Greenberg, I., & Colby, D. K. (this volume). Creativity, consciousness and AI in organizations.

Maheshwari, A. K., Nandram, S., & Kumar, P. (this volume). Dharma matrix in the age of artificial intelligence.

Mullainathan, S., & Spiess, J. (2017). Machine learning: An applied econometric approach. *Journal of Economic Perspectives, 31*(2), 87–106.

Nader, T. (2015). Consciousness is all there is: A mathematical approach with applications. *International Journal of Mathematics and Consciousness, 1*(1), 1–65.

Runco, M. A. (2014). *Creativity: Theories and themes: Research, development, and practice*. Academic Press.

Searle, J. R. (1980). Minds, brains and programs. In D. R. Hofstadter & D. C. Dennett (Eds.), *The Mind's I*.Basic Books.

Sha, Z. G., & Xiu, R. (this volume). Fulfilling the higher purpose and meaning of human life with Tao science and AI.

Tegmark, M. (2018). *Life 3.0: Being human in the age of artificial intelligence*. Vintage.

CHAPTER 2

V-Theory of Transcendence for Achieving Peace in the Age of Artificial Intelligence (AI)

Anil K. Maheshwari

Introduction

Healthy living in the age of AI encompasses a balance between leveraging technological advancements for improved quality of life and managing the potential health risks associated with increased digital dependency (Tegmark, 2018). Digital literacy, balanced use of time, physical activity, healthy eating, proper sleeping, meditation etc., can help with maximizing the benefits of technology while minimizing its drawbacks. Lederach (2005) states that achieving world peace requires creating peace at the individual level, as well as having the moral imagination for creating peace at the collective level. Anderson (2018) calls for developing social consciousness to the next level, using Wilber's Integral Theory as a key framework. Gelot (2018) claims the primacy of the transcendent in

A. K. Maheshwari (✉)
Maharishi International University, Fairfield, IA, USA
e-mail: akmaheshwari@miu.edu

A. K. Maheshwari (ed.), *AI and Consciousness in Organizations and Society*, Palgrave Studies in Workplace Spirituality and Fulfillment,
https://doi.org/10.1007/978-3-031-91470-6_2

creating the common ground for deep peace, drawing on teachings from Christianity. Transcending regularly, using V-theory, to connect with pure consciousness can create deep inner peace and bliss at the individual level (Maharishi, 1963; Maheshwari, 2023). Maharishi (1963) developed Transcendental Meditation™ (TM) technique from *Yoga Sutras* for personal development and world peace. An increasing corpus of empirical scientific research shows that group practice of TM can create coherence in collective consciousness that enables social harmony and peace (Maharishi, 1995; Orme-Johnson et al., 1983; Hagelin et al., 1999; Dillbeck & Cavanaugh, 2017). We will present *Yoga Sutras*, a branch of the Vedas, that provides an 8-limbed path to unite with the unbounded transcendent reality. The nature of human development through V-theory of transcendence will be described. We will share select scientific evidence on generating coherence in collective consciousness for achieving positive results at the collective level. Implications and recommendations for design and the use of AI will be presented.

Consciousness is Primary

The Vedas state that consciousness is all there is (Nader, 2015). Consciousness is an absolute, self-referral totality that can express itself in an infinite number of ways at the relative level. Vedic knowledge is presented recursively, from revealing the central wholeness to the unfolding of successive outer levels of observed reality. Consciousness is an infinite generative source, that curves back into itself to manifest everything (Bhagavad Gita 9:8). Consciousness is the unmanifest sap flowing through the rose that can manifest itself in the form of flat green leaves, hard brown thorn, and the soft beautiful pink flowers. Similarly, Consciousness is the unmanifest potential in the tiny hollow seed that can manifest itself into a huge banyan tree. The totality of Vedas can be experienced in the human physiology through the techniques of union with consciousness, described in *Yoga Sutras* (Nader, 1994). Yoga is defined as *Chitta Vritti Nirodha* (YS: 1:2) or the settling down of mental perturbations. Consistent practice of transcendence can help increasingly quieten the mind and effortlessly connect with and become the Oneness of the Unified Field of all the laws of nature (Maheshwari, 2021). Connecting with pure consciousness thus can provide human beings with the right sets of thoughts and actions, which will be completely in tune with nature, and will attract full support of nature for world peace (Maharishi, 1963; Maheshwari, 2023).

As the Bhagavad Gita (2:48) says: *Yogasthah Kuru Karmani*. "Established in Being, perform action." Maharishi clarifies further.

> If the mind is without Being, the process of thinking is as though lifeless, and, when the mind is not familiar with Being, the process of thinking and the thought force are very weak. If these are weak, so will be the resultant activity, and as a result of weak activity, the accomplishments are not satisfying, and the fulfillment of life is not gained. So, it is the art of Being while thinking that is the basis of all accomplishments and fulfillment in life. (Maharishi Mahesh Yogi, 1963, p. 89).

States of Consciousness

Knowledge is structured in consciousness, and knowledge is different in different states of consciousness (Maharishi, 1963). What one sees depends upon one's state of consciousness. There are ordinary states of consciousness, like waking, sleeping, and dreaming.[1] Then there are higher states of consciousness, beginning with the pure or transcendental consciousness (TC). These four states of consciousness are represented in Fig. 2.1 using two dimensions.

On the horizontal axis is the contents of thought, and on the vertical axis is the awareness of those thoughts. In the sleeping state, there are no thoughts, and there is no awareness of the self. In the dreaming state, there is an awareness of the contents of thought, but there is no awareness of the self. In the waking state, there is an awareness of the self and there is also awareness of those thoughts. The fourth state is the transcendental state, where there is full awareness of the self, but there is no awareness of thoughts. This is called Transcendental Consciousness (TC) or *turiya*. Vedic wisdom calls it the true self that is worth knowing. *Shivam Shantam advaitam chaturham manyante, sa atma, sa vigyeya (Mandukya Upanaishad, 7).* "Shiva is pure silence, it is the non-dual transcendental state. That is *atma*, and is worth knowing." This fourth and settled state of pure consciousness is naturally peaceful and blissful.

[1] There are also impaired states of consciousness such as vegetative state and coma, and altered states of consciousness such as hallucinating, and hypnosis. However, we are not concerned with them at this time.

		Self-Awareness	
		No	Yes
Thoughts	Yes	**Dreaming**	**Waking**
	No	**Sleeping**	**Pure Consciousness**

Fig. 2.1 Four major states of consciousness

There are many higher states of consciousness. In the next higher state, one retains awareness of the *turiya* even while operating in the relative world. This is the state of Cosmic Consciousness, where there is awareness of pure consciousness even while one is awake and engaged with the objects of waking consciousness. The blissful peace and creativity of pure consciousness is available while operating in a day-to-day life. With continued practice, one develops a finer and finer ability of direct perception of the ultimate reality. People in higher states report increased feelings of bliss, and there is also a measurable calming of the physiological processes. This process of refinement of perception continues to grow until one reaches the ultimate, non-dual, state of consciousness, also called Unity Consciousness. In this state, everything is a part of the self and is seen as fluctuations within the field of the self. One sees no distinction between oneself and the other. All the states of consciousness are shown in Table 2.1.

It is important to note that the higher states of consciousness are subjective experiential states. The experiences of the highest states can mostly be judged by qualified masters who can specify what state has been reached.

Table 2.1 Seven states of consciousness

State of consciousness	*Self-awareness*	*Content of experience*
Sleep state	None	None
Dream state	None	Illusory
Waking	Individual Ego (Lower self)	Perceptions, thoughts, feelings
Transcendental consciousness	Unbounded (Pure Consciousness: Higher Self)	None
Cosmic consciousness	Unbounded (Pure Consciousness: Higher Self)	Perceptions, thoughts, feelings
Refined cosmic consciousness (god consciousness)	Unbounded (Pure Consciousness: Higher Self)	Finest Relative Perception, brought about by most refined development of the heart
Unity consciousness or Brahman consciousness	Unbounded (Pure Consciousness: Higher Self)	...fluctuations within pure consciousness "...all things in terms of the Self."

Yoga Sutras

There are several paths of *Yoga* (or Union) according to ancient Indian scriptures (Maharishi, 1969). *Karma yoga* places primacy on action, *Jnana Yoga* places primacy on knowledge of the Absolute pure consciousness, and *Bhakti Yoga* places loving surrender to the higher reality. Seekers can follow the principles and practices of Yoga at all these levels to achieve their goal. The path to spiritual development can be through transcending the surface reality and experiencing the totality of existence, or pure consciousness. Maharishi Mahesh Yogi says:

> The crucial mistake that has dogged mankind for countless centuries is the loss of understanding of the primary importance of the field of pure consciousness. It is this field alone which is the field of all possibilities and the home of all the laws of nature. Unless thought and action are experienced from this field, life remains incomplete and plagued by ups and downs, plagued by imbalance. Only direct experience can re-establish the importance of pure consciousness as the field that we must contact before we can be successful in whatever interests us. (1978: 39).

Patanjali's *Yoga Sutras* is a short 196-verse scripture in the ***karma yoga*** tradition that offers ***ashtanga yoga*** or a proven 8-limbed path to union with pure consciousness. *Yoga Sutras* can guide an individual on how to attain union and to lead others in their spiritual journeys. "Yoga is achieved by the cessation of all the impulses of the mind" (*Yoga Sutra*: 1:2) says. Stillness of mind creates the conditions and the opportunity to connect with the infinite unbounded unmanifest Being, the all-knowing field of consciousness. Maharishi Patanjali cognized the *Yoga Sutras* in Sanskrit in about 500BC to 400CE. *Yoga Sutras* are terse and they can be interpreted both as a state to be reached and as a process to be followed. Its pithy 196 verses are organized in 4 chapters. They describe the goal of life as realizing the self where only consciousness exists.

Yoga Sutras (2:29) is a long phrase that provides a comprehensive eight-limb formula to facilitate a range of possibilities. (Table 2.2). Briefly the 8 limbs of *Yoga* are:

1. *Yama* is the administrator that helps keep all limbs together. There are five *yamas*.
2. *Niyama*, or the rules through which the administrator leads. There are five *niyamas*.
3. *Asanas* are the third limb that forms the basis for stability, at the level of body and mind.
4. *Pranayama* is fourth limb, which is activity or dynamism of the breath.
5. *Pratyahara*—is the fifth limb, and a subtle one. It is the process of digesting the experiences gathered through the sense organs.
6. *Dharana* means to hold or grasp a certain thought or state of Being.

Table 2.2 8 limbs of Yoga Sutras

Limb #	*Sanskrit term*	*Area of focus*
1	*Yama*	Administrator
2	*Niyama*	Laws
3	*Asana*	Physical
4	*Pranayama*	Breath
5	*Pratyahara*	Senses
6	*Dharana*	Mind
7	*Dhyana*	Intellect
8	*Samadhi*	Being

7. *Dhyana* is a deeper value of holding and is usually translated as meditation. It is the silent field in which all holding and sustaining of the mind takes place.
8. *Samadhi* is the total stillness of mind, where all is Being. This is the state of *Sat-chit-anand* or bliss consciousness.

The first two limbs of *Yoga Sutras* are sets of behavioral principles for social and personal conduct. The next two limbs relate to the health of the body and the breath. The last three limbs relate to calming and organizing the sensory mind and being in the Absolute Oneness with perfect equanimity.

Yamas: This first limb of *Yoga* is characterized as the administrator role. The relative world can be thought of in terms of the rules that govern relationships between individuals. The *Yama*, the master administrator, uses those rules to govern and see who has done how much good and should receive how much happiness. *Yama* has five sub-limbs. The five *yamas* are *Satya* (truth), *Ahimsa* (non-violence), *Asteya* (non-attachment), *Brahmacharya* (celibacy), and *Aparigraha* (non-possession). These five *yamas* structure the unity of natural laws to govern (Table 2.3).

Truth refers to realizing one's own nature as being pure consciousness. Non-violence in thought and deed comes naturally when the self is established in pure consciousness: there is no other, so hurting anyone else is hurting the self. These two principles of truth and non-violence were key to Mahatma Gandhi's effective spiritual and political advocacy through the technique of *satyagraha* or pursuit of truth using non-violent non-cooperation with untruth. Non-attachment to any objects comes easy when one realizes that even one's body and mind are temporary and will pass. *Brahmcharya* (literally means living like a *Brahman*) means dissolving any temptation for materials and carnal pleasures. The desire to

Table 2.3 5 yamas of Yoga Sutras

Yama #	*Sanskrit term*	*English*
1	*Satya*	Truth
2	*Ahimsa*	Non-violence
3	*Asteya*	Non-attachment
4	*Brahmcharya*	Celibacy
5	*Aparigraya*	Non-possession

Table 2.4 5 niyamas of Yoga Sutras

Niyama #	*Sanskrit term*	*English*
1	*Shauch*	Cleanliness or purity
2	*Santosh*	Contentment, Satisfaction
3	*Tapas*	Purification, Glowing
4	*Swadhyaya*	Self-learning
5	*Ishawarpranidhan*	God awareness

possess material things falls off with the realization of infinite inner bliss. It is notable that these five *yamas* are the same as five precepts required for Buddhist spiritual programs.

Niyamas: The second limb is *niyama*, or a set of rules for personal conduct. The five main *niyamas* are *Shauch* (cleanliness or purity), *Santosh* (contentment or satisfaction), *Tapas* (purification), *Swadhaya* (self-learning), and *Ishawarpranidhan* (bringing God into one's awareness). (Table 2.4).

Cleanliness in thought and action is the first rule for a healthy life. To live with contentment is to enjoy life as a state of prosperity, fulfillment, glory, and grace. *Tapas* is to purify oneself, through disciplined living. When something heats up, it glows and radiates brilliance, and the impurities fall off. *Swadhaya* means self-study, or always working on realizing the higher self. *Pranidhana* means going deeper into bringing God deeper within oneself and living with humility. Almost all of the *niyamas* are also found in the Buddhist canon.

Asana: The 3rd limb of *Yoga Sutras* relates to the body. *Yoga Sutras* (2:46) says that "Steadiness in pose" is *asana*. *Yogis* typically sit in a lotus pose for long periods without moving, to concentrate their attention. However, *asana* can mean any pose whatsoever. Maharishi *yoga asanas* is a system of poses that help flexibility of the whole body and all muscle groups. Swami Ramdev has utilized *yoga asanas* to new levels to help provide relief from chronic diseases to people across India (Maheshwari & Pandey, 2022).

Pranayama: The 4th limb is about bringing attention to the *Prana*, or flow of life energy through the breath. *Pranayama* literally means regulation of life-breath. These are physical exercises where the inhalation and exhalation can be regulated in terms of their speed, holding, and which nostril. There are breathing exercises focused on inhaling, and others on exhaling. These practices are used by hermits to control their physiological parameters such as heart rate, metabolic level, hormonal system, etc. *Prana* flows more easily in a physical body made supple through the practice of *asanas*. Regular practice of *Pranayama* provides almost complete control of the body and can be used to heal the body and make it healthy and disease-free.

Pratyahara: The 5th limb, *Pratyahara,* is a subtle activity that works on the sensory aspects of mind. It is a largely mental activity of reversing the flow of inputs or sensory "nutrition." In western mode of thinking and doing, one's attention is usually directed outside, on acquiring sensations through the five senses of seeing, touch, hearing, taste, and smell. All the sense organs are shut off and one sits in complete silence with eyes and ears closed. It helps the mind to digest and assimilate the accumulated sensory objects from worldly activity. It is akin to reflecting upon one's impressions, perceptions, and thoughts. It is a first step in calming down the mind, by bringing attention to the self, and not be controlled by the vagaries of the external world. *Pratyahara* also marks the transition of *yoga* practices from the external activity to the three internal limbs of *Yoga*—*Dharana*, *Dhyana* and *Samadhi*—that are increasingly subtle mental practices for experiencing the infinite self, or pure consciousness. There is little equivalence for these steps in western thought traditions, but they can be understood from a quantum field theory perspective. Intellect is involved in holding thoughts at many levels.

Dharana: The 6th limb means "holding the intellect" in the field of Being. This can be considered as concentration or holding the mind steady, and keeping the mind focused on the here and now.

Dhyana: The 7th limb is popularly translated as meditation. Maharishi Mahesh Yogi says that the intellect has two values: the ego value, which is relevant for relative functioning, and Being value that is the Absolute restful state. The refinement of thought in the intellect happens due to the intellect itself. *Dhyana* can lead to complete control over the rational mind by the mind itself.

Samadhi: The 8th limb is being in the transcendental state. It means "evenness of intelligence," or complete balance between all opposites. This is an experience beyond time and space, and is called the 4th state of consciousness, or Transcendental Consciousness (TC). TC is different from the waking, sleeping, and dreaming states of consciousness. This state is considered the "*Atma*" or the soul.

Transcendence

When consciousness is left free to experience itself, that is transcendence (Maharishi, 1969). The intellect becomes aware of itself through transcending itself. By direct unmediated experience one can *realize* the true self as beyond time and form, beyond thoughts and objects. Universality and individuality are two simultaneous aspects of the intellect. There are impulses of the transcendent as much as there are impulses of ego. Our V-Theory of Transcendence (Maheshwari, 2021) shows that the universe can be alternately experienced at two different levels: in its dynamic diversity of impulses of the ego at the top of the V, and its silent transcendental unity at the bottom of the V (Fig. 2.2). The upper level is the level of diverse dynamic action. The bottom level is the level of the transcendent, the source of pure potential. The path to understanding and participating in the continuous transformation of the world at the top of the V is through experiencing the silent unity at the bottom of the V. Both levels are important in their own ways.

The first step is to choose a path or practice to transcend surface reality and connect with the pure consciousness at the bottom of the

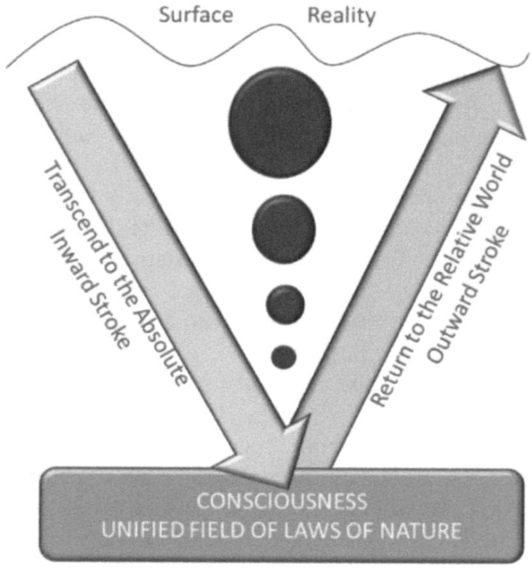

Fig. 2.2 V-Theory: A 2-step model of Transcendence. *Source* Maheshwari (2023)

V. It is called the inward stroke. Staying for a certain period of time at the bottom of the V helps bring deep rest and energy to the individual mind. The second step of the V is to return to the multi-valued dynamic surface reality. This is called the outward stroke. We recognize that multiple practices may be considered in the context of a simple 2-step V-model of an inward and outward stroke. Transcendence can be achieved effectively through Transcendental Meditation (TM) (Travis & Shear, 2010). Other traditions of transcendence too could be conceived through V-theory with the premise that the consciousness at the bottom of the V is primary, self-referral, and independent of matter.

Almost all spiritual traditions prescribe their own means of transcending (Wilber, 1993). Some suggest prayer and devotion as a way of reaching God. Others suggest sacred practices to cleanse oneself and reach the transcendent states. There are many techniques of meditation coming from many different traditions including Vedic, Buddhist, Chinese, Zen, and others. Daniel Goleman (1996) categorizes meditations into two major kinds. Some meditation techniques such as the Vedic ones are premised on their being an ultimate reality. These meditative practices lead to the achievement of that ultimate reality. Some meditations assume that there is no ultimate reality, for example, the Buddhist view of the world. These mediation practices lead to the achievement of liberation from all surface attachments, into nothingness. In addition, there are many innovative meditations offered as applications on mobile phones and other devices.

Transcendental Meditation

Transcendental Meditation™ is a mantra-based meditation based on the ancient Vedic scriptures. The technique is easy to learn and requires no change in lifestyle or beliefs. It is normally practiced for 20 minutes twice daily sitting quietly with eyes closed. In this technique, a specific sound or mantra is repeated to bring attention inwards. There is no intellectual effort involved in transcending. The TM mantra is a meaning-free Vedic sound that has the potential to transcend surface reality and lead one to the transcendent source of thought. The mantra is carefully chosen by a trained TM teacher according to the prescribed process. Effortlessly repeating the mantra begins to calm down the mind. It is not necessary to hold on to the mantra all the time; if the mantra goes away for some time, that is alright. Surface-level thoughts come and go. One gradually drops down from the surface level of thoughts to a deeper, quieter absolute state where the mind is totally at rest. At this bottom layer the mind is pure consciousness, the transcendent state—"a state of inner wakefulness with no object of thought or perception, just pure consciousness aware of its own unbounded nature" (Maharishi, 1976: 123). Maharishi has taught that TM and advanced TM-Sidhi techniques are the technologies of consciousness.

TM is a general-purpose technique for solving many problems. Research has shown benefits from TM at every level of body and mind. There are significant positive changes in physiology and psychology at the individual level. "No other stress management technique has anywhere close to this amount of hard data in support of its claims to reduce stress," Rosenthal (2009). Regular practice of TM has been shown to help with reduction in stress and anxiety,[2] total brain integration,[3] improvement in cardiac health,[4] and reduction in negativity in society.[5] Many researchers have confirmed the reality of transcendental consciousness. TM and TM-Sidhi program provides enormous psychological benefits[6] as well. Research has shown that regular practice of TM habituates the mind to restful alertness and leads to broad comprehension and improves the ability to focus sharply. It leads to a reduction in anxiety, depression, and anger.[7] The meditator gets established in Transcendental Consciousness and can stay stable and creative under the most extreme of external circumstances. Meditators tend to perceive the world more positively and holistically. They are better able to see another person's perspective, without being easily swayed by social pressure to do something which they judge to be wrong. Creativity increases, as measured by tests of both verbal and pictorial fluency, flexibility, and originality. Perception becomes more accurate and less driven by preconceptions and misconceptions. Basic memory processes improve.

[2] David Orme-Johnson and Vernon Barnes (2013).

[3] Fred Travis (2011).

[4] Robert Keith Wallace (1970).

[5] Orme-Johnson et al. (1988).

[6] Refer to various research articles by Charles Alexander and associates.

[7] Nidich et al. (2018)

Collective Consciousness and World Peace

Tat Sannidhau Vaira Tyagah (*Yoga Sutras*: 2:35) means: "In the vicinity of *Yoga* (or unity) negative tendencies are eliminated." The combined effect of many people meditating together on the environment creates a powerful force for reducing hostilities. Research has demonstrated that advanced meditation practices based on *Yoga Sutras* can enliven that deep peaceful quality within oneself, which can lead to deep bliss and spontaneous feeling of lightness, appropriately called *Yogic Flying* (Orme-Johnson, 2023). When people practice *yoga* together from that transcendental state, the entire world comes into a state of least excitation, and the result can be defined as deep peace.

> My calculation is that the day one-tenth of the adult population of the world begins to meditate a half-hour morning and evening and begins to emit an influence of peace and harmony from the deepest level of consciousness – from that day, the atmosphere of the world, this negative atmosphere of the world, will be neutralized, and from that day will dawn the chance of no war for centuries to come. This is our practical plan based on the most scientific basis for lasting peace. Maharishi (1963).

When a group of people meditates together, not only do they develop coherence individually, but their collective coherence also exponentially rises. This Super-radiance effect, also called the "Maharishi Effect," is the phenomenon that a small group of trained and committed meditators, a tiny fraction of the overall population, can generate enough coherence to counter negative forces and bring peace to the entire population. Scientific research has proven this as a "Super-Radiance effect" (Orme-Johnson, 2023). This effect states that collective transcendence is possible with less than 1% of people practicing TM and TM-Sidhi techniques. Furthermore, the Maharishi Effect is stronger nearer its source and diminishes further away from the source. There is thus a dosage effect: the larger the group, the greater the influence on social variables (Orme-Johnson & Fergusson, 2018).

Scientific Evidence

Even though the Maharishi Effect seems non-intuitive, the statistical analysis of the findings is irrefutable and undeniable. A growing corpus of published papers from researchers across many universities has established strong validity to this phenomenon (Orme-Johnson, 2023). Here are a few of the prominent research projects in brief.

1. *The International Peace Project in the Middle East*. Trained TM Siddha meditators were sent to Israel in 1983 to reduce the conflict and improve life in the region. The results showed that the Quality-of-Life Index in the region followed the change in size of the TM group at a day-to-day level (Fig. 2.3). In other words, when the number of meditators was larger, the quality of life improved much more (Orme-Johnson, 2016; Orme-Johnson et al., 1988).

2. *Peace-making Project in Washington DC*. A number of TM-Sidhis meditators were proactively sent to Washington DC to demonstrate this phenomenon in 1993 (Fig. 2.4). The local police department was involved in this experimental research design and they were told about the predicted reduction in crime. Crime fell by 23%, much more than what the police considered would be magical (Goodman et al., 1997; Hagelin et al, 1999).

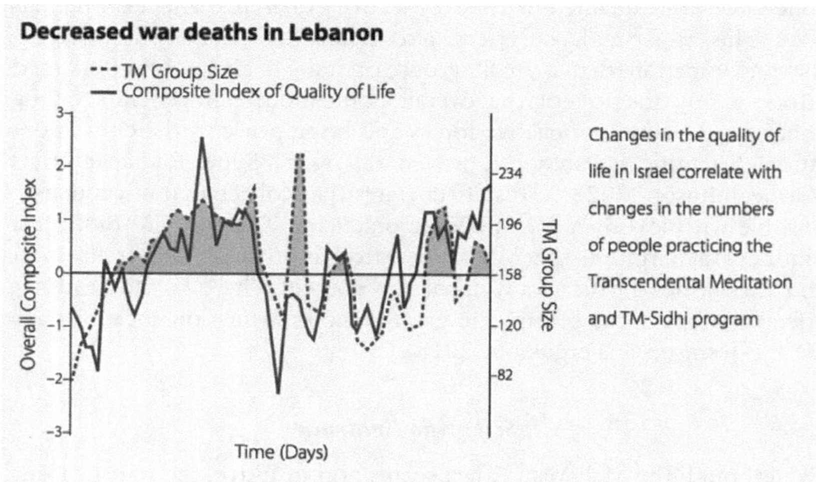

Fig. 2.3 Lebanon Peace Project

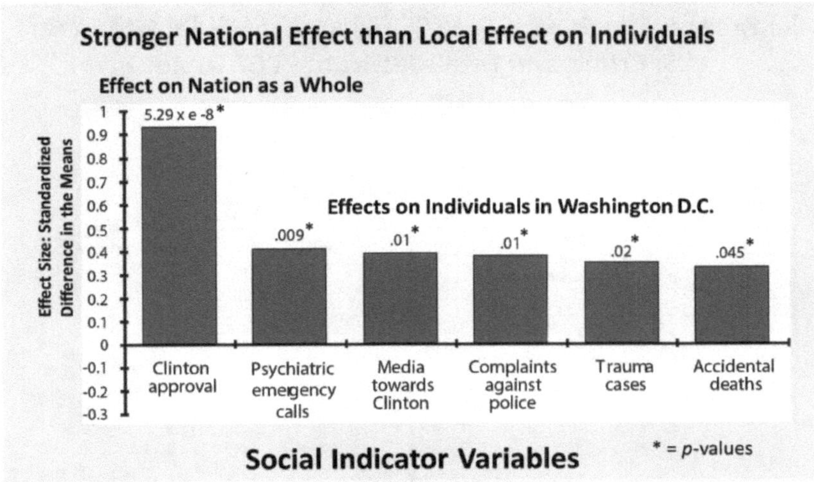

Fig. 2.4 Washington Peace Project

3. *The Invincible America Assembly (IAA) Project in Fairfield Iowa.* In one of the latest experiments, almost two thousand TM-Sidhas meditated together regularly in Fairfield, Iowa, from 2007 to 2011 (1% of the total US population). During that period, all the indicators of crime in the United States began to fall. Figure 2.5 shows the results from this multi-year, prospective super-radiance experiment in the United States (Cavanaugh & Dillbeck, 2017). This study shows that crime, drugs, and mortality rates dropped when the meditating group was in place. However, when the meditating group was removed, the numbers climbed back up again (Orme-Johnson, 2023).

The Interplay of AI and Yoga Sutras

The increasingly AI-driven world needs a countervailing force to create a sense of balance in life. *Yoga Sutras* provides the intellectual understanding of the various mechanisms to reach peace within oneself and in the world. As AI becomes increasingly integrated into various facets of life, this interplay can help us rethink the role of AI in enhancing human

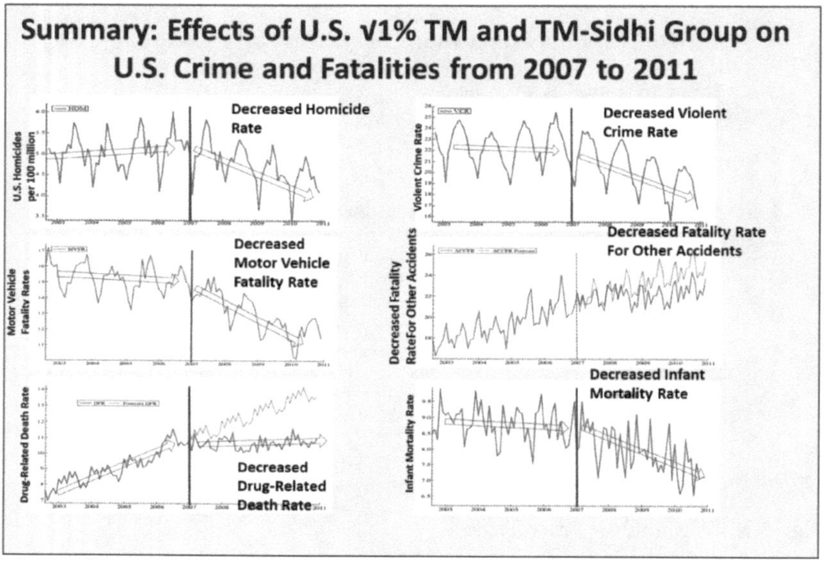

Fig. 2.5 Super-radiance effect: coherent collective consciousness improves Quality of Life

well-being, guiding ethical decisions, and fostering personal growth in the digital age. AI could support mental discipline by providing tools for mindfulness and meditation practices (Maheshwari & Biberman, 2024). On the other hand, AI may excite the mental tendencies, that the *Yoga Sutras* warn against—encouraging constant stimulation and external validation rather than inner peace and contentment. Through AI-driven meditation apps, personalized routines, and biofeedback devices, individuals can cultivate focus, reduce distractions, and develop deeper concentration. Similarly, AI algorithms can analyze brain activity or physical responses to suggest personalized meditation techniques, helping practitioners track their development of mental clarity and alignment. Balancing the use of AI with mindfulness and ethical reflection could allow individuals to benefit from AI without becoming overly reliant on it.

The *Yamas* and *Niyamas* can provide clear ethical guidelines for the design and deployment of AI systems. For instance, the principle of

Ahimsa can inspire AI to avoid harm, ensuring that AI technologies do not contribute to biases, surveillance, or unethical manipulation of data. Likewise, *Satya* can encourage transparency and honesty in AI algorithms, fostering trust in technology by prioritizing truth and openness in data handling and decision-making processes. The *Niyamas*, which focus on personal discipline, including *Tapas* (austerity) and *Svadhyaya* (self-study), can inform the way AI interacts with users. AI could encourage austerity and self-reflection through data-driven insights about behavior, health, and learning, through AI fitness trackers. Ethical AI can also help with the ultimate goal of the Yoga Sutras to achieve Samadhi, or a state of oneness (Maheshwari & Biberman, 2024).

Looking Ahead

Ideally, all life on earth would be guided by the timeless principles of *Yoga Sutras* for a healthy and peaceful world. By regularly transcending, one can experience peace within oneself. Enlightenment and bliss make it easier to continue to practice meditation and enjoy the enormous personal benefits of health and prosperity. The indirect benefit of more harmonious collective consciousness makes the world a better place and brings purpose and joy to everyone's life. Governments and business organizations around the world should pay attention to and invest in developing collective consciousness for a more just and harmonious society. Business organizations should encourage their employees to transcend regularly and together to create a harmonious and peaceful environment within the organization. Initiating youth into TM-Sidhis could lead to a large permanent transcending group, that would very rapidly transform the world into a peaceful place for all to enjoy.

The interplay between *Yoga Sutras* and AI creates an opportunity for enhancing the peace in the world by integrating ancient spiritual wisdom with modern technological advancements. When AI is guided by the principles of yoga, it can help humanity reach greater inner peace, ethical clarity, and higher consciousness. As we move forward into an increasingly AI-driven future, applying the teachings of the *Yoga Sutras* can ensure that AI is developed and used in ways that enhance personal and collective well-being, promoting both spiritual and technological harmony.

References

Anderson, G. L. (2018). The evolution of social consciousness and modern political theory. *International Journal of World Peace, 35*, 1.

Cavanaugh, K. L., & Dillbeck, M. C. (2017). Field effects of consciousness and reduction in U.S. urban murder rates: Evaluation of a prospective quasi-experiment. *Journal of Health and Environmental Research, 3*(3–1), 32–43.

Dillbeck, M. C., & Cavanaugh, K. L. (2017). Group practice of the Transcendental Meditation® and TM-Sidhi® program and reductions in infant mortality and drug-related death: A quasi-experimental analysis. *SAGE Open, 7*(1), 2158244017697164.

Gelot, L. M. (2018). Reclaiming the transcendence of positive peace against the violence of post-liberal peace. *International Journal of World Peace, 35*, 2.

Goleman, D. (1996). *The meditative mind: The varieties of meditative experience*. Tarcher. VFIM.

Goodman, R. S., Orme-Johnson, D. W., Rainforth, M. S., & Goodman, D. H. (1997). *Transforming political institutions through individual and collective consciousness*. Annual Meeting of the American Political Science Association; American Political Science Association.

Hagelin, J. S., Rainforth, M. V., Cavanaugh, K. L., Alexander, C. N., Shatkin, S. F., Davies, J. L., & Orme-Johnson, D. W. (1999). Effects of group practice of the transcendental meditation program on preventing violent crime in Washington, DC: Results of the National Demonstration Project, June–July 1993. *Social Indicators Research, 47*(2), 153–201.

Lederach, J. P. (2005). *The moral imagination: The art and soul of building peace*. Oxford University Press.

Maharishi, M. Y. (1963). *Science of being and art of living*. Signet.

Maharishi, M. Y. (1969). *On the Bhagavad-Gita: A new translation and commentary. Chapters 1–6*. Penguin.

Maharishi, M. Y. (1976). *Creating an ideal society: A global undertaking*. MERU Press.

Maharishi, M. Y. (1995). *Maharishi University of Management: Wholeness on the move*. MUM Press.

Maheshwari, A. K. (2021). Higher consciousness management: Transcendence for spontaneous right action. *Journal of Management, Spirituality & Religion, 18*(6), 77–91.

Maheshwari, A. K., & Pandey, N. (2022). Yoga sutras and spiritual entrepreneurship. In *WORLD SCIENTIFIC ENCYCLOPEDIA OF BUSINESS SUSTAINABILITY, ETHICS AND ENTREPRENEURSHIP* (pp. 291–314).

Maheshwari, A. K. (2023). Wholeness of consciousness-based leadership and management. In *Consciousness-based leadership and management, Volume 1:*

Vedic and other philosophical approaches to oneness and flourishing (pp. 3–25). Springer.

Maheshwari, A. K., & Biberman, J. (2024). Artificial oneness: Bridging the human machine divide. *Journal of Management, Spirituality & Religion.*

Nader, T. (1994). *Human physiology: Expression of Veda and the Vedic literature: modern science and ancient Vedic science discover the fabrics of immortality in human physiology*. Maharishi Vedic University.

Nader, T. (2015). Consciousness is all there is: A mathematical approach with applications. *International Journal of Mathematics and Consciousness, 1*(1), 1–65.

Nidich, S., Rainforth, M., Schneider, R., Salerno, J., & Gaylord-King, C. (2018). Non-trauma-focused meditation versus exposure therapy in veterans with post-traumatic stress disorder: A randomized controlled trial. *Lancet Psychiatry, 5*(12), 975–986.

Orme-Johnson, D. W. (2016). Factor analysis of social indicators in the Middle East: Effects of cultural, military, political, and climatic events and group practice of the Transcendental Meditation and TM-Sidhi programs. *Journal of Maharishi Vedic Research Institute, 1*(1), 5–39.

Orme-Johnson, D. W. (2023). Creating coherence in collective consciousness for universal flourishing: Automatic self-transcending for reducing conflicts and improving the quality of life in society. In *Consciousness-based leadership and management, Volume 1: Vedic and other philosophical approaches to oneness and flourishing* (pp. 121–149). Springer.

Orme-Johnson, D. W., Alexander, C. N., Davies, J. L., Chandler, H. M., & Larimore, W. E. (1988). Peace project in the Middle East: Effects of the Maharishi Technology of the Unified Field. *Journal of Conflict Resolution, 32*, 776–812.

Orme-Johnson, D. W., & Fergusson, L. (2018). Global impact of the Maharishi Effect from 1974 to 2017: Theory and research. *Journal of Maharishi Vedic Research Institute, 8*, 13–79.

Orme-Johnson, D. W., & Barnes, V. A. (2013). Effects of the transcendental meditation technique on trait anxiety: A Meta-analysis of randomized controlled trials. *The Journal of Alternative and Complementary Medicine., 19*, 1–12.

Rosenthal, N. (2009). *Transcendence: Healing and transformation through transcendental meditation.* Tarcher.

Tegmark, M. (2018). *Life 3.0: Being human in the age of artificial intelligence.* Vintage.

Travis, F. (2011). States of consciousness beyond waking, dreaming and sleeping: Perspectives from research on meditation experiences. In D. Certkovik & I. Cosvic (Eds.), *States of consciousness: Experimental insights into meditation, waking, sleep and dreams.* Frontier collection.

Travis, F., & Shear, J. (2010). Focused attention, open monitoring and automatic self-transcending: Categories to organize meditations from Vedic, Buddhist and Chinese traditions. *Consciousness and Cognition, 19*, 1110–1119.

Wallace, R. K. (1970). Physiological effects of transcendental meditation. *Science, 167*, 1751–1754.

Wilber, K. (1993). *The spectrum of consciousness*. Quest Books.

CHAPTER 3

Dharma Matrix: An Open Architecture for Ethical Decision-Making in the Age of AI

Anil K. Maheshwari, Sharda S. Nandram, and Payal Kumar

Introduction

Dharma is a foundational Vedic concept for upholding the universe, and approximately translates to righteousness and duty. It is a semi-normative concept that helps balance the external context along with inner consciousness to exercise discretion and action in a role. *Dharma* is facilitated by imbibing the norms and expectations of one's role(s) and learning all about the situation. *Dharma* ultimately helps with upholding the cosmic order while also guiding the individual in evolving oneself

A. K. Maheshwari (✉)
Maharishi International University, Fairfield, IA, USA
e-mail: akmaheshwari@miu.edu

S. S. Nandram
Nyenrode University, Breukelen, Netherlands
e-mail: S.Nandram@nyenrode.nl

P. Kumar
Indian Institute of Hospitality, Gurgaon, India

A. K. Maheshwari (ed.), *AI and Consciousness in Organizations and Society*, Palgrave Studies in Workplace Spirituality and Fulfillment,
https://doi.org/10.1007/978-3-031-91470-6_3

toward a higher consciousness. Unlike rigid prescriptive systems, *Dharma* functions as an open architecture framework, allowing for flexibility and adaptation to diverse contexts and personal circumstances. This paper further compares various *dharma* perspectives with Western ethical frameworks, including Aristotelian Virtue Ethics, Kantian Deontology, and Utilitarianism. Unlike Western models that often lean toward moral absolutism, *dharma's* open architecture accommodates diverse moral realities, making it applicable in various situations (Sharma, 2021, Mishra & Kalagnanam, 2022; Srinivas, 2021). Through practical examples, such as workplace dilemmas and classroom misconduct, this paper demonstrates how *Dharma's* seven modes of determining ethical action—including scripture, tradition, conscience, and reason—supported by AI tools and techniques, can help individuals practically navigate ethical challenges within a delicate moral relativistic framework (Clooney, 2013; Miller, 2020).

Dharma Sources

Dharma is a central and holistic concept to uphold the universe. It can be found across many branches of the vast Vedic philosophical literature, and encompasses a vast swath of norms including duties, rights, laws, conduct, virtues, and the right way of living. Many Vedic texts and traditions offer slightly different perspectives on dharma. The primary Vedic book, the *Rigveda*, associates *dharma* with the concept of "*ṛta*," or the cosmic order that regulates the universe. Thus, maintaining harmony with this cosmic order is considered the primary duty for everyone. The *Dharma Shastras* offer a prescriptive, structured approach to *Dharma*, grounding it in societal roles and duties based on caste and life stages (Doniger, 2020). The *Upanishads* emphasize the inner, spiritual aspect of *dharma*, and that understanding one's true self (Atman) and realizing its unity with Brahman (the ultimate reality) is the highest *dharma* (Ganeri, 2019). *Manusmriti* is a socially oriented text that describes *dharma* as duties and responsibilities for individuals based on their stage of life (*ashrama*) and caste (*varna*). The *Bhagavad Gita* offers a practical perspective on *dharma*, emphasizing the importance of performing one's personal duty (*svadharma*) without attachment to the results of the actions. It defines *karma yoga* (the path of selfless action) as a means to uphold *dharma*. The *Mahabharata*, which includes the *Bhagavad Gita*, considers numerous context-dependent complexities of *dharma* (Schroeder, 2018).

Lead characters like Yudhishthira, Arjuna, and Bhishma all face moral dilemmas and paradoxes, demonstrating that *dharma* can be contextually determined. Patanjali's *Yoga Sutras* define *dharma* through the *Yamas* (ethical restraints) and *Niyamas* (personal habits), focusing on moral and ethical conduct for spiritual growth. The *Puranas,* such as the ancient story of lord Rama in the *Ramayana,* use stories and fables to illustrate *dharma*. They show by example how deities and sages uphold *dharma* in a strict and absolutist sense of morality.

Dharmasastras

The *Dharma Shastras* are ancient Vedic texts that serve as legal and ethical manuals. All of these Dharma Shastras, composed over centuries, reflect the dynamic and evolving nature of *dharma* (law, duty, and righteousness) in ancient India. They are attributed to various sages and are not the work of a single author. The most famous among them include:

1. *Manu Smriti* (Laws of Manu): Traditionally attributed to the sage *Manu*, it is one of the earliest and most influential of the Dharma Shastras. It covers topics ranging from daily rituals to the duties of kings.
2. *Yajnavalkya Smriti*: Attributed to the sage *Yajnavalkya*, this text is known for its concise form and unique approach to dharma (moral and duty). It's particularly noted for its advancements in the understanding of inheritance laws.
3. *Narada Smriti*: Ascribed to the sage *Narada*, this text is primarily focused on judicial procedures and has been influential in shaping legal practice in ancient India.
4. *Parashara Smriti*: Attributed to the sage *Parashara*, it is considered important for understanding the transition periods between the different Yugas (eras) as it adapts dharma to the changing times.
5. *Vishnu Smriti*: Attributed to Lord Vishnu or sages who followed his teachings, this text focuses on religious duties, social laws, and rituals. It is relatively concise but is known for its detailed regulations on law and punishments.

6. *Katyayana Smriti*: Often attributed to the sage Katyayana, this text is more focused on judicial matters, laying down detailed rules on legal procedures, contracts, property laws, and the punishment for various offenses.
7. *Gautama Dharma Sutra*: One of the earliest texts in this genre, attributed to the sage Gautama. It is part of the Kalpa Sutras (ritualistic texts) and lays down rules for daily conduct, civil law, and punishment, serving as a guide for the duties of different castes and life stages.
8. *Baudhayana Dharma Sutra*: Attributed to the sage Baudhayana, it provides insights into legal norms, rituals, and societal duties, including rules for marriage, inheritance, and penance.
9. *Apastamba Dharma Sutra*: Attributed to the sage Apastamba, this text is known for its pragmatic approach, emphasizing both the spiritual and social aspects of life. It contains teachings on moral behavior, rituals, and family laws.
10. *Vashistha Dharma Sutra*: Ascribed to the sage Vashistha, this work is another early text outlining rules for personal conduct, ethical behavior, and the duties of different social groups, especially regarding religious observances.

Dharmasastras collectively provide a holistic framework of moral, legal, and social principles and laws, around the concept of *Dharma*, to guide all sections of society in pursuit of a just and harmonious society. Each text was meant to be adaptable, and their ethical and moral principles included the flexibility and moral relativism to taking into account the different needs of individuals and society to suit diverse contexts and eras (Clooney, 2013). Here are 10 key principles of *Dharmasastras*.

1. *Dharma* (Righteous Duty): The concept of *Dharma* itself represents moral and ethical duties, obligations, and responsibilities that an individual should discharge to uphold society, family, and self. It emphasizes righteous conduct, promoting truthfulness and non-violence, and fairness in all actions, to ensure that people act in ways that uphold ethical standards.
2. *Varna* and *Ashrama* System: Moral relativism of righteousness comes in two major ways. The varna system categorizes society into four groups: *Brahmins* (priests), *Kshatriyas* (warriors), *Vaishyas*

(merchants), and *Shudras* (laborers), each with distinct duties. Alongside this, the *ashrama* system describes four life stages—*Brahmacharya* (student), *Grihastha* (householder), *Vanaprastha* (retiree), and *Sannyasa* (renunciate)—each with specific responsibilities.

3. *Karma* (Action): *Dharma* never permits shirking of righteous duties. *Karma* is an individual's actions, whether good or bad, that directly shape their future. Righteous actions in alignment with *Dharma* yield positive outcomes, while negative actions bring adverse consequences.
4. Raja *Dharma* (Duties of a King): The duties of a king focus on maintaining justice, law, and order. A ruler is responsible for ensuring security, administering justice, and leading with righteousness, while always guided by *Dharma*.
5. *Nyaya* (Justice): Justice is founded on fairness, truth, and equity. The texts address legal matters like property rights, inheritance, and criminal law, emphasizing the protection of the weak and ensuring justice is accessible to all, regardless of status.
6. *Ahimsa* (Non-Violence): Non-violence toward all living beings is a core principle of peaceful coexistence. *Ahimsa* is regarded as a superior ethical practice, encouraging individuals and rulers to pursue peace and minimize violence in their actions and decisions.
7. *Yajna* and *Dana*: Sacred rituals (*yajna*) and charity (*dana*) are considered key duties. Performing these acts is believed to foster spiritual development and betterment of society, thus blending personal growth with social responsibility.
8. Punishment and Redemption: Punishment is viewed as a corrective tool to restore order in society. *Dharma* includes the possibility of redemption. Wrongdoers are given opportunities for repentance, ensuring that punitive justice is balanced with compassion and moral recovery.
9. Women and Family: *Dharma* outlines familial roles and responsibilities emphasizing the respectful treatment of women, and the protection of vulnerable family members, such as children and the elderly, underlining the family's foundational role in society.
10. Spiritual Progress: Beyond fulfilling material and social duties, *Dharma* encourages individuals to seek personal spiritual growth through meditation, discipline, and detachment from material

desires. The ultimate aim is *moksha*, or liberation from the cycle of rebirth.

Dharmasastras are a primary source for moral and ethical behavior guidance that incorporates elements of moral relativism, and prescribing duties, rights, and justice according to social roles, life stages, and contexts.

Dharma in Other Scriptures

Other major scriptures such as the *Upanishads, Yoga Sutras, Mahabharata*, and *Ramayana*, also present different or nuanced perspectives on moral obligations, social order, and spiritual goals. This creates an open architecture for *dharma*, with moral relativism, that may have helped the Vedic philosophy persist over the millennia.

Ramayana presents an idealized version of *Dharma*. It portrays *Dharma* as absolute, focusing on fulfilling societal and familial responsibilities. Lord Rama embodies unwavering commitment to duty, regardless of the personal cost and circumstances. However, even here, moral relativism subtly appears as characters like *Sita* and *Bharata* face unique moral challenges that differ from traditional expectations.

The *Upanishads* offer a transcendental view of *Dharma*, focusing less on societal roles and more on self-realization and spiritual liberation for all individuals. *Dharma* here is universal, guiding individuals to understand the Oneness of *Atman* and *Brahman*, over-riding the adhering to social structures. This view presents a much more absolutist norm of dharma by valuing inner spiritual truth over external societal duties, emphasizing personal transformation over collective norms.

The *Yoga Sutras* do not take a rigid view of *Dharma*, but one that is deeply intertwined with the principle of contextual morality. The *Yoga Sutras* recognize that right action can be situational, requiring discernment and adaptability according to *Viveka* (discernment), a refined sense of judgment that helps navigate the often-ambiguous path of *Dharma*, ensuring that actions contribute to both personal and collective well-being. The *Sidhis* require supreme adherence to principles, so Yoga Sutras provide for variable interpretation, depending upon one's goals.

In the *Mahabharata*, *Dharma* becomes highly context-driven. Characters like Arjuna and Yudhishthira face conflicting duties and complex dilemmas, which necessarily require moral relativism. What is "right" shifts based on one's perception of the totality of the context? The *Mahabharata's* open architecture allows *Dharma* to adapt to real-world challenges, highlighting the ambiguity and pragmatic nature of righteous action, which is very ably conveyed by the *Bhagavad Gita*, which forms the core of the *Mahabharata*.

Table 3.1 summarizes the varying perspectives on Dharma across these texts, illustrating the balance between fixed principles and moral relativism.

Determining *Dharma* in Context

There are seven primary sources for *Dharma*. These include scriptures, tradition, conscience, reason, guidance from wise individuals, examples of virtuous people, and divine inspiration. Here is how one might approach making decisions based on these sources:

1. Scriptures (*Shruti* and *Smriti*): As discussed above, Vedic texts like the *Upanishads*, *Dharmasastras*, *Mahabharata*, and *Ramayana* offer guidelines on *Dharma*, providing clarity on ethical and social duties. Scriptures serve as a foundational reference for traditional principles but require flexible interpretation for modern contexts.
2. Tradition (*Sampradaya*): Tradition refers to customs and societal norms passed through generations. It is useful in decisions involving social roles, family duties, and community rituals. While tradition holds value, it is important to assess its contemporary contextual relevance.
3. Conscience (*Atma Santushti*): Conscience is the inner voice that guides individuals through personal moral dilemmas. It is essential when no external guidance is available, and decisions are best made by reflecting inwardly while aligning with ethical principles.
4. Reason (*Yukti*): Reason involves logical thinking to navigate complex dilemmas where scripture or tradition may not provide clear answers. Rational analysis helps determine the consequences of actions, emphasizing long-term effects on oneself and society.
5. Guidance from Wise Individuals (*Gurus*, Elders, or Mentors): Consulting experienced individuals offers insights based on wisdom. Their guidance is valuable; however, it should be combined with personal judgment and ethical reflection.

Table 3.1 Comparing the concept of Dharma across Dharmasastra, Mahabharata, Upanishads, and Ramayana

Aspect	*Dharmasastra*	*Mahabharata*	*Upanishads*	*Ramayana*
Nature of Dharma	Morally relative. Based on caste and life stage	Context-driven. Adapting to practical situations	Transcendental. Focused on self-realization	Idealized. Strict adherence to societal and familial duties
Social Order	Fixed. Promote social harmony through well-defined roles	Flexible. Moral dilemmas lead to ambiguity	More focus on spiritual liberation	Fixed. Strict adherence to societal roles and responsibilities
Spiritual Focus	Spiritual progress through *Dharma*	Balance social duty with spiritual wisdom	Self-realization based on the unity of *Atman* and *Brahman*	More focus on societal harmony
Karma (action) vs. *Jnana* (wisdom)	Focus on *Karma* (righteous action, duty)	Balance between *Karma* and *Jnana* (action with wisdom)	Focus on *Jnana* (self-knowledge, realization)	Focus on strict *Karma* (perfect fulfillment of duties)
Role of the Individual	Fixed. Defined by social identity	Complex. Balancing personal and social duties	Transcendental self (Atman). Beyond social identity	Fixed. Strict adherence to social role and identity
Moral Relativism	Duties vary by caste and stage	Right action shifting based on context	Inner spiritual truth over external duties reflects relativism	Low flexibility
Open Architecture	*Dharma* tied to societal roles, norms	High flexibility. Adapt Karma to real dilemmas	Dharma focused on universal truth and self-realization	Strict Dharma, but allows subtle moral complexity

Aspect	*Dharmasastra*	*Mahabharata*	*Upanishads*	*Ramayana*
Ultimate Goal	Righteous living, better rebirth or eventual *Moksha*	*Svadharma* (personal duty) balanced with spiritual growth	*Moksha* (liberation through self-realization)	Strict adherence to Dharma, for personal and cosmic harmony
Dharma in Practice	Follow prescribed duties, social and moral laws	Complex and ambiguous. Manage conflicts with morality	Transcendence of material world through meditation & wisdom	Ideal adherence to duty. Minimal deviation from societal roles

6. Virtuous Role Models (*Sadachara*): Learning from the actions of virtuous individuals provides real-life models of ethical behavior. However, it should also be adapted to one's unique context.
7. Divine Inspiration: Spiritual intuition and divine guidance, experienced through meditation or prayer, can offer deep insights during moments of spiritual crisis or when seeking moral clarity.

Dharma Matrix

We find personal and social elements in *Dharma*. There are also real-world and transcendental elements in *Dharma*. Inspired by Wilber's four quadrant model, we encapsulate the complexity and richness of *Dharma* in a 2 × 2 *Dharma Matrix*. One dimension is material needs versus spiritual evolution. The other dimension is focusing on individual needs versus the needs of society (Table 3.2).

Table 3.2 Dharma matrix

	Swadharma *(Personal)*	Sanatana *Dharma (Social)*
Material (*Artha/ Kama*)	Material *Swadharma* *Shouldering responsibility*. Fulfilling one's material duties and responsibilities according to role in society. For example, a businessperson focusing on ethical profit-making	Material *Sanatana Dharma* *Loka-sangraha*. Upholding universal material duties, contributing to society's economic and social welfare, engaging in charitable actions, and ensuring social justice
Spiritual (*Moksha/ Dharma*)	Spiritual *Swadharma* *Yama - Niyama*. Pursuing one's spiritual path according to one's personal inclinations and role. This might include spiritual practices, meditation, or self-study aligned with personal growth	Spiritual *Sanatan Dharma* or *Life as Yagya*. Adhering to universal spiritual duties, such as compassion, non-violence, truthfulness, and love, which are universally applicable regardless of personal inclination

1. Material *Swadharma*: *Artha* is the individual's duty to fulfill their personal material responsibilities. It focuses on the specific roles one plays in society (such as a student's duty to study, a parent's duty to provide for their family) and performing these duties ethically and to the best of one's ability.
2. Material *Sanatan Dharma*: *Kama* covers universal duties in the material realm. It emphasizes the idea that while fulfilling one's material duties, one should also adhere to principles like fairness and justice, and social service and charity, which are considered universal principles applicable to all.
3. Spiritual *Swadharma*: The personal spiritual evolutionary journey is the small d—i.e., *dharma*. It focuses on selecting and following a unique path toward spiritual growth and self-realization, which might include meditation, worship, and other spiritual practices that align with one's individual nature and inclinations.
4. Spiritual *Sanatan Dharma*: *Moksha*, the universal spiritual goals and principles that apply to all beings. It encompasses duties like compassion, truth, non-violence, and the pursuit of spiritual wisdom. These are principles that transcend individual paths and are considered eternal and universal.

The *Dharma* Matrix can be useful in navigating through a maze of considerations for effective decision-making in context. This matrix provides a way to think about how different aspects of life—both material and spiritual—intersect with individual and universal duties. Each cell should be tended to different levels in different contexts.

Dharma vs Western Ethics and Virtues

Western notions of ethics and virtues are an important contemporary driver for decision-making. A western reader who has no knowledge of the Vedas may end up feeling confused, as *dharma* is presented in different ways in many of the ancient texts. We may need to emphasize that all these views are complementary, rather than contradictory. A comparison between *Dharma* traditions and Western ethics and virtues traditions highlights both similarities and key differences in their approaches to personal and social development. Whereas *Dharma* traditions emphasize duty, social roles, spiritual growth, and situational ethics.

Western traditions are more individual-oriented and offer frameworks that focus on individual virtues, moral duties, and consequences.

1. Duty vs Virtue: In *Dharmasastra* and *Mahabharata*, *Dharma* is morally relative and specific to one's social role, caste, or context (Sharma, 2021). In Aristotle's Virtue Ethics, there is emphasis on developing character traits (virtues) like courage, temperance, and justice. Virtue is cultivated through practice and leads to a fulfilling life (eudaimonia).
2. Absolutism vs. Relativism: In *Ramayana* and *Dharmasastra*, *Dharma* is often portrayed as absolute, with clear rules and expectations for each social group and role. However, in *Mahabharata*, *Dharma* is fluid and can adapt to complex moral dilemmas. Kantian Deontology asserts that moral duties are absolute and universal. Kant's categorical imperative demands that actions be guided by maxims that could be universal laws, emphasizing duty over consequences (Schroeder, 2018).
3. Consequences of Actions: In *Upanishads* and *Mahabharata*, *Dharma* is tied to the concept of *Karma*—doing the right actions without worrying about their consequences. This ties closely to spiritual progress and the ultimate goal of *Moksha* (liberation) Utilitarianism, on the other hand, focuses on the consequences of actions. The ethical value of an action is to maximize happiness or utility for the greatest number (Schroeder, 2018).
4. Role of Self vs Community: The *Upanishads* focus on self-realization and inner growth, viewing *Dharma* as the duty to transcend the material world and realize one's unity with *Brahman*. The *Ramayana*, however, places greater emphasis on fulfilling one's duties to the community, family, and society, with personal sacrifice often required for the greater good. Western traditions also focus on the self and community. Aristotle emphasizes personal virtue development as a path to individual flourishing, while Kant focuses on fulfilling moral duties toward others out of respect for their autonomy (Schroeder, 2018).
5. Spiritual Goals vs Secular Ethics: Spiritual liberation (*Moksha*) is the ultimate goal in Eastern traditions. *Dharma* is a means to achieve both personal spiritual growth and societal harmony (Sharma, 2021). The *Mahabharata* shows that worldly actions, when aligned with *Dharma*, can lead to spiritual evolution. In contrast, Western

ethical systems are largely secular. Aristotle's virtue ethics aims for *eudaimonia* (flourishing) in a worldly sense, while Kant and Mill focus on moral duty and the consequences of actions (Schroeder, 2018).

Table 3.3 summarizes the *Dharma* traditions and Western moral frameworks. *Dharma* has multiple perspectives in the *Dharma Matrix*. There are also many overlapping perspectives from the Western ethics and virtues traditions. In a nutshell, *Dharma* traditions emphasize a balance between social roles, ethical duties, and spiritual growth, often reflecting moral relativism in complex situations. Western ethics emphasize personal virtue and universal duties, often grounded in secular reasoning and individual rights. Here are a few key parallels between the two.

1. *Dharmasastras* align with Kantian Deontology in terms of its duty-based approach to ethics, where one must follow specific rules and obligations based on their social role. However, the social context in *Dharmasastras* is more rigid, while Kant emphasizes individual autonomy.
2. *Upanishads* parallel the idea of transcendence and inner contemplation found in Virtue Ethics (*eudaimonia*, or flourishing). However, while Virtue Ethics emphasizes character development, the *Upanishads* emphasize self-knowledge leading to liberation (*moksha*).
3. *Mahabharata* offers a more situational view of ethics, closer to Virtue Ethics, where decisions are made based on wisdom applied to the complexity of real-life scenarios. Its pragmatic approach, where context shapes the right action, resonates with Aristotelian practical wisdom (phronesis).
4. *Ramayana* reflects a strict adherence to duty and moral principles, aligning with Deontological Ethics, but with an idealized focus on maintaining cosmic and social order.

Dharma and AI

The rise of AI has the potential to significantly alter how the concept of *Dharma* and virtues are understood and applied in organizational and ethical decision-making. AI's capacity to process vast amounts of data and provide personalized insights can complement and transform *Dharma's*

Table 3.3 Comparing Eastern *Dharma* traditions with Western ethics and virtues frameworks

Aspect	*Eastern Dharma traditions*	*Western ethics and virtue frameworks*
Concept of duty and virtue	Dharma is role-specific and tied to social order. Moral relativism in Mahabharata reflects context-dependent Dharma	Aristotelian Virtue Ethics focuses on developing virtues like courage, temperance, and justice, leading to a fulfilling life (eudaimonia)
Absolutism vs. relativism	Dharma can be absolute in Ramayana. Mahabharata introduces moral relativism based on context	Kantian Deontology emphasizes absolute, universal moral duties via the categorical imperative
Consequences of actions	Actions (Karma) directly impact spiritual progress and future outcomes	Utilitarianism (Mill, Bentham) is based on the consequences of action, aiming to maximize overall happiness
Role of self and community	Primary focus is on self-realization (Atman-Brahman) while fulfilling social responsibilities for the greater good is also emphasized	Aristotle emphasizes personal virtue for flourishing, while Kant stresses moral duties toward others
Spiritual goals vs. secular ethics	Dharma leads to Moksha (spiritual liberation) alongside societal harmony	Largely secular goals, focusing on personal flourishing (eudaimonia) and fulfilling moral duties without spiritual dimensions

open architecture, allowing for more nuanced and adaptive approaches to ethical dilemmas in modern contexts.

1. Personal Assistant: AI's ability to offer customized feedback also aligns with the *Dharmic* emphasis on context-sensitive decision-making. AI could provide tools that allow individuals to analyze the ethical implications of their actions within specific contexts. For example, AI could help leaders evaluate the long-term impact

of their decisions on various stakeholders, enabling them to better fulfill their duties (*Svadharma*) while balancing moral relativism and universal ethical principles.

2. Virtual advisor: *Dharma* traditionally draws upon multiple modes of determining ethical action, such as scripture, conscience, and guidance from wise individuals. AI can act as a new virtual "wise advisor," offering data-driven insights and recommendations based on ethical frameworks programmed into its algorithms. For instance, AI systems could help identify potential biases, legal risks, or ethical concerns in business decisions, allowing individuals to align their actions with broader *Dharma* principles such as fairness (*Nyaya*) and non-harm (*Ahimsa*). This can support Spiritual *swadharma* of the *Dharma* Matrix.
3. Spiritual development: Additionally, AI can facilitate a greater alignment of ethical decision-making with personal spiritual growth. As AI platforms increasingly incorporate consciousness-based education and mindfulness practices, individuals can integrate *Dharma's* spiritual dimensions, such as the pursuit of *Moksha* (liberation), with their professional roles. AI can recommend meditative or reflective practices to help individuals cultivate self-awareness (*Atma Santushti*), aligning personal growth with ethical decision-making.
4. Cosmic compassion: AI has the potential to democratize access to virtuous role models and ethical guidelines. By integrating vast databases of historical examples and virtuous leaders from various cultural traditions, AI can provide users with personalized suggestions on how to emulate virtuous behavior in a given situation. This feature could encourage individuals to adapt ethical behavior tailored to their specific roles and responsibilities, much like *Dharma* adjusts according to caste and life stage.

However, the integration of AI into *Dharma* presents challenges as well.

1. The reliance on AI for ethical guidance may risk reducing the role of personal conscience and critical reasoning, which are fundamental to the *Dharmic* process.
2. The programming of AI with ethical frameworks may raise concerns about whose interpretation of *Dharma* or virtue ethics is being

encoded, potentially reinforcing specific biases. It often hallucinates and can make things up, as things are currently.

How should a management practitioner, from the East or the West, know how to follow their *dharma*, especially in the fast-changing age of AI? Here are two scenarios of how *Dharma* and AI may help with ethical decision-making.

Scenario 1: Woman of Color Facing a Difficult Decision at Work

Maya, a senior manager and woman of color at a tech company, is confronted with a difficult decision as her team prepares to launch a new AI-driven product. Upon reviewing the product's algorithm, Maya discovers a bias that disproportionately affects marginalized communities, particularly people of color. The leadership team, focused on deadlines and profitability, pushes to move forward with the launch, downplaying the issue. Maya's conscience, however, urges her to address the bias before the product goes live, forcing her to balance corporate expectations, ethical obligations, and her own personal values.

Dharma Matrix suggests that Maya's responsibility is to act in alignment with both her professional role and her personal sense of duty toward social justice. Drawing on the principle of *Ahimsa* (non-harming) from ancient Vedic texts, she is guided to avoid causing harm, especially to vulnerable groups. *Dharma* teaches that one's actions should benefit the larger good, and Maya recognizes that releasing a biased product would violate her ethical duty to protect marginalized users. Her *Dharma*, therefore, calls her to speak up and address the issue, even if it risks tension within the company.

From an ethics and virtues perspective, Maya faces a moral dilemma. Kantian deontology would suggest that Maya has a duty to ensure fairness and equality, as allowing the biased algorithm to launch would violate the principle of justice. From an Aristotelian perspective, Maya is called to cultivate courage and integrity in her actions, standing up for what is right despite the potential personal and professional risks. She also considers utilitarianism, weighing the consequences of her actions: while delaying the launch might have short-term financial implications, correcting the bias would benefit society in the long run by ensuring that the product serves all users fairly.

From an AI perspective, data-driven objective solutions can support Maya in her decision-making and implementation processes. From a *dharma* matrix's material *swadharma* perspective, AI-driven auditing tools could be employed to analyze the algorithm for bias, providing concrete data that Maya can use to present her case to the leadership team. These tools can help identify where and how the bias occurs, offering a clear path for remediation before the product is launched. AI's capacity to provide an evidence-based argument strengthens Maya's position, showing that addressing the bias now would not only align with ethical standards but also mitigate potential long-term reputational and legal risks for the company. From a Spiritual *swadharma* perspective, AI tools designed for ethical decision-making can help Maya model different scenarios, analyzing the potential outcomes of launching the product with or without adjustments. Such tools could quantify the risk of negative press, user dissatisfaction, and even legal action, offering a comprehensive view of how the decision could impact the company's bottom line and societal reputation. From a material *sanatan dharma* perspective, AI-enhanced mindfulness and reflection tools can help Maya align with her inner sense of Dharma through meditation and reflective practices. These tools provide Maya with the mental clarity needed to navigate the stress and uncertainty of challenging the status quo, ensuring that her actions are rooted in both ethical reasoning and spiritual grounding. From a spiritual *sanatan dharma* perspective, AI can help Maya navigate the organizational dynamics and cultural resistance she may face. AI-driven platforms that facilitate communication across teams can assist Maya in framing her concerns in a way that resonates with her colleagues and superiors, emphasizing the business case for ethical AI. These platforms can guide Maya in developing communication strategies that bridge the gap between her ethical concerns and the company's financial goals, allowing her to advocate for a more socially responsible approach without alienating her leadership. AI-powered diversity and inclusion tools could assist Maya in tracking the long-term impact of her actions.

Ultimately, Maya chooses to speak up and advocate for addressing the algorithm's bias before launching the product. She uses AI tools to support her argument, presenting evidence of the bias and offering data-driven solutions. Her actions align with her *dharma*, ethical principles, and the long-term well-being of the company. Maya's decision not only reflects her personal integrity but also inspires a shift toward more inclusive practices within the organization. Through this experience, Maya's case demonstrates how *dharma*, ethics, and AI can work together to guide decision-making in complex corporate environments, while promoting fairness and justice for all.

Scenario 2: Professor Facing Student Misconduct

Dr. Williams, a senior professor teaching data science, faces a dilemma regarding declining student engagement, rampant plagiarism, and an increasing sense of entitlement among students who expect high grades without demonstrating mastery of the material. Faced with maintaining academic integrity and ensuring that her students genuinely learn, Dr. Williams must decide how to address these issues in a way that upholds her ethical responsibilities while fostering an environment of growth.

From a *Dharma* perspective, Dr. Williams is guided by the principles of truthfulness and fairness, which demand that she confront the issue of plagiarism directly. *Dharma* emphasizes the importance of integrity and justice, reminding Dr. Williams that allowing dishonest practices to persist would harm not only the individual students but the academic community as a whole. Her role as an educator carries the duty to uphold the highest standards of academic rigor and ethical behavior, which requires addressing misconduct with clarity and fairness. Tradition demands that Dr. Williams follow University guidelines and policies which uphold these values and advocate for strict enforcement of rules against plagiarism and academic dishonesty.

From an ethical perspective, Dr. Williams feels a moral obligation to help students develop not only academically but also as ethical individuals. Allowing plagiarism to go unchecked would leave her students unprepared for future challenges. Her conscience pushes her to create an environment where students can learn the value of hard work, honesty, and responsibility, knowing that these qualities will serve them far beyond the classroom. Dr. Williams also recognizes that ignoring plagiarism would have long-term negative consequences for students who graduate without having truly earned their degrees. By enforcing academic integrity, she protects both the institution's standing and the students' prospects. Addressing these issues now is the logical choice, ensuring the long-term success of the students and the university. Dr. Williams consults with her colleagues and mentors who have faced similar challenges. These discussions help her balance discipline with compassion, offering her insights on how to address plagiarism without alienating students. Finally, through spiritual reflection and meditation, Dr. Williams connects with her deeper sense of purpose as an educator. She realizes that her Dharma involves nurturing her students' personal and ethical development. This spiritual insight reinforces her commitment to ensuring that students leave her class with not only the knowledge they need but also the moral framework to navigate future challenges with integrity.

From an AI perspective, it provides Dr. Williams with tools to address these challenges more effectively. From a *dharma* matrix's material *swadharma* perspective, AI-driven plagiarism detection tools, for instance, allow her to quickly identify instances of academic dishonesty, ensuring that students are held accountable for their work. From a *spiritual dharma* perspective, AI-based learning analytics can help Dr. Williams better understand why students may be disengaged or resorting to dishonest practices. This insight allows Dr. Williams to tailor her teaching methods, offer additional resources, or even suggest personalized learning pathways for students who need extra support. AI can also assist Dr. Williams in implementing a flipped classroom model, where students engage with materials outside of class and use in-person sessions for deeper discussions and problem-solving. From a material *sanatan dharma* perspective, AI can assist Dr. Williams in aligning with her inner *Dharma* through meditative practices which she also recommends to her students to help them clear their minds of external pressures and temptations to cut corners and focus on greater and joyful learning. From a spiritual *sanatan dharma* perspective, AI-powered communication tools enable Dr. Williams to maintain continuous dialogue with her students and peers and administrators, offering feedback in real-time on ethical issues like plagiarism in a larger context.

By integrating *Dharma*, ethics, and AI, Dr. Williams creates a balanced approach that not only enforces academic integrity and standards but also offers students the support and resources they need to succeed. She opts to use stricter plagiarism detection alongside workshops on honesty and study skills, ensuring that her students understand the value of academic integrity. Dr. Williams demonstrates how *Dharma* and ethics, complemented by technology, can create a more responsible and effective educational environment.

Discussion

The exploration of *Dharma* as an open architecture for ethical decision-making reveals its unique adaptability and makes it a powerful framework for navigating the complexities of organizational ethics. The introduction of the novel *Dharma* Matrix provides four different perspectives on how *dharmic* decisions should be made and implemented with help from AI tools and technologies. The integration of *Dharma* with AI technologies presents an innovative approach to addressing ethical challenges in dynamic environments. This discussion highlights how the flexible yet structured nature of *Dharma*, when combined with the power of AI, can facilitate ethical decision-making in organizations.

Dharma's ability to accommodate both moral relativism and universal ethical principles is one of its greatest strengths. Unlike rigid ethical systems that impose absolute rules, Dharma considers the context and social roles of individuals, as seen in the *Dharmasastras'* prescriptive, duty-based approach and the *Mahabharata's* depiction of complex, situational ethics. This flexibility allows decision-makers to adapt ethical principles to their specific circumstances, making *Dharma* particularly relevant in organizations where diverse ethical dilemmas arise. In the workplace, for example, individuals are often faced with competing duties: loyalty to the company, fairness to employees, and responsibility to society. *Dharma's* framework, which includes scripture, tradition, conscience, reason, guidance from wise individuals, examples of virtuous people, and divine inspiration, offers multiple pathways for ethical reflection. AI further enhances these pathways by providing data-driven predictions that align with Dharma's core principles, enabling decision-makers to make well-rounded, informed choices.

AI's Role in Supporting Ethical Decision-Making

The integration of AI into ethical decision-making offers new possibilities for applying *Dharma* in organizational contexts. AI's ability to process vast amounts of data, detect biases, and simulate ethical scenarios complements *Dharma's* emphasis on contextual decision-making. For instance, AI can provide predictive analytics and risk assessments, helping individuals understand the long-term consequences of their actions, much like the reasoning (*Yukti*) mode in *Dharma*. In the case study of Maya, a senior manager discovering bias in an algorithm, AI tools could support her ethical decision-making by analyzing the algorithm's impact on marginalized communities. This data would enable Maya to present a more compelling, evidence-based argument to her leadership team, aligning her actions with the *Dharmic* principles of fairness and collective well-being. In this way, AI not only aids in identifying ethical issues but also strengthens the ethical reasoning process. Furthermore, AI's ability to customize ethical feedback and provide tailored recommendations is aligned with *Dharma's* context-sensitive nature. By mapping *Dharma's* seven modes of determining ethical action to specific scenarios, AI can offer personalized guidance that resonates with an individual's role and duties. The intersection of *Dharma* and AI thus creates a more adaptive, responsive ethical framework that can evolve alongside organizational needs and challenges.

While AI can enhance ethical decision-making, the reliance on AI for ethical guidance should not overshadow the human capacity for reflection, conscience, and wisdom—that are the central tenets of *Dharma*. AI's role should be complementary, providing data and predictions while leaving the final ethical decision to human judgment. This ensures that the spiritual and personal growth aspects of *Dharma*, such as self-realization and moral responsibility, are not diminished in favor of efficiency or automation. Moreover, the training of AI with ethical principles introduces the question of which interpretation of *Dharma* or virtue ethics is being encoded. Ethical frameworks programmed into AI should be inclusive, reflecting a diverse range of cultural and philosophical perspectives to avoid reinforcing specific biases. The ethical governance of AI should therefore align with the universal principles of fairness and equity that Dharma advocates.

Implications for Organizations

For organizations, the combination of *Dharma* principles and AI tools presents a holistic approach to navigating ethical challenges. AI can assist in aligning corporate actions with ethical standards, while *Dharma* provides a deeper, spiritual foundation that goes beyond mere compliance. By integrating both, organizations can foster environments that promote both ethical rigor and compassion. Leadership development is another area where *Dharma* and AI can converge. AI-powered tools can help leaders make more informed, ethical decisions by offering real-time feedback on the impact of their choices. Meanwhile, *Dharma's* focus on the inner development of virtues like courage, integrity, and fairness can guide leaders toward a more holistic, ethical leadership model. This approach not only enhances organizational ethics but also contributes to personal and professional growth.

Future Directions

The open architecture of *Dharma* offers a flexible and comprehensive platform for ethical decision-making. A key area for further investigation is how the *Dharma* Matrix can be effectively applied to contemporary organizational ethics, particularly within multinational corporations operating across diverse cultural contexts. Studying how *Dharma's* inherent adaptability to different social roles and life stages can lead to more inclusive, context-sensitive ethical policies will be crucial for advancing global business ethics. Furthermore, the integration of *Dharma* into leadership development programs offers an opportunity to cultivate a new model of ethical leadership—one that balances moral relativism with universal principles, fostering leaders who are both compassionate and effective across multicultural environments.

Comparative studies between *Dharma* and Western ethical systems should be expanded to include case studies from diverse sectors—such as education, healthcare, and governance—to assess the practical application of *Dharma's* ethical framework in real-world dilemmas. Continued exploration of *Dharma's* unique blend of moral relativism and universal principles will contribute to the development of a more holistic and inclusive approach to ethics, in the increasingly globalized and interconnected world. This research will ultimately enhance the understanding of how ethical frameworks can be both context-sensitive and universally grounded, supporting more ethical and sustainable decision-making across various industries. Another significant direction for future research is the ethical dilemmas related to fairness, bias, and transparency in the realm of AI and machine learning. Examining how *Dharma's* flexible ethical principles can inform AI ethics offers the potential for developing more nuanced, responsible approaches to technology development and deployment. Research could focus on how *Dharma's* emphasis on personal spiritual growth may enhance employee well-being and contribute to organizational sustainability.

Future research could focus on how AI can support *Dharma's* flexible approach to ethical leadership, fostering leaders who balance moral relativism with universal principles, while navigating diverse, multicultural settings. By continuing to explore the integration of *Dharma* and AI, scholars and practitioners can contribute to a more holistic, inclusive, and effective framework for ethical decision-making, grounded in both spiritual and technological progress. This evolving framework will support more ethical leadership and decision-making, ultimately fostering sustainable and just outcomes in a rapidly changing world.

Conclusion

Dharma, across Vedic philosophical traditions, offers a unique open architecture that balances moral relativism and universal principles. *Dharmasastras'* duty-based approach contrasts with the *Upanishads'* focus on spiritual liberation, while the *Mahabharata* introduces situational ethics, and the *Ramayana* portrays strict adherence to duty. This flexibility, when compared with Western ethical frameworks such as Virtue Ethics and Kantian Deontology, allows *Dharma* to function as an adaptable ethical system, accommodating various contexts and moral dilemmas. Whether in academia, corporate settings, or technology-driven industries, *Dharma's* seven modes of determining ethical action provide a comprehensive framework for ethical reflection.

The integration of AI into the ethical decision-making framework of *Dharma* offers a powerful, context-sensitive approach for addressing modern organizational challenges. AI's ability to analyze data, predict outcomes, and provide personalized ethical guidance complements *Dharma's* flexible architecture. This combination allows for greater inclusivity, fairness, and integrity in decision-making, ensuring that both individuals and organizations act in alignment with their ethical duties while navigating the complexities of today's rapidly changing world. However, it is crucial that AI enhances rather than replaces human reflection and moral responsibility, maintaining the central role of conscience and wisdom in ethical deliberation.

In a rapidly changing and complex world, individuals must navigate multiple roles in society, each demanding different priorities and actions. *Dharma*, which upholds everything that exists, embraces this complexity by encompassing diverse roles, contexts, spaces, and times. This is why *Dharma* manifests differently across various scriptures, with each scripture serving a distinct purpose tailored to specific life goals and stages.

Comparing all ways *Dharma* is described in these texts misses the point of their unique roles and intentions.

Unlike many ethical frameworks that lean toward universal principles, *Dharma* uniquely integrates an observer-centric perspective, balancing universality with contextuality. This duality—being both universal and situational—sets *Dharma* apart. The *Dharma* Matrix offers a simplified, practical tool to guide behavior by focusing on the core principles of *Swadharma* (personal duty) and *Sanatan Dharma* (universal duty). However, it is not a rigid, one-size-fits-all framework. Instead, it serves as a reflective guide, honoring *Dharma's* open architecture, which allows adaptability to diverse contexts while remaining rooted in ethical integrity.

By blending AI's analytical capabilities with *Dharma's* ethical principles, organizations can develop more nuanced and adaptable ethical frameworks, making *Dharma* even more relevant for addressing complex, real-world dilemmas. By adopting the *Dharma Matrix*, businesses are encouraged to create environments that promote individual well-being, organizational integrity, and societal harmony. This holistic perspective can transform traditional business practices by embedding timeless ethical principles into the core of organizational strategies and operations. Future research should continue exploring how *Dharma* and AI together can enhance ethical decision-making across various sectors, further testing this innovative framework's robustness in contemporary organizational contexts.

References

Clooney, F. X. (2013). *Hindu God, Christian God: How reason helps break down the boundaries between religions*. Oxford University Press.

Doniger, W. (2020). *The Hindus: An alternative history*. Penguin Books.

Ganeri, J. (2019). *The self: Naturalism, consciousness, and the first-person stance*. Oxford University Press.

Miller, R. E. (2020). *Ethics and the multicultural classroom: Challenges and opportunities for pluralistic pedagogy*. Routledge.

Mishra, P., & Kalagnanam, S. (2022). *Managing by dharma: Eternal principles for sustaining profitability*. Springer.

Schroeder, M. (2018). *Virtue ethics and the emotions*. Oxford University Press.

Sharma, A. (2021). *Hindu ethics: Purity, abortion, and euthanasia*. State University of New York Press.

Srinivas, T. (2021). *The postcolonial Indian state and the transformation of dharma*. Cambridge University Press.

CHAPTER 4

AI and Consciousness: Adding Spiritual to Scientific Perspectives

Tom Culham, Jyoti Bachani, and Chris Laszlo

Introduction

There is an ongoing and raging debate in society, particularly in the field of science, regarding the nature of consciousness and the impact of Artificial Intelligence (AI) on it. Spirituality as a domain of study has dealt with consciousness as a core concept. This chapter contributes to the debate on the role of Artificial Intelligence and consciousness by providing a review of the prevalent scientific views and adds spiritual perspectives from a variety of faith traditions. The spiritual perspectives are based on the

T. Culham (✉)
Simon Fraser University, Vancouver, Canada
e-mail: thomas_culham@sfu.ca

J. Bachani
St Mary's College, Moraga, CA, USA

C. Laszlo
Case Western Reserve University, Cleveland, USA
e-mail: cpl8@case.edu

A. K. Maheshwari (ed.), *AI and Consciousness in Organizations and Society*, Palgrave Studies in Workplace Spirituality and Fulfillment,
https://doi.org/10.1007/978-3-031-91470-6_4

academic and personal experiential knowledge of the authors, all of whom are professors with a long-standing interest in Management, Spirituality, and Religion. The chapter is an informed and shared inquiry into the matters of Spirituality and specifically focuses on consciousness and how it might relate to Artificial Intelligence (AGI).

There are a variety of perspectives on consciousness which are important to acknowledge for the purpose of this chapter. For some time, beginning with western enlightenment, it has been theorized that consciousness arises out of the physical brain. This is known as material monism which sees consciousness as the product of the brain upon reaching a threshold level of complexity (Dennett, 1988). Although this theory dominates to the extent that this is considered an assumption by most, the reality is that no one in the field of science or philosophy has been able to logically support this proposition. It remains a leap of logic that the brain, as physical matter, is the foundation of consciousness. The alternate view, neutral monism or panpsychism, (Chalmers, 2015) holds that consciousness is an essential property of the universe and that the human brain may be more like a receiver or transmitter that is able to "tune into" this field. These two views, material monism and neutral monism aka panpsychism, are the primary dividing lines in the debate that still continues. Although science and neuroscience perspectives on consciousness are grounded in the materialist paradigm, over a hundred scientists called for a more open approach in scientific inquiry regarding the nature of consciousness (Cardeña, 2014). Based on our research and long-standing engagement with different faith practices, we enrich this debate by offering an informed spiritual perspective.

If a person holds the material monism view, then one could extrapolate that Artificial General Intelligence (AGI) might possibly achieve consciousness one day by virtue of reaching the threshold level of complexity. If a person holds the neutral monism view, then it becomes more difficult to imagine that AGI would ever be able to achieve the human capacity to tune into the universal field of consciousness. In the panpsychist view, AGI might have its own degree of consciousness, much as a tree or a mouse can be seen to have consciousness, but it will never achieve *human* consciousness because it is not, and never will be, human.

A Scientific Perspective on Consciousness as a Property of the Universe

Let us consider one scientific view consistent with panpsychism. Donald David Hoffman, professor in the Department of Cognitive Sciences at the University of California, Irvine, is a cognitive psychologist and philosopher. In his research, he professes that the idea of the brain as giving rise to consciousness has not been proven by science. Rather he and other colleagues (Gefter et al., 2016) propose that consciousness causes brain activity and creates all objects and properties of the physical world. Their rationale is that evolution provides perceptions that enabled survival, and it also hides information that is not needed for survival. If all of reality were available to our brain, we would spend too much time trying to figure it out and be eaten by tigers as we did that. Therefore, the world we perceive is nothing like reality.

Plato's allegory of the cave suggests that the world is an illusion of reality. Adding mathematical modeling to it, Gefter, et al. further propose that the world can be considered to be a set of conscious agents. Consciousness exists in the individual and yet when two individuals interact this too becomes a conscious agent. As more individuals' consciousness interact, a unified consciousness arises. This theory is called conscious realism. An example of two consciousness becoming one occurs with the brain and its two hemispheres. In split brain experiments, it is possible to observe two different consciousness related to each side of the brain. However, when the hemispheres are connected, there is one consciousness.

Based on his work and on the emerging ontology of quantum science, Hoffman challenges the traditional scientific view of objective reality. In this view, reality is founded on the basis that different individuals can measure the same object and draw similar conclusions. Quantum mechanics "tells us that there are no public physical objects" (Gefter, et al., 2016, p. 4), that is, physical objects are an illusion, rather they are fields of energy and even space time may be an illusion (Hoffman, 2019). In addition, quantum mechanics has demonstrated that the observer influences objects, suggesting they are not independent from the act of observation (Wojciech et al., 1988). Publicly shared concepts such as headaches, the moon, and sun, etc. appear to be the same, however, our individual perceptions and experiences of phenomena are unique to each person (Gefter et al., 2016).

Several important conclusions arise from Hoffman's claims that are relevant to consider in the context of AI's role from spirituality perspective. The first is that consciousness is primary, that it isn't derived from objective physical matter. Hoffman states:

> As a conscious realist, I am postulating conscious experiences as ontological primitives, the most basic ingredients of the world. I'm claiming that experiences are the real coin of the realm. The experiences of everyday life — my real feeling of a headache, my real taste of chocolate — that really is the ultimate nature of reality (Gefter et al., 2016, p. 4).

From this statement, it can be concluded that subjective conscious experience is the foundation of reality. A second observation is the reality that we perceive is not the truth; rather, it is an illusion based on our observation of reality as we perceived it. The third and related consideration is that consciousness is subjective, that is knowledge is always from a certain point of view.

Consciousness and the Brain

Next, let us consider Iain McGilchrist's thesis on consciousness. Drawing on his expertise in neuroscience, he claims that the brain has two different kinds of consciousness related to the left and right hemispheres of the brain. It is important to note that this is not functional differences, rather it is a difference in consciousness which can be observed when the operation of one of the consciousness is shutdown through medical means or brain damage. Two of McGilchrist's claims regarding hemisphere consciousness parallel Hoffman's. The first is the epistemology of the right and left hemispheres. The left hemisphere relies on abstract information, or information that is a representation of reality for the purpose of getting, and manipulating things while the right hemisphere relies on first-hand, subjective, lived experience for the purpose of seeing the whole picture and relating to the world. In addition, the left hemisphere is self-referential and is only prepared to accept its point of view. Due to these attributes, the left hemisphere has the tendency to dominate and overrule the perspective of the right hemisphere which is open to multiple perspectives. Since our brains are plastic, they are modified through repeated patterns of use; therefore, since the enlightenment and particularly in the last fifty to a hundred years, left hemisphere consciousness has been emphasized and valorized in society.

By construction, AI is based on left hemisphere epistemology. AI relies on data abstraction and representation of reality rather than lived experience. Thus, it is derived from second-hand knowledge at best and may or may not reflect reality (as described by Hoffman). Representation is second-hand knowledge. It can take the form of language, verbal or written, mathematical formulas, video, music, etc. however, it is not first-hand lived experience, the epistemology of the right hemisphere. Like left hemisphere epistemology while it can mimic awe, wonder, joy, sadness, anger, etc. it does not ***know*** the embodied experience of these phenomena.

Proponents of AI have the perspective that AI will improve on human knowledge, because it is capable of drawing from multiple sources, across time and cultures. Therefore, AI has the capacity for finding patterns that a single person could not. Thus, it is likely able to develop creative solutions to problems that a human would miss (Youvan, 2024). Perhaps this is the case. However, this view misses some important aspects of the human discovery processes: intuition and related constructs such as presencing and sensing.

Intuition as a Means of Knowing

In philosophic terms, intuition can be thought of as a priori knowledge defined as:

> A non-inferential knowledge or grasp, as of a proposition, concept or entity that is not based on perception, memory, or introspection; also, the capacity in virtue of which such cognition is possible (Audi, 2006, p. 442).

Neuroscientists define it as:

> Any sudden comprehension, realization, or problem solution that involves a reorganization of the elements of a person's mental representation of a stimulus, situation, or event to yield a nonobvious or nondominant interpretation (Kounios & Beeman, 2014, p. 74).

Intuition originates in the right hemisphere of the brain. It plays a significant role in one of the two ways in which scientific progress is achieved. The first means of scientific progress is achieved through normal science, the purpose of which is to describe, reduce ambiguities, elucidate, and expand the number of problems solved within a given paradigm. A majority of work and problems solved by scientists fall within the realm of normal science. The other manner in which progress occurs is through revolutions which occur when one paradigm replaces another. The revolutionary process that scientists go through of changing from one paradigm to another is far from logical or predictable. Kuhn states normal science only leads to the recognition of anomalies or problems with the current paradigm (1970).

The shift from one paradigm to another is a relatively sudden and unstructured event like the gestalt switch. Although unresolved anomalies in an existing scientific paradigm can accumulate slowly, they eventually reach a crisis point or threshold beyond which a revolution in paradigms takes place. In describing the discovery of a new paradigm, scientists often speak of "the scales falling from the eyes" or of "the lightning flash" and that "inundates" a previously obscure puzzle, enabling its components to be seen in a new way that for the first time permits its solution. On other occasions, the relevant illuminations come in sleep. No ordinary sense of the term interpretation or logic fits these flashes of intuition through which a new paradigm is born. Though such intuitions depend upon the experience gained with old paradigms, they are not logically or piecemeal linked to particular items of that experience as an interpretation would be. Instead, they gather up large portions of that experience and transform them to the rather different bundle of experience that will thereafter be linked to the new paradigm but not the old (Kuhn, 1970, p. 123).

Scientific progress depends on scientist's first-hand, embodied, intuitive insights which are not logically connected or related to previous paradigms and are often described in terms that are associated with spirituality: e.g., "scales falling from the eyes"." AI uses second-hand knowledge to generate information based on probabilities. That means that there is a relationship between information that is available to AI and the supposedly new information that it produces. AI works within existing paradigms. As Kuhn (1970) observes, there is little or no logical connection between paradigms such as Newtonian and Quantum physics.

Given the nature of the operation of AI, it is highly doubtful that it might become capable of intuiting or sensing new paradigms as described here. Further, it does not have an embodied unconscious, nor does it embody the unconscious history of humanity. Einstein noted the significance of intuition in scientific discovery in the following statement: "The intuitive mind is a sacred gift, and the rational mind is a faithful servant. We have created a society that honors the servant and has forgotten the gift". Further, he felt that scientific discovery originated from the heart, with the mind state of a "religious worshipper or lover". Einstein and Kuhn's statements convey the sense of the presence of spirit and devotion to a practice or topic that intuitively reveals knowledge that is logically unknowable and yet new and useful in logical rational terms. We consider the spiritual traditions next.

Consciousness in the Spiritual Traditions of Buddhism, Daoism, and Confucianism

The spiritual traditions of Buddhism, Daoism, and Confucianism are known as the three teachings. They share important concepts that align well with panpsychism. The first is that there is a universal mind, known as Dao in Daoism and Confucianism and supreme ultimate in Buddhism (Crowe, 2010). The second is that all humans come into the world with an innate nature which is "not born and never destroyed" or is "original or fundamental nature" and is one with the universal mind (Crowe, 2010, p. 69). Awareness of one's innate nature is not consciously available in ordinary life; awareness of it is achieved through cultivation of silence, tranquility, and limiting of selfish desires (Crowe, 2010).

This is epistemologically significant because innate nature is one with the source of everything (Dao, Supreme Ultimate, God, Brahman, etc.). By enhancing one's awareness of one's innate nature, access to the knowledge of the universe is revealed. For the purposes of this discussion, it is important to note that these traditions, particularly Buddhism make a distinction between everyday ordinary or conceptual knowledge gained through the usual forms of education and training and real knowledge that is obtained intuitively and experientially through contemplative practices that focus on eliminating thought.

Huang Po an influential Zen Buddhist during the Tang Dynasty in the ninth-century China said: "Give up all indulgence in conceptual thought and intellectual processes. When such things no longer trouble you, you will unfailingly reach Supreme Enlightenment" (Blofeld, 1958, p. 130). In other words: if you give up conceptual thought, which is a (left-brain) process of creating duality through judgment and distinguishing this from that, one will achieve oneness and a non-dual (whole brain) awareness where there is no distinction between the self and the universe. In this state, the individual merges with universal mind and has access to the knowledge of the universe. An important aspect of Daoist philosophy is its emphasis on lived experience over and above conceptual thought (Kirkland, 2004).

Indian contemplative religions as well as Christian mysticism traditions have similar ideas. Sister Jean Marie Dwyer is a member of the Dominican monastery in British Columbia, Canada. She chronicles and compares the recognition of the God Within, of Etty Hillesum, a woman of Jewish upbringing caught up in the holocaust, with Meister Eckhart's doctrine "birth of the word in the soul" (p, 82). Eckhart was a thirteenth-century German Catholic theologian, philosopher, and mystic who belonged to the Dominican Order. While this story is told in the context of Catholicism, where divinity is seen to be separate and outside the person, in the Dominican view, divinity is immanent, within where development involves an inner journey resulting in union with God within (Dwyer, 2014). This illustrates how the phenomena observed in the East Asian three teachings, Indian traditions and Dominican mysticism, while using different terms, point to the same experiential phenomena.

The phenomenon of oneness, where subject and object merge, is also experienced in everyday life. For example, dedicated athletes, dancers, or musicians have reported that when they are in the midst of their performance or sport, they become one with the activity. It is possible to experience oneness or nonduality on an incremental basis through certain practices and can be introduced into secular education practices (Czikszentmihalyi, 1990).

Consciousness in the Hindu Spiritual Traditions

The ancient Hindu philosophical beliefs and different schools of thoughts from the Vedas to the Gita—were studied and synthesized in the twentieth century in the context of the dominant scientific methods that prevailed. Among the scholars who studied and practiced these beliefs were Sri Aurobindo, Swami Vivekananda, a disciple of Sri Ramakrishna, and several others. Using Sri Aurobindo's teachings about consciousness, as per the Hindu and Vedantic philosophy in the context of European and American scientific methods—we will make some observations about AI and conjectures on its implications for researchers.

In Aurobindo's book, The Life Divine (1940/2005), the concepts from ancient Hindu texts of the *Rig Veda* and *Upanishads*, in *Sanskrit*, are described in English using ideas from modern Psychology, in an attempt to convey the rather different philosophical perspective of the indigenous traditions. One of the ways to understand consciousness is that there are different levels of it. *Yoga* has popularized the seven *chakras* as the seats of the seven levels of conscious awareness that potentially exist within each one of us. These seven centers of consciousness where force, action, and awareness reside in different levels. The highest is located above the crown—where intuition is most open and inspiration occurs, and through which mind can have illumined thoughts and direct contact with the overmind—an even higher level of consciousness. The next chakra is behind the pineal gland and governs the dynamic mind, will, vision, and mental formation. The third chakra is at the throat, the expressive and externalizing mind. It expresses thoughts and inspiration coming from above as well as vital feelings coming from below, concerning itself with creative work. The heart chakra governs the emotional being, with sophisticated human emotions of love and compassion. The next one at the solar plexus houses the power and ambition and is considered having guts. Below it in the pelvic cavity is the chakra for lower vital consciousness seeking personal comfort, including sexuality. The final chakra is at the base of the spine and where consciousness resides as the seat of *Kundalini* and sub-consciousness starts just beyond it. Subconsciousness provides abrupt, involuntary, and mostly automatic to feed the needs of the conscious waking human sense. Above the waking consciousness is the superconscient mind, including the higher consciousness. Table 4.1 below offers one summary of the various levels of consciousness within the Hindu belief system, including where the center for each is in different parts of the body.

In addition to the levels of consciousness, the Hindu belief system also holds the belief that consciousness occurs not just at certain levels, but also in the dynamic between that conscious awareness and either vertically or concentrically adjacent levels of consciousnesses. Our true human nature is the same as that of the all-pervasive consciousness—the way a candle has the same light as the sun. The ultimate true nature of humans is the same as the divine cosmic energy "*sat chit anand*," loosely translated as "truth awareness bliss." This "chit" is akin to the concept of consciousness, although in practical use, the word might be better translated as awareness. Anand is bliss—so consciousness with awareness

Table 4.1 Hindu levels of consciousness and knowledge

Consciousness	*Consciousness descriptor*	*Corresponding Chakra*[1] *and location*	*Knowledge*
Divine consciousness	Super mind[2]	Crown	True Knowledge
Higher consciousness	Intuitive mind		Mixed true knowledge and ignorance
Ordinary consciousness	Thinking mind	Third eye	Ignorance[3]
	Emotional mind	Throat	Ignorance
	Physical body	Heart Navel Sex organs	Ignorance
Subconscient[4] (the inconscient in the process of becoming conscient)	Matter		Absence of knowledge
Inconscient[5] (mindless)			

leads to recognizing our true nature of cosmic bliss—of oneness with the universal energy.

Consciousness might be assumed to exist independently as a foundational epistemological basis but in choosing the word awareness—it adds the critical dimension of human experience and choice, as to where we as living beings choose to focus our awareness. A parallel might be the human life-critical function of breathing—which is autonomous and continues without any effort on our part, and yet it can also be controlled

[1] Chakras are psychic centers co-located within the physical body that are commonly accepted concepts across Indian traditions (Pradhan, 2014; White, 2012). In this view, human life unfolds in two dimensions: the physical body, and the subtle body consisting of psychological, emotional, mind, non-physical aspects of being (Sharma, 2006).

[2] Supermind is similar to *de* or virtue in Daoism meaning the dynamic manifestation of the undifferentiated Divine. It is the intermediary between the Divine and the manifest world (Aurobindo, 1977).

[3] Ignorance, unwisdom, or incorrect knowledge is a misunderstanding of metaphysical reality that includes: ignorance out of darkness, misconceptions, mistaking illusion to be reality, etc. (Wayman, 1957). Also see (Gefter et al., 2016).

[4] The subconscient is the inconscient in the process of becoming conscient. It includes the unconscious mind but includes much more than the unconscious of contemporary psychology (Parni, 2007).

[5] Inconscient Matter is the lowest presence of spirit (Parni, 2007).

with our own will—as we choose to breathe deeply or let out a sigh, taking charge of the vital life-force, and through experience—change our state of mind. The seven yoga chakras are also sites where the energy can be moved with various moves of the breath, body, and awareness.

The Hindu philosophy rests on the idea that the human soul is made in the form of the one universal energy that all creation comes from. If one believes in a Creator, then every human also has the capacity to attain Godhood, through cultivating good practices, as action is the dynamic that shifts consciousness. The various spiritual practices, contemplative, ritualistic, ascetic, etc. are all meant to lead humans toward that fulfillment by providing time and space for detaching from the illusory world, which is considered akin to a simulation, the projection of one's entangled mind state. The practices are a way to cultivate the detachment from the material world, and to be reminded of and practice the recognition of our own true nature. These are recommended as mental hygiene to regularly remove the many layers of ignorance that surround our mind.

This perspective is in sharp contrast with the ideas that rely primarily on the physical reality as being the basis for everything else, including experience. The denial of primacy of physical and material realm, and instead shifting the locus to consciousness as a dynamic between the individual and its context—the particular and the universal—changes the epistemology. The subjective and objective disappear. This non-dual perspective is confusing for perspectives grounded in Western philosophical traditions that rely on material reality or even experience alone. A few scholars have tried to bridge this.

Let us consider the scholarship of Michael James, a devotee of an Indian Hindu sage, the late *Ramana Maharshi*. The purpose here is to further supplement the earlier claims by adding James' views on spiritual development from a practice tradition, where cultivating a return to source or oneness is practiced. *Ramana Maharishi* was known as a *jīvanmukta*, literally meaning "liberated while living," which in *Vedānta* philosophy is a person who has gained complete self-knowledge and self-realization and attained enlightenment or liberation while living. The teachings of *Ramana Maharshi* are simple in that the means of development is to enquire within to know oneself or one's innate nature. And yet these are difficult to put into practice. According to James' (2024), description of *Ramana Maharshi's* teachings, source, or pure consciousness is available within everyone. While the mind and ego arise out of source, their orientation is external and away from inner knowledge of source. While ego's awareness originates in source, it mistakenly identifies itself with the body. Knowing source involves the effort of reversing the attention of the mind and ego from external phenomena to the inner self revealing knowledge like no other. Dedicated practice and lived experience of the teachings are indispensable and studying the teachings supports practice. These teaching and practices align with Daoism and Buddhism in being focused on inward inquiry for self-realization.

James (2024) perspective is that AI is an advanced form of *information processing*. It is good for solving problems in the world, which only creates more problems. As stated concisely by Ehrenfeld (2024), "The ills and failings of modernity spring from an excess of left-brain domination." For spiritual development, this kind of information does not bring clarity because AI cannot help us know (experience) what is real within.

As a Hindu sage, *Ramana Maharshi* drew upon the conceptual framework of Hindu consciousness. Hindus believe that consciousness is present in everything, from inert rocks that have no mind to the creatures who can attain the highest level of divine or pure consciousness. The Hindi or Sanskrit words for consciousness are "Chetna" and "Chitta." In the Hindu belief system, our true human nature is the same as that of the Supreme Being who made us in likeness of the divine—the way a candle has the same light as the sun. Humans are born with a true nature that is described as "sat chit anand" "truth awareness bliss." This "chit" is "chitta" or awareness, same as the concept of consciousness. The human soul gets entangled in the material world's trappings and forgets their truth, of being blissful at their very core. The various spiritual practices, contemplative, ritualistic, ascetic, etc. are all different paths that lead humans back to their true nature, as these are reminders that help with recognition of our own true nature, by removing the various layers of ignorance that surround our minds.

Adding Spirit to the Science of Consciousness

Hinduism, Daoism, Buddhism, and Confucianism traditions all claim that everyday knowledge is associated with ordinary consciousness, while true and real knowledge is associated with divine consciousness. In contrast, AI relies on abstract knowledge recorded by humans in one form or another. The generative AI models produce language by predicting the most likely sequence of words based on records of language in its memory. That is, AI relies on existing knowledge across numerous domains to predict or propose solutions. It may generate new knowledge within a specific domain based on its vast store of knowledge across domains, but it doesn't generate knowledge that hasn't been already developed and stored in some shape or form. Therefore, AI is limited to what can be generated by ordinary consciousness and data about it that is stored in the prevalent digital form. Some of these limitations are spelled out next.

While the amount of data in digital form from ordinary knowledge is vast and beyond what any human could possibly access, it is still finite and limited in several ways. Not all knowledge is recorded and even when it is, it may or may not be available in the prevalent form. New formats as well as new knowledge are being developed on an ongoing basis. All that has not been entered into databases is not available to AI tools. Relying on existing ordinary knowledge, AI also suffers from a magnified version of human failings of ordinary knowledge. As an illustration, consider the 2020 documentary film Bias that shows how AI learns from data. When past data is full of inaccuracies or human failings or terrible ideas that the society has since outgrown, the best outcome from such AI is that it learns from the bad behaviors of humans to amplify all the past ills in its own extrapolations from it. AI systems have systemic bias built into them, as in the case of how the past court records and rulings led to biased algorithms. Historically, in the US, there were judges who held racist views and had no compunctions about passing unfavorable judgments with racial biases interfering with their ability to be fair judges. Minorities would be convicted in these cases beyond what they deserved. When AI was built using these judgments, it led to AI with court heuristics based on legal precedents that eventually favored convicting the minorities, beyond what they deserved. These implications of AI are far from conscious or even intentional, but far too common. These can lead to unintended consequences like institutionalized racism.

Limitations of the AI-Based View of Consciousness

Intuition is an important human attribute that contributes to the development of new knowledge. Intuition along with imagination enables humans to go beyond existing possibilities and recorded knowledge. See Table 4.1 for various levels of consciousness as per the Hindu traditions. Intuition is associated with a higher level of consciousness. Intuition inverts our traditional conception of knowledge in that it relies not on language but appears as wordless first in the form of embodied gut feel, flashes of insight, instantaneous, non-rational visions, and or dreams. AI systems will have to be designed rather differently from the currently dominant machine-learning-algorithms that extrapolate future from the past, to have anything resembling intuition or imagination. These are qualities that, like the so-called gut-feeling are distributed and embodied, in ways that are purely experiential. AI cannot have experiences, the way humans or sentient beings can. That is a fundamental difference—that marks a point of departure between the machine consciousness and human consciousness.

Another limitation of AI can be found in comparing the human response to being in the presence of a moving piece of art, music, dance, or theater. This kind of response is embodied resulting in changes at the physiological level. Such responses might be calming, arousing, inspiring, provocative, or even cathartic, as varied and individualistic as the observers. AI is disembodied and therefore incapable of both having experiences as well as developing the consciousness that might respond to the experiential stimuli.

AI is limited only to abstract knowledge recorded by ordinary disembodied consciousness. It does not have access to the intuitive mind or super mind as the knowledge produced by these types of consciousness is obtained through lived experience and is usually impossible to describe in abstract form such as language. The classic Daoist text, the Daodejing states: "The Way (Dao) that can be Spoken is not the constant Way (Dao)". AI also does not have any access to consciousness below the mind in the form of emotional and embodied consciousness. This knowledge is felt through the senses first and even though machines with sensors exist, their responses of making sense of the sensory input are still based on past data and machine learning. There is no way for the sensors in the machines to make fresh meaning of the sensory data, and definitely no ability to create the expressions in language, as humans will most certainly attempt to do. The ability to abstract up from experience to express in language is a human quality that requires human consciousness, that machines and algorithms cannot match yet. The body and sense are important pathways to spiritual development. "If spiritual progress is bliss, and bliss is accomplished through the body, by embodied beings, the spiritual senses are the channels of this bliss, through which the practitioner and the divine are lured into an eternal game of union" (Cattoi, 2011, p. 235) Thus, from a spiritual perspective, these are some of the significant limitations of AI when it comes to understanding consciousness.

Conclusion

This chapter began with the observation that there is a debate regarding whether matter is the foundation of consciousness or consciousness is itself the foundation. This debate has not been settled, yet the scientific community has increasingly tended to support the view that consciousness is foundational (Chalmers, 2015; Radin, 2013). The science-based discussion on the difference in consciousness of the left and right hemisphere of the brain was used to focus our attention on their differing epistemology. The left hemisphere relies on abstract information, or information that is a representation of reality for the purpose of getting, and manipulating things while the right hemisphere relies on first-hand, subjective, lived experience for the purpose of seeing the whole picture and relating to the world. AI, by its nature and design, is based on left hemisphere epistemology, which is an abstraction or representation of reality rather than lived experience itself. With the help of advanced sensors, AI based on the left hemisphere epistemology can mimic awe, wonder, joy, sadness, anger, etc., but it still does not know the embodied experience of these phenomena. The spiritual traditions offer a perspective that allows for right hemisphere epistemology. The different spiritual traditions include embodied experiences and practices that through ritual and repetition, through abstract meaning-making, might eventually be expressible in language, but are primarily felt and sensed in ways that machines cannot experience and express yet. The whole brain, heart, and spirit, and their interrelationships embedded within the larger cosmos view is still a human endeavor. In this, the human consciousness still remains primary to artificial intelligence and consciousness it might contribute.

It was noted that intuition originates in the right hemisphere of the brain and is capable of producing knowledge that is not logically or stepwise related to previous knowledge. It was concluded that AI is able to develop knowledge within existing frameworks but is unlikely capable of intuiting new paradigms. Further, it does not have an embodied unconscious, nor does it embody the unconscious history of humanity.

The authors review four ancient spiritual traditions based on their own practices and using the practice-based expertise, they add a perspective on how and where spirituality might explain what consciousness is and how it adds to the debate on scientific understanding of consciousness and the role of AI in that. A common theme across these traditions is that there are different levels of consciousness and associated knowledge.

Of particular interest to understand the implications of AI is the view that there is ordinary consciousness and related knowledge that humans have from the matters of everyday life to the abstract knowledge represented by such disciplines as science, philosophy, etc. In the spiritual traditions, this knowledge is considered a certain kind of ignorance because it is a self-limiting knowledge, which gets in the way of diving in to deeper richer self-inquiry to uncover the true spiritually relevant knowledge that makes us aware of our role and place as part of the cosmos.

The ordinary knowledge is what arises with exclusive concentration in a single field. This is the only kind of knowledge AI can use and build on. This is limited and limiting by design, in a number of different ways; predominately, it relies on digital forms of conceptual abstract knowledge that excludes embodied experience and intuition. The other type of knowledge is true knowledge associated with divine consciousness which is obtained through contemplative practices that enable intuitive insight beyond the limits of currently available abstract knowledge.

Finally, with respect to spiritual development, it was concluded that AI is not ideally suited to this endeavor as it relies on abstraction of knowledge which itself is not real knowledge in spiritual terms and real knowledge is obtained only through embodied lived experience. Maheshwari and Biberman (2024) reviewed the matter of AI and spirituality and concluded that while AI might help people make progress toward spiritual development, in its current state of development AI is not capable of achieving real knowledge or Oneness consciousness. However, the authors held out the possibility that future versions of AI could do so provided the developers writing the algorithms were themselves advanced in their consciousness. It is our view that even these conditions violate the premise proposed in this paper that AI is based on abstraction of ordinary knowledge and that real knowledge can only be experienced directly. This is consistent with the Daoist claim that The Way (Dao) that can be Spoken is not the constant Way (Dao)" meaning that language is a representation and a mere shadow of lived experience.

References

Audi, R. (2006). *The Cambridge dictionary of philosophy*. Cambridge University Press, 11th printing.

Aurobindo, S. (1977). *Life divine book* I, ch.14–16.

Blofeld, J. E. C. (1958). *The Zen teaching of Huang Po: On the transmission of the mind*. Grove Press.

Cardeña, E. (2014). A call for an open, informed study of all aspects of consciousness. *Frontiers in Human Neuroscience, 8*, 17.

Cattoi, T. (2011). Conclusion: The virtues of sensuality. In T. Cattoi & J. McDaniel (Eds.), *Perceiving the divine through the human body: Mystical sensuality* (pp. 223–235). Palgrave MacMillan.

Chalmers, D. (2015). Panpsychism and panprotopsychism. *Consciousness in the Physical World: Perspectives on Russellian Monism, 246*(2003), 102–154.

Crowe, P. (2010). Nature, motion, and stillness: Li Daochun's vision of the three teachings. *Journal of Daoist Studies, 5*(5), 61–88.

Czikszentmihalyi, M. (1990). *Flow: The psychology of optimal experience* (pp. 75–77). Harper & Row.

Dennett, D. C. (1988). Quining qualia. *Consciousness in Contemporary Science*, 42–77.

Dwyer, J. M. (2014). *The unfolding journey. The God within: Etty Hillesum & Meister Eckhart*. Novalis.

Ehrenfeld, J. (2024). To reach flourishing, turn right sharply at the next corner. *Journal of Management Spirituality and Religion, 21*(3), 264–287.

Gefter, A., & Hoffman, D. D. (2016). The evolutionary argument against reality. *Quanta Magazine, 21*.

Hoffman, D. (2019). Do we see reality? *New Scientist, 243*(3241), 34–37.

James, M. (2024). *The blind intelligence of AI cannot help us to see what is real*. Ramana Foundation UK. https://www.youtube.com/watch?v=sM_A79mjGIc Downloaded 2024-04-13

Kirkland, R. (2004). *Taoism: The enduring tradition*. Routledge.

Kounios, J., & Beeman, M. (2014). The cognitive neuroscience of insight. *Annual Review of Psychology, 65*, 71–93.

Kuhn, T. (1970). *The structure of scientific revolutions* (2nd ed.). University of Chicago Press Ltd., London.

Maheshwari, A. K., & Biberman, J. (2024). Artificial oneness: Bridging the human machine divide. *Journal of Management, Spirituality & Religion*. https://doi.org/10.51327/RZRA6516

Pradhan, B. (2014). *Yoga and mindfulness based cognitive therapy: A clinical guide* (pp. 154–155). Springer. ISBN 978-3-319-09105-1.

Pani, R. N. (2007). *Integral education: Thought & practical* (p. 9788131302866). APH Publishing.

Dean Radin, D. (2013). *Supernormal: Science, yoga, and the evidence for extraordinary psychic abilities*. Deepak Chopra Publishing.

Sharma, A. (2006). *A primal perspective on the philosophy of religion* (pp. 193–196). Springer. ISBN 978-1-4020-5014-5.

Wayman, A. (1957). The meaning of unwisdom (Avidya). *Philosophy East and West, 7*(1/2), 21–25.
White, D. G. (2012). *Yoga in practice.* Princeton University Press.
Wojciech, H. Z. (1988). Quantum mechanics demolishes the view that the universe exists out there. In A. van der Merwe & W. A. Miller (Eds.), *Between Quantum and Cosmos: Studies and Essays in Honor of John Archibald Wheeler.* Princeton University Press.
Youvan, D. C. (2024). AI Tulpas and the future of consciousness: Exploring emergent phenomena and digital thought forms.

Part II

CHAPTER 5

Transforming Consciousness-Based Education in the Age of AI

Anil K. Maheshwari

Introduction

Grand challenges facing humanity require a higher level of consciousness to operate from the level of total interconnectedness of life (Johansen, 2020; Laszlo et al., 2021; LaLoux, 2014; Maheshwari, 2021a; Polman & Winston, 2021; Tsao & Laszlo, 2019). Business organizations are undergoing revolutionary changes from exponential development of technologies of production, distribution, and consumption in what has been called the fourth industrial revolution (Diamandis & Kotler, 2020; Schwab, 2017). Recognizing that more of the same won't work anymore, management schools have also been evolving rapidly to engage with the opportunities and threats posed by the rapidly evolving socio-technical environment (Datar et al., 2010). The COVID-19 pandemic has further disrupted business schools providing an opportunity to innovate (Krishnamurthy, 2020).

A. K. Maheshwari (✉)
Maharishi International University, Iowa, USA
e-mail: akmaheshwari@miu.edu

A. K. Maheshwari (ed.), *AI and Consciousness in Organizations and Society*, Palgrave Studies in Workplace Spirituality and Fulfillment,
https://doi.org/10.1007/978-3-031-91470-6_5

The qualities needed in the exemplary manager of the future could be the empathizing and synergizing quality, the visionary and transformative quality, the moral quality (Laszlo et al., 2021), and more. These and similar qualities can be subsumed under the idea of an integral (Wilber, 2014), holistic (Dhiman, 2017), higher consciousness (Maheshwari, 2021a), total interconnectedness (Tsao & Laszlo, 2019), and oneness view of the world (Laloux, 2014). The new manager ideally would be self-aware, self-organizing, and self-regulating (Maheshwari, 2021a). A new model of leadership based on the convergence of quantum sciences and spirituality may be key to development of innovative pro social and environmental behaviors toward oneness and flourishing in the world (Tsao & Laszlo, 2019). Managers need to develop a higher level of consciousness where they can experience their own infinite potential (Maharishi, 1995). They need to *unboundarize* from their self-limiting beliefs and tap into the unbounded potential of themselves and their teams (Maheshwari, 2021a).

Higher education has been the cornerstone of personal, social, and economic development. However, in recent decades, growing concerns have emerged regarding its effectiveness in delivering on its promises. Students, educators, and policymakers have voiced frustrations about increasing costs, rigid curricula, a disconnect between education and the real-world job market, and a failure to foster critical thinking and innovation. The mental demands of modern life require not just "a new set of skills to be put in" but a new threshold of consciousness (Kegan, 1998). Educational institutions have been criticized for focusing on narrow, discipline-specific knowledge while neglecting broader developmental aspects, such as the growth of consciousness, emotional intelligence, and holistic well-being (Schmidt-Wilk et al., 2000). Students frequently feel disengaged and alienated by curricula that do not reflect their unique learning styles, interests, or life goals, nor do they experience all the learned knowledge (Dillbeck, 1977). Employers often report that recent graduates lack the critical thinking, problem-solving, and interpersonal skills needed in the modern workforce. This has led to concerns about the employability of graduates and the overall value of a college degree. AI is presenting both challenges and opportunities for educational reform. This chapter explores how to raise students' consciousness and how AI technologies could provide the right tools and resources to adapt more rapidly. Through interdisciplinary research, this integration could lead to a more personalized, holistic, and effective model of education that better aligns with the evolving demands of the twenty-first century.

This chapter explores the potential of merging CBE and ABE to create a more adaptive, responsive, and holistic learning environment. It examines the benefits of this integration for both educators and students, highlights potential downsides, and proposes future research directions to ensure its successful implementation. Ultimately, this new educational framework holds the promise of fostering well-rounded, emotionally intelligent, and ethically grounded individuals capable of thriving in an increasingly complex world.

Challenges to Management Education

Huisman and Wende (2022) highlight contemporary issues and concerns in higher education system. Expansion of diversity can be experienced as fragmentation by some. Similarly, promoting access & equity can be experienced differently by meritocratic elitist communities. It can be challenging to optimize for micro (teaching), meso (organizational), and macro (system) levels simultaneously. Doyle and Brady (2018) suggest that the higher education system should be reframed as an evolving system with emergent business models. They make a case for alternative organizational theories or models that perceive higher education organizations as emergent entities in which change is continuous, often unpredictable, and arising mainly from local interactions. The higher education system needs to evolve to meet the emergent needs of the local marketplace in a strategic and continual manner (Manning, 2017).

Evolving Nature of Work

> *Four people working on a construction site were asked what they were doing. One said, "laying bricks". The second said, "erecting a wall". The third said, "building a cathedral". The fourth said, "making the world peaceful and blissful."*

Arendt (2005) differentiates the spectrum of effort as labor, work, and action. From laboring for one's personal needs, to working to produce artifices and services for others, to creative action that is fulfilling for oneself and simultaneously evolutionary for the world, there is a range of perceptions and motivations that depend upon one's level of consciousness. There is a concomitant difference in levels of commitment, satisfaction, and personal alignment in one's work between doing a job, building a career, and following one's calling. A higher purpose helps connect with a reality greater than ourselves, infuse greater meaning and energy into our work and lives, and create new ecosystems for human flourishing (Laszlo et al., 2021; Nader & Maheshwari, 2023).

Workers will need to become **problem solvers** who are **Adaptive, Creative,** and **Entrepreneurial** (PACE) (Bolles, 2021). However, creative actions driven by intrinsic motivation can be easily killed by over-control (Amabile, 1998). Management education would need to ensure that students are equipped with the skills and knowledge that employers are looking for in the evolving globalized workplace, and yet the students should retain a strong sense of personal creative agency. The education system will need to evolve to cater to an increasingly diverse set of students at all career stages who need to learn continuously to evolve their skillsets (Bolles, 2021). Business schools can also incorporate critical thinking, problem-solving, and leadership skills into the curriculum, along with a wide range of skills through providing students with opportunities to practice these skills. Great attention needs to be paid to sustainability and social responsibility (Polman & Winston, 2021). Management education would need to sensitize students with sustainability (Rimanoczy, 2020), empathy (Heaton & Travis, 2013; Pavlovich, 2019), and other mindsets to address these challenges in a responsible manner. Educators can incorporate sustainability mindset and social responsibility (Kassel & Rimanoczy, 2018) into immersive learning opportunities. Workers need to be freely able to practice their self-development and personally meaningful spiritual practices (Fry, 2003) to develop their own higher sense of purpose in life (Nader & Maheshwari, 2023). TM and mindfulness are among the practices that have been shown to promote relaxation, focus, and overall well-being (Cranson et al., 1991; Travis & Shear, 2010).

Value of Higher Education

In the age of AI, the necessity of a college degree is nuanced and depends on the career path and individual goals. It needs to be balanced with the time and opportunity cost of earning at work. Certain professional fields, such as medicine, law, and engineering, still require formal education and accredited degrees for licensing to practice. However, the rise of AI is shifting how skills and expertise are valued in other areas. Many industries are now prioritizing practical skills, problem-solving abilities, and adaptability over traditional credentials. Online courses, certifications, and hands-on experience with AI tools can offer viable pathways to careers in technology, data science, and creative industries. On the other hand, a college degree provides structured learning and networking opportunities. It also promotes a broader understanding of interdisciplinary topics and helps cultivate soft skills such as communication and collaboration. A college degree thus remains valuable for comprehensive development, deeper learning, and opening doors to leadership roles that require holistic thinking and ethical grounding. Students taking loans for their college education can cultivate a positive mindset by focusing on the long-term value and opportunities their education will bring. They can make the most of the college experience by engaging in courses, networking, internships, and extracurricular activities that enhance skills and future employability. Cultivating gratitude for the opportunity to learn and grow, and focusing on future possibilities that higher education unlocks, can shift the mindset from one of burden to one of empowerment.

Technological landscape is growing and evolving exponentially through a convergence of technologies including AI, robotics, metaverse, genetics, and more (Diamandis & Kotler, 2020). Management education will need to adapt to ensure that students are rapidly skilled with the necessary theories, tools, experiences, and meta-skills to succeed at work. The rapidly rising cost of higher education puts pressure on student finances as well as on the viability of business schools. Management schools may need to develop tiered education models, such as onsite and online with different cost structures. There have been suggestions that driven by market pressures, the vertically integrated business model of universities may be unbundled along the lines of instruction, testing, credentialing, and social skills. For example, MOOCs present severe challenges as an alternative marketplace for higher education, that changes the delivery, certification, and economics of these innovations and could be rapidly disseminated globally (Dieleman et al., 2022).

Reframing Management Education

If I had an hour to solve a problem I'd spend 55 minutes thinking about the problem and five minutes thinking about solutions. - Einstein.

It is important to identify the right issue that lies at the core of the problem. The question becomes: How would management education add value to students and managers who wish to operate from a higher purpose and seek to harness and flourish in an exponentially changing technology-assisted environment? McBride & Hackney (2003) called out the meta-need for developing integrative principles for teaching, such as:

1. Establish a series of generic frameworks or patterns in pedagogical approaches that can be applied to changing technologies and business practices. Derive these bottom-up from observing practice, and top-down drawing on theories across disciplines.
2. Educate the students in critical thinking. Apply critical thinking to the selection of topics and sources.
3. Seek to provide a psychologically safe learning environment where the students come to their own understanding and generate ownership of principles and practices for themselves.

The solution may lie in shifting focus away from imparting knowledge to developing the knower themselves. This can include cultivating meta-skills such as critical thinking, problem-solving, emotional intelligence, and self-directed learning in students. Students can be encouraged to take responsibility for their own learning by setting personal learning goals, creating their own learning plans, and evaluating their own progress. Students could further reflect upon and refine their own personal goals based on their self-identified strengths and weaknesses. Flexible personalized curricula could be adaptable to changing needs, interests, and trends for every student. Close mentorship relationships and work opportunities can guide and support their developing a deeper understanding of their chosen field and gaining insight into career paths.

CBE emphasizes the development of one's consciousness as the primary means to enhance learning and personal growth (Heaton & Heaton, 2018). Eastern spiritual traditions as well as quantum field theory provide significant support to the proposition that consciousness is all there is, and that the universe is one unbounded ocean of consciousness (Maharishi, 1963; Nader, 2021). Everything is a manifestation of that unbounded consciousness. Further, consciousness as the source of all the laws of nature is accessible in one's own physiology (Nader, 1994). Building upon the principles of consciousness-based leadership and management (Maheshwari, 2023a, 2023b), here are three principles of CBLM:

1. Holism: CBE views the world as a whole rather than as a collection of parts. This holistic approach incorporates academic, personal, and professional development to create a well-rounded individual. CBE incorporates interdisciplinary approach that links different academic disciplines together and integrates knowledge across different fields. CBME aims to develop social responsibility, by encouraging students to act and to contribute to the well-being of society (Heaton & Heaton, 2018).
2. Collaboration and Empathy: CBE emphasizes the development of self-awareness, which helps develop the ability to understand one's own thoughts, feelings, and behaviors, and strengths and weaknesses. CBE aims to develop resilience by helping students to deal with stress, anxiety and other negative emotions (Orme-Johnson & Barnes, 2014; Travis et al., 2009).
3. *Unboundarize* oneself: The regular practice of transcendence is the key to the effectiveness of CBE. The techniques of transcendence help students transcend their normal thinking process to reach a state of inner unbounded peace and calm, which can improve self-awareness, focus, and creativity (Maharishi, 1995). CBE can thus help unleash student creativity, by helping students to tap into their inner infinite potential and to think in new and innovative ways (So & Orme-Johnson, 2001; Travis, 1979).

Consciousness-Based Education (CBE)

Based on the teachings of Maharishi Mahesh Yogi (1995), a consciousness-based system of education (CBE) places primary emphasis on the knower, i.e., on developing the knower's potential for learning from within (Fig. 5.1). In comparison, the Learning paradigm focuses on improving the student's process of knowing/learning, and the Instruction paradigm focuses on efficiently communicating the known/knowledge to the students. Consciousness-based education (CBE) paradigm proposes that all knowledge should be integrated in the consciousness of the student/learner/knower. The quality of perception and knowledge is different in different states of consciousness. CBE principles have been

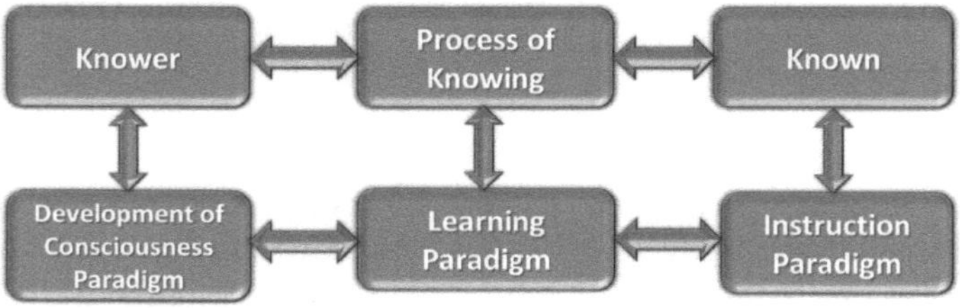

Fig. 5.1 Paradigms of education (Adapted from Llewellyn & Pearson, 2011)

applied to deliver integrated learning for students for even technical subjects (Maheshwari, 2021b). With greater awareness of their interests and capabilities, students may dive into their chosen fields of management with a holistic perspective as well as a specific point of view and develop their leadership skills (Heaton, 2006).

CBE seeks to develop in students a deeper understanding of themselves and their place in the world, through self-awareness, holistic thinking, and purposeful living. The goal is to empower them with the tools and knowledge to achieve personal growth, resilience, and mindful decision-making, fostering a positive impact in their communities and beyond. This approach nurtures not only intellectual and professional skills but also emotional and spiritual well-being, promoting balanced, compassionate, and conscious leaders capable of driving meaningful change in an interconnected world.

Development of Consciousness

Development of Consciousness (DC) has gained traction in the fields of psychology, education, and leadership studies as a transformative approach to creating more meaningful and engaged learning experiences (Schmidt-Wilk et al, 2000; Wilber, 2014). Emotional intelligence (EI) and Spiritual intelligence (SI) are critical components of DC that involve the ability to recognize, understand, and manage emotions in oneself and others, and finding deeper meaning and purpose in life (Goleman, 1998; Zohar et al., 2000). Higher levels of EI and SI tend to lead to more resilient, empathetic, and capable decision-makers. DC involves cultivating ethical awareness, a sense of social responsibility from a systems thinking perspective (Ebert & Alfonso, this volume). Students must develop not only intellectual competence but also commitment to ethical reasoning and civic engagement. Programs that emphasize DC aim to help students critically examine their values and motivations and integrate all the knowledge within their own higher selves.

Human beings can experience higher states of consciousness beyond the normal experience of waking, dreaming, and sleeping states of consciousness. Waking state is the common state of consciousness that we experience when one is awake and engaged in daily activities. Sleeping state is the state of consciousness that one experiences when asleep. Dreaming is the state of consciousness that one experiences during REM sleep, when one has vivid dreams. There is a fourth and higher state of consciousness called Transcendental Consciousness (TC). It is a state of pure consciousness, where one is aware of oneself but not aware of any contents of the mind. Maharishi (1978) describes TC (4th state) as the absolute, non-changing, non-variable, eternal, infinite, unboundedness—which is the inner core of everyone's life. During transcendence, the intellect becomes aware of itself through transcending itself. By direct unmediated experience one can realize the true self as beyond time and form, beyond thoughts and objects. Universality and individuality are two simultaneous aspects of the intellect. There are impulses of the transcendent as much as there are impulses of ego. TC is physiologically described as a state of "restful alertness" and inner peace (Wallace, 1970). TC can be reached through the practice of transcendence achieved using contemplation practices such as Transcendental Meditation (TM). There are further higher states such as cosmic consciousness (CC), when the absolute reality of TC is available even when one is in waking state. The highest state is of Unity Consciousness, where everything is perceived as reverberations of oneself. This is the state that is reported by seers as the ultimate state of oneness. The states are described in terms of awareness of self and the world in Table 5.1.

V-theory of Transcendence

V-theory provides a simple 2-step framework for how one could transcend and develop their consciousness to higher levels (Maheshwari, 2021a). V-Theory shows that the universe can be alternately experienced at two different levels: in its dynamic diversity of impulses of the ego at the top of the V, and its silent transcendental unity at the bottom of the V (Fig. 5.2).

Table 5.1 States of consciousness

State of consciousness	*Self-awareness*	*Content of experience*
Sleep state	None	None
Dream state	None	Illusory
Waking	Individual ego (lower self)	Perceptions, thoughts, feelings
Transcendental Consciousness	Unbounded pure consciousness (higher self)	None
Cosmic consciousness	Unbounded pure consciousness (higher self)	Perceptions, thoughts, feelings
Refined cosmic consciousness	Unbounded pure consciousness (higher self)	Finest relative perceptions of infinite correlations in everything
Unity consciousness or Brahman consciousness	Unbounded pure consciousness (higher self)	Fluctuations within pure consciousness "...all things in terms of the Self."

Source Maheshwari (2021a)

Fig. 5.2 V-theory: a 2-step model of transcendence

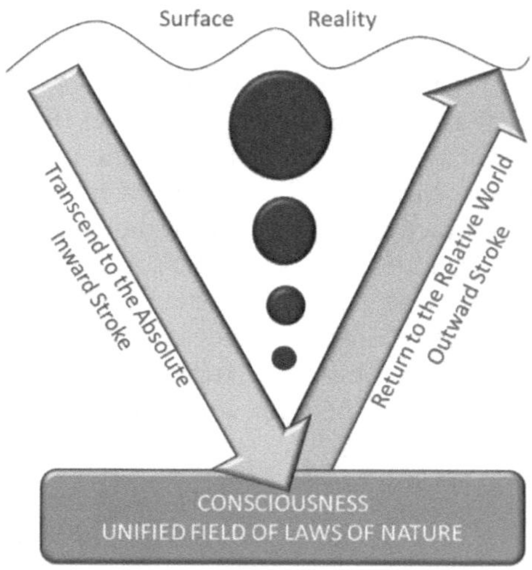

The upper level is the level of diverse dynamic action. The bottom level is the level of the transcendent, the source of pure potential. The path to understanding and participating in the continuous transformation of the world at the top of the V is through experiencing the silent unity at the bottom of the V. The first step is to choose a path or practice to transcend surface reality and connect with the pure consciousness at the bottom of the V. It is called the inward stroke. Staying for a certain period of time at the bottom of the V helps bring deep rest and order to the individual mind. The second step of the V is to return to the dynamic surface reality. This is called the outward stroke. Multiple practices may be considered in the context of a simple 2-step V-model of an inward and outward stroke. Transcendence can be achieved effectively through TM (Travis & Shear, 2010). Other approaches from other traditions of transcendence too could be conceived through V-theory with the premise that the consciousness at the bottom of the V is primary, self-referral, and independent of matter.

Almost all spiritual traditions prescribe their own means of transcending (Wilber, 2014). Some suggest prayer and devotion as a way of reaching God. Others suggest sacred practices to cleanse oneself and reach the transcendent states. There are many techniques of meditation coming from many Eastern traditions including Vedic, Buddhist, Chinese, Zen, and others. Some meditations are premised on their being an ultimate reality, for example, Vedic and Yoga Sutras-based meditations. Regular practice of TM technique by college students has been shown to lead to higher brain integration score, which is indicative of lower stress and higher creativity (Travis et al., 2009). Once the student develops higher creative capacity, they can naturally grow their knowledge organically and holistically, with the least amount of effort and a great sense of accomplishment and fulfillment. The way to enhance integrative learning is thus to enliven the student's consciousness. TM helps individuals experience the deep silence within, which helps achieve a state of deep relaxation and inner calm, and enhance educational effectiveness (Cranson et al., 1991; Rosaen & Benn, 2006).

CBE Principles

CBE offers a transformative approach that goes beyond traditional academic knowledge, aiming to develop the full spectrum of a person's inner potential—creativity, intelligence, moral development, emotional resilience, and spiritual growth (Heaton, 2016; Maheshwari, 2023a, 2023b). This holistic approach focuses on self-awareness and the expansion of consciousness, paving the way for both personal and societal transformation (Dillbeck & Dillbeck, 1987). Here are some key principles of CBE.

1. Principle of Wholeness: Rooted in consciousness-based approach and systems thinking, it encourages leaders and managers to view their roles not in isolation but as integral components of a larger system. In the context of management education, it emphasizes the interconnectedness of all aspects of an organization, individuals, and the broader environment. The principle of wholeness advocates balancing economic goals with social, ethical, and ecological responsibilities. By integrating analytical thinking with emotional intelligence, spirituality, and ethical awareness, it fosters decision-making that aligns with long-term well-being and sustainability. The Principle of Wholeness cultivates leaders capable of navigating complexity with wisdom, compassion, and a commitment to collective growth.
2. Principle of Growth in Layers: This principle recognizes that individuals, teams, and organizations evolve through incremental learning, experience, and self-awareness. In the context of management education it emphasizes nurturing foundational skills and values before advancing to more complex competencies, ensuring sustainable and authentic growth (Schmidt-Wilk et al., 2000). Water the root and enjoy the fruit. In leadership, this approach fosters a deeper understanding of personal and organizational goals, aligning inner development with outward actions. By embracing this layered progression, management education encourages continuous improvement, adaptability, and the integration of diverse perspectives to achieve holistic and enduring success.
3. Principle of Knowledge Structure: It asserts that knowledge is intrinsically linked to the state of consciousness in which it is experienced. In management education, this principle recognizes that understanding and decision-making vary across levels of awareness—from routine cognition to deeper states of insight. As consciousness expands, individuals perceive more holistic connections, leading to profound insights and innovative solutions. This principle highlights the dynamic and evolving nature of knowledge, emphasizing practices like meditation and self-reflection to elevate awareness. By aligning knowledge acquisition with consciousness development,

it fosters adaptive, ethical, and visionary leadership in complex environments.

4. Principle of Effortless Effort: It emphasizes that achieving optimal results comes from aligning actions with natural laws and focusing on the right approach rather than sheer force (Schneider et al., 2005). *Yogasthah Kuru karmani*, or established in Self, perform action. In management education, purposeful, well-directed efforts rooted in clarity of vision and inner alignment can lead to efficient outcomes. It underscores the importance of working smarter, not harder, by identifying the "right angle" or the most harmonious way to approach a task. By cultivating practices like mindfulness, focus, and strategic thinking, managers can reduce friction, increase flow, and achieve sustainable success with less strain and greater effectiveness.

AI-Based Education (ABE)

AI systems have the potential to revolutionize how education is delivered, making it more personalized, efficient, and responsive to the needs of individual learners (Baker & Siemens, 2014). AI can be particularly effective when integrated with the development of consciousness, creating learning environments that foster both cognitive and emotional growth. One of the most significant contributions of AI is its ability to personalize learning experiences. This personalized approach overcomes the limitations of the one-size-fits-all model that dominates traditional college education systems. AI-powered systems can

1. Analyze student activity data and provide personalized recommendations for learning topics, materials, activities, and assessments.
2. Assess student work and provide instant, detailed, and personalized feedback, allowing students to understand areas needing improvement immediately.
3. Adapt the level of difficulty of assessments to the individual student's level of understanding and can help to ensure that students are challenged but not overwhelmed. AI can adjust the difficulty level and type of content in real-time.

4. Predict which students are at risk of falling behind in which aspects and provide early interventions to help them succeed. Predictive analytics enables educators to anticipate learning challenges and prevent disengagement.
5. Support the development of emotional intelligence by creating interactive learning environments that encourage self-reflection and empathy.
6. Create virtual tutors or chatbots that simulate real-world social interactions, helping students practice communication, conflict resolution, and emotional regulation in safe, controlled settings.
7. Improve mental health by analyzing students' behavior and emotional states, providing real-time feedback and guidance to help them manage stress and anxiety (Kashihara, 2020).
8. Analyze vast amounts of data to tailor instruction to individual learners' strengths, weaknesses, and learning preferences (Luckin et al., 2016).
9. Support students progress at their own pace and focus on areas where they need the most support (Holmes et al., 2019; Zawacki-Richter et al., 2019).
10. Create natural language processing (NLP) systems for real-time translation, making educational content accessible to non-native speakers globally (Zawacki-Richter et al., 2019).
11. Democratize learning by breaking down barriers related to disabilities using assistive technologies for students with disabilities, such as speech-to-text and adaptive learning platforms.
12. Deliver immersive experiences using virtual reality (VR) and augmented reality (AR) offer students dynamic ways to explore content, such as virtual science labs or historical simulations (Murtaza et al., 2022).
13. Enhance student engagement through interactive learning gamified environments and incorporating quizzes, challenges, and rewards.
14. Assist teachers in managing large classes by automating administrative tasks like grading and tracking student performance (Baker & Siemens, 2014).
15. Support educators to focus on the more interpersonal aspects of teaching, such as providing mentoring, coaching, and creating a more engaging and inclusive classroom environment.

16. Enable lifelong learning by creating flexible, adaptive learning environments that cater to individuals at different stages of their careers.
17. Provide customized resources reskilling and upskilling that enable learners to continuously acquire new knowledge and skills through microlearning.
18. Provide a constantly available knowledge and personalized tutor to suit the schedules of working professionals.
19. Revise content in real-time to ensure that the educational program stays relevant to learners' needs and the demands of the future job market.
20. Diffuse high-quality education availability for students across diverse socioeconomic backgrounds, in underfunded schools or developing countries (Zawacki-Richter et al., 2019).
21. Foster continuous innovation by constantly analyzing student performance data and adjusting teaching methods and curricula in real-time (Baker & Siemens, 2014).
22. Be grounded in constructivist and behaviorist or other preferred theories of learning, to support individual learning and feedback preferences.

The rapidly rising cost of higher education puts pressure on student finances as well as on the viability of business schools. Thus, AI-based systems can also:

1. Help business schools develop tiered education models, such as onsite and online with different cost structures.
2. Help address market pressures by unbundling the vertically integrated business model of universities, along separate lines of instruction, testing, credentialing, and social skills.
3. Enable Massively Open Online course systems (MOOCs) as an alternative low-cost marketplace for education and skill development (Dieleman et al., 2022).
4. Enable the low-cost scalability of personalized learning experiences to global audiences.

There are several AI platforms available at the time of this writing. AI-based intelligent tutoring systems like Khanamigo—an AI tutor integrated into the Khan Academy platform—empower learners by tailoring educational experiences to their individual needs. Khanamigo is a leading platform that serves as interactive learning environment, providing constructive real-time feedback, personalized exercises, and adaptive learning paths based on student performance. By offering constant, context-aware assistance. Khanamigo can explain complex concepts, quiz students, and track their progress. It leverages machine learning to continuously adapt content based on students' responses, ensuring that the material is neither too easy nor too difficult. This adaptive feedback loop aligns with the behaviorist theory of learning, where reinforcement and feedback shape behavior. Some tools even display "mindful" capabilities (Delcker et al., 2024).

From a connectivism and social learning perspective, some other AI-based tools foster collaboration among students and teachers by providing platforms where knowledge can be shared, and discussions can take place. These platforms can integrate AI to provide intelligent recommendations on assignments, resources, and collaboration opportunities based on a student's learning history. MOOC platforms use AI to connect learners with personalized learning resources, quizzes, and global peers to expand knowledge networks. They also support the idea that AI can serve as a tool for facilitating lifelong learning and reskilling, particularly in an era where knowledge is rapidly evolving. Other AI-based tools use AI to tailor curriculum pathways for each student, ensuring that educational content is accessible and adaptable to all learners, regardless of their initial knowledge base. This supports the notion of equity in education, where AI's scalability can help bridge gaps in access to quality education, particularly for students in underserved areas.

Considering the above, management education will need to evolve rapidly to ensure that students can cost-effectively acquire the necessary theories, tools, experiences, and meta-skills to succeed in an exponentially evolving work environment. While AI offers numerous opportunities, it also raises important ethical questions. The use of AI in education must be governed by principles that prioritize student autonomy, privacy, and fairness. Even though education systems based on generative AI tools have been heralded as the future of education, research suggests that it could also harm learning because it is biologically impossible for humans and AI to develop mutual empathy. Overuse of AI systems can also impact foundational thinking abilities such as critical thinking and creative thinking. AI tools need to be supplemented by DC approaches.

Synergizing CBE and ABE

The alignment of CBE and ABE systems can create a powerful holistic system that integrates the strengths of both approaches, fostering intellectual, emotional, and spiritual growth. By combining personalized AI-driven learning with the focus on self-awareness and inner development of consciousness-based education, this integration enhances the potential for learners to become well-rounded individuals capable of addressing complex global challenges. This synergy could be manifested in several ways.

1. Development of consciousness: Guide students through mindfulness and meditation practices, analyzing biometric data such as heart rate variability and brainwave activity to provide real-time feedback on their progress toward higher states of consciousness (Schneider et al., 2005). Meditation apps can be tailored to individual needs offering personalized guidance based on students' current mental and emotional states (Schmidt-Wilk et al., 2000).
2. Personalized learning: Individualized and adaptive pathways can be designed not only to adjust based on the student's academic performance and relate the subject matter to the knowledge of the self, enhancing both cognitive and emotional well-being (Maheshwari & Biberman, 2024).
3. Adaptive Education: Analyze student behavior and recommend mindfulness exercises or reflective practices when signs of stress or disengagement are detected. Suggest mindful breaks or meditation practices based on students' stress levels or attention spans, ensuring a balanced learning experience. One can track emotional intelligence, stress management, and self-awareness, offering a holistic view of student development (Travis & Arenander, 2006).
4. Moral development: Enhance group learning dynamics, supporting collective consciousness by monitoring interactions, and nudging them toward collaboration, empathy, and shared reflection (So & Orme-Johnson, 2001). It could offer insights into group behavior and suggest practices to foster better communication and collective well-being through reflective exercises (Schneider et al., 2005).

5. Balanced Learning: Pair with ethical reflection exercises to help students consider the broader implications of their actions. AI could present data on real-world challenges, while CBE could guide reflection on the ethical dimensions of potential solutions (Holmes et al., 2019). Create environments to balance cognitive skills and sessions of meditation and reflection to ensure a holistic learning experience (Murtaza et al., 2022).
6. Influence future AI development: Students can influence how AI systems are designed so that algorithms focus not only on academic productivity but also promote ethical values such as compassion, mindfulness, and integrity and holistic well-being in mind (Maheshwari & Biberman, this volume).

There are thus several levels of integration of CBE with ABE that can offer a balanced and holistic learning model that nurtures both intellectual and emotional intelligence.

Benefits and Challenges

The merger of ABE with CBE presents a holistic approach that supports the intellectual, emotional, and spiritual growth of learners. This integration could revolutionize how we educate, ensuring that the development of the whole person is prioritized alongside academic success. Merging AI with CBE creates benefits such as:

1. Ensures that learning addresses the whole person, integrating intellectual, emotional, and spiritual growth. Traditional education often focuses on academic success, neglecting emotional intelligence and ethical development (Maheshwari & Biberman, 2024). CBE ensures personalized learning paths that are integrated with personal preferences of consciousness-based practices for mental and emotional well-being.
2. CBE encourages and learners to make decisions that are compassionate and socially responsible, and prepares students to balance technological advancements with human-centered decision-making (Holmes et al., 2019). AI-based gamification and adaptive learning tools can increase engagement, but when combined with reflective practices, students are less likely to experience burnout or mental

fatigue (So & Orme-Johnson, 2001). Students consistently working at the challenge appropriate to their level of consciousness can help reduce stress and enhance mental focus (Schmidt-Wilk et al., 2000; Travis & Arenander, 2006).

3. AI's ability to scale can be applied to deliver personalized consciousness-based solutions for ethical, emotional, and spiritual development. This creates opportunities for holistic education across geographic and economic boundaries (Zawacki-Richter et al., 2019). CBE equips students with the tools for ethical leadership and emotional intelligence, essential for addressing global challenges like climate change and inequality. AI provides the technical skills and data-driven insights needed to find solutions (Maheshwari & Biberman, 2024).
4. Finally, ABE and CBE together have the potential to significantly enhance autonomy in education, through self-driven self-paced self-oriented education within and outside formal educational institutions (Luckin & Holmes, 2016). AI can automate administrative tasks, such as grading and lesson planning, freeing teachers to focus on mentoring and providing emotional support to students.

The merger or ABE with CBE also presents several challenges and potential downsides.

1. An overreliance on technology could reduce opportunities for human interaction and emotional learning, that could erode students' critical thinking and independence in problem-solving. A heavy reliance on AI could reduce student–teacher interactions, weakening the sense of community as well as effectiveness of development (Zawacki-Richter et al., 2019). ABE relies heavily on gamification and external rewards to engage students, which could undermine their intrinsic motivation for personal growth and learning, which is central to CBE (Travis & Arenander, 2006).
2. The "digital divide" or unequal access to advanced AI-based educational could widen the gap between privileged and underprivileged learners. The integration of AI and CBE requires significant financial investment in technology, infrastructure, and training (Zawacki-Richter et al., 2019). AI algorithms can embed biases, leading to decisions based on flawed data or favoring certain demographics

(Baker & Hawn, 2021). AI's collection of student data raises privacy concerns, especially if this data is used inappropriately or accessed by unauthorized parties (Holmes et al., 2019). Excessive AI surveillance may create a controlled environment that contradicts the principles of self-development (Zuboff, 2019).

3. If not properly integrated, AI's emphasis on measurable outcomes may conflict with the subjective and introspective nature of consciousness-based practices (Schmidt-Wilk et al., 2000). Teachers may lack the expertise to combine both approaches effectively. The complexity of merging AI and consciousness-based practices could overwhelm students, leading to information overload, confusion, and disengagement. AI's mechanistic approach might struggle to fully support the emotional and ethical growth that CBE emphasizes (So & Orme-Johnson, 2001). Merging AI-based and CBE presents practical challenges in curriculum design, teacher training, and integrating AI tools with spiritual practices (Schneider et al., 2005).

Merging AI-based and CBE offers the potential for a personalized, holistic learning experience, it also introduces several ethical concerns, conflicts between technological and humanistic approaches, overreliance on AI, and inequality in access. The merger of AI-based and CBE offers the potential to both reduce and increase the cost of education, depending on how it is implemented. The net impact on cost will depend on how well institutions balance AI's efficiency with the resource demands of consciousness-based practices, ensuring that education remains both affordable and holistic. Table 5.2 summarizes the challenges and benefits.

The Integration Path

The path forward therefore involves careful planning, phased integration, and aligning innovation with the institution's core values. The goal is to gradually incorporate the strengths of both systems while maintaining the educational institution's mission and capacity for growth. Below is a suggested approach for such an institution:

Table 5.2 Benefits and challenges of merging AI-based and consciousness-based education

Benefits	*Challenges*
Holistic development: merging AI and CBE ensures that learning addresses intellectual, emotional, and spiritual growth	Overreliance on technology: heavy integration of AI could reduce human interaction and critical thinking
Enhanced personalization with inner growth focus: AI-driven personalized learning paths combined with mindfulness and reflection reduce stress and enhance learning outcomes	Loss of human connection: AI might depersonalize education, weakening student–teacher relationships and emotional development
Ethically informed use of technology: CBE integrates ethical decision-making with AI-based learning	Inequality and access: the digital divide could widen as underserved regions may not have access to advanced AI tools
Increased engagement and mental well-being: combining AI tools with mindfulness prevents burnout, enhancing engagement and retention	Ethical concerns with AI: AI algorithms may perpetuate biases, and privacy concerns arise from data collection
Scalable ethical and emotional support: AI ensures scalability, providing holistic support to students across socioeconomic boundaries	Loss of intrinsic motivation: reliance on external rewards through AI could undermine students' intrinsic motivation for learning
Preparing students for complex global challenges: AI provides technical skills while CBE promotes ethical leadership to solve global challenges	Conflict between technological and humanistic approaches: AI's focus on efficiency might clash with consciousness-based education's emphasis on personal growth
Improved Teacher Support: AI automates administrative tasks, allowing teachers to focus on mentoring and student relationships	Reduced emphasis on emotional and ethical dimensions: AI may not fully support emotional and ethical growth, potentially weakening moral development
Reducing stress while maximizing learning efficiency: AI ensures the appropriate challenge level, while mindfulness reduces stress, creating optimal learning conditions	Complexity of integration: merging AI with consciousness-based practices presents challenges in curriculum design and teacher training
Scalable learning: AI allows personalized, scalable learning across large groups, maintaining collective well-being	Cost and resource constraints: significant financial investment in technology and training is needed, especially for schools in developing regions

(continued)

Table 5.2 (continued)

Benefits	*Challenges*
Ethical leadership: students will be equipped with both technological and ethical skills, fostering responsible leadership in a globalized world	Over-monitoring and surveillance: AI's tracking of student behavior may infringe on privacy, conflicting with consciousness-based principles of self-awareness and freedom
Self-driven learning: AI allows learners to explore content at their own speed, while consciousness-based practices like meditation help balance academic progress with self-care, reducing burnout	Difficulty in self-regulation: self-driven learners without the structure of traditional environments may struggle with discipline, leading to disengagement despite AI's personalized content

1. Assess Institutional Readiness: Begin by conducting a needs assessment to evaluate the institution's current state, including its technological infrastructure, faculty expertise, student demographics, and administrative capacity to offer consciousness and AI-based holistic education.
2. Faculty Training and Development: Provide professional development for educators on both AI and consciousness-based practices like mediation and emotional intelligence.
3. Introduce Consciousness-Based Practices: Start by introducing meditation and well-being programs in non-academic areas, such as wellness centers or extracurricular activities.
4. Experiment with AI-Based Tools: Use AI-powered adaptive learning platforms for specific subjects like math, science, or language learning to offer personalized learning paths for students. Experiment with AI-driven administrative tools, such as for grading and attendance tracking.
5. Create a Roadmap for Integration: Develop a clear roadmap that includes pilot programs and milestones for the 1-year, 3-year, and 5-year phases.
6. Foster a Culture of Holistic Learning: Promote ethical and emotional development through integrated AI and consciousness-based education.
7. Develop Partnerships and Collaborations: Partner with AI developers and CBE experts to help implement cutting-edge technologies and create a strong research base.

8. Continuous Feedback and Improvement: Maintain flexibility in implementation, regularly assessing the effectiveness of both AI and consciousness-based practices.

A phased, thoughtful approach by starting with faculty development and pilot programs, followed by phased integration of both systems, can create a holistic learning environment that addresses both intellectual and emotional needs.

Discussion

An AI-backed view of consciousness-based education (AI-CBE) can open a wide canvas for imagination and research. Imagine management students in higher states of consciousness in a friendly learning environment where every student can flourish (Maheshwari, 2021a). Imagine management students as leaders guiding their teams to do their work with joy and creativity, driven by a higher purpose (Nader & Maheshwari, 2023). Imagine an entire flourishing enterprise operating in harmony and effectiveness where the future leaders would be both emotionally grounded and highly adaptable to change (Laszlo & Brown, 2014). Imagine where students can learn to adapt to environmental changes, integrate new ideas, purify those ideas and influences that are not helpful, and grow their own selves in a healthy way. How can one better enable students to lead with emotional intelligence and fully embrace and exhibit exemplary leadership practices: model the way, inspire a shared vision, challenge the process, enable others to act, and encourage the heart (Kouzes & Posner, 2003). How can one better enable students to exhibit high self-efficacy and embrace the concept that giving is the basis for receiving? How can one better enable students to practice gratitude on a regular basis, and practice a sense of balance in life?

Imagining transitional scenarios for a merged AI-CBE system allows us to envision how to revolutionize the learning experience across different life stages. We can see how this hybrid approach offers personalized, meaningful education while promoting emotional resilience, ethical decision-making, and professional success. Through AI's capacity to tailor learning experiences and consciousness-based practices that foster self-awareness and emotional intelligence, individuals at various stages of life can achieve personal and professional fulfillment. Whether it's a young student seeking engagement, or a professional expanding global opportunity, or an educator striving to stay relevant and secure, the merged system transforms how individuals learn and grow. Through continuous learning and self-reflection, they become capable of contributing positively to society while maintaining personal well-being and professional excellence.

Conclusion

A merged AI-CBE system could represent a profound shift in how learning systems can be designed to meet the needs of both students and educators in the twenty-first century. By merging the precision of personalized AI-driven learning with the holistic development offered by consciousness-based practices, this integrated educational model can foster not only academic achievement but also emotional resilience, ethical decision-making, and personal growth. This hybrid system can provide educators essential tools to stay professionally relevant while managing cognitive overload and work-life balance through AI-driven automation and mindfulness. This approach addresses the increasing complexity of fields like business education, enabling teachers to integrate cutting-edge trends such as AI, sustainability, and leadership into their curricula without sacrificing the humanistic values at the core of education. Students benefit from engaging, personalized learning experiences that are not only academically enriching but also promote emotional well-being and ethical consciousness—skills essential for navigating the challenges of a globalized and technologically advanced world. By reducing administrative burdens, increasing accessibility, and offering scalable learning environments, the merged system presents an opportunity to make high-quality education more affordable and widely available. It prepares both educators and students to thrive in a future where adaptability, lifelong learning, and ethical leadership are paramount. This forward-thinking model stands as a promising blueprint for evolving education into a system that equips individuals with the knowledge and character needed to address global challenges with confidence, compassion, and integrity.

AIs will teach a hyper-personalized curriculum in a gamified fashion, utilizing your favorite sports stars, film stars, and teaching modalities (Selwyn, 2019). Imagine learning directly from an AI version of Aristotle or Einstein? An AI educator that is infinitely patient and knowledgeable. This is now possible. Next, rather than just reading or listening to a lesson, imagine "experiencing a lesson." Imagine entering a photo-realistic virtual world where you engage with AI agents that are indistinguishable from humans. You are now learning through experience.

The integration of ABE and CBE into an AI-CBE system offers significant potential for transforming paradigms in management education, but it also presents numerous avenues for further research (Pavlovich, 2010; Wang et al., 2024; Weisbrod et al., 2024). A critical area of study is the long-term impact of this merged approach on student outcomes, including not only academic performance but also emotional well-being, ethical decision-making, and life satisfaction (du Boulay, 2022). Future research should explore the effectiveness of combining AI's personalized learning capabilities with DC practices in fostering holistic growth (Lagrosen & Lagrosen, 2020).

Another key research area is how this hybrid model can be scaled for broader adoption, in diverse educational contexts such as K-12, higher education, and professional training. Investigating the accessibility and affordability of implementing AI-CBE across different socioeconomic backgrounds is essential to ensuring its equitable deployment (Shneiderman, 2022). The ethical considerations of using AI in education need further exploration. Researchers should examine how AI systems can be designed to avoid biases and support inclusive learning environments. Additionally, understanding the potential privacy concerns and implications of using AI to track emotional and cognitive states is crucial for developing responsible educational environments. Finally, future research should delve into how teachers and educators can best adapt to these evolving tools. Studies could explore professional development programs that merge AI training with emotional intelligence and reflective practices, empowering educators to embrace innovation while maintaining human-centered learning (Nader & Maheshwari, 2023). Overall, a multidisciplinary approach that incorporates pedagogy, psychology, ethics, and technology will be vital in guiding the future of this transformative educational model. Ultimately, the integration of AI and CBE could lead to a new paradigm for higher education that prioritizes the holistic development of individuals as ethical, socially responsible, and emotionally intelligent citizens. This AI-CBE system would prepare students not only for the workforce but also for the challenges of living in an interconnected, rapidly changing world.

References

Amabile, T. M. (1998). *How to kill creativity* (Vol. 87). Harvard Business School Publishing.

Arendt, H. (2005). *Essays in understanding, 1930–1954: Formation, exile, and totalitarianism*. Schocken.

Baker, R. S., & Hawn, A. (2021). Algorithmic bias in education. *International Journal of Artificial Intelligence in Education*, 1–41.

Baker, R., & Siemens, G. (2014). Learning analytics and educational data mining. In *Cambridge handbook of the leaning sciences* (pp. 253–272).

Bolles, G. A. (2021). *The next rules of work: The mindset*. Kogan Page.

Cranson, R. W., Orme-Johnson, D. W., Gackenbach, J., Dillbeck, M. C., Jones, C. H., & Alexander, C. N. (1991). Transcendental meditation and improved performance on intelligence-related measures: A longitudinal study. *Personality and Individual Differences, 12*(10), 1105–1116.

Datar, S. M., Garvin, D. A., & Cullen, P. G. (2010). *Rethinking the MBA: Business education at a crossroads*. Harvard Business Press.

Delcker, J., Heil, J., Ifenthaler, D., Seufert, S., & Spirgi, L. (2024). First-year students' usage of and attitudes towards mindless and mindful AI-technology. In *Artificial intelligence for supporting human cognition and exploratory learning in the digital age* (pp. 25–40). Springer Nature Switzerland.

Dhiman, S. (2017). *Holistic leadership: A new paradigm for today's leaders*. Springer.

Diamandis, P. H., & Kotler, S. (2020). *The future is faster than you think: How converging technologies are transforming business, industries, and our lives*. Simon & Schuster.

Dieleman, M., Šilenskytė, A., Lynden, K., Fletcher, M., & Panina, D. (2022). Toward more impactful international business education: A teaching innovation typology. *Journal of Teaching in International Business, 33*(4), 181–202.

Dillbeck, M. C. (1977). The effect of the Transcendental Meditation technique on anxiety level. *Journal of Clinical Psychology, 33*(4), 1076–1078.

Dillbeck, M. C., & Dillbeck, S. L. (1987). The Maharishi technology of the unified field in education: Principles, practice, and research. *Modern Science and Vedic Science, 1*(4), 383–431.

Doyle, T., & Brady, M. (2018). Reframing the university as an emergent organization: Implications for strategic management and leadership in higher education. *Journal of Higher Education Policy and Management, 40*(4), 305–320.

du Boulay, B. (2022). Artificial intelligence in education and ethics. In *Handbook of open, distance and digital education* (pp. 1–16). Springer Nature Singapore.

Ebert, L., & Montero, A. (this volume). Systems thinking mindset and AI.

Fry, L. W. (2003). Toward a theory of spiritual leadership. *The Leadership Quarterly, 14*(6), 693–727.

Goleman, D. (1998). *Working with emotional intelligence*. Bantam Books.

Heaton, D., & Heaton, C. (2018). Consciousness-based education: Cultivating sustainable minds. In K. Kassel & I. Rimanoczy (Eds.), *Developing a sustainability mindset in higher education* (pp. 277–296). Routledge.

Heaton, D. (2016). An innovative approach to cultivate responsible next generation leaders: Transcendental Meditation in management education. In S. Tiwari & L. Nafees (Eds.), *Innovative management education pedagogies for preparing next-generation leaders* (pp. 139–160). IGI Global.

Heaton, D. P. (2006). Consciousness-based education: A foundation for teaching and learning in the academic disciplines. *Journal of Consciousness-Based Education, 2*(1), 1–8.

Heaton, D. P., & Travis, F. (2013). Consciousness, empathy, and the brain. In *Organizing through empathy* (pp. 17–33). Routledge.

Holmes, W., Bialik, M., & Fadel, C. (2019). *Artificial intelligence in education: Promises and implications for teaching and learning*. The Center for Curriculum Redesign.

Huisman, J., & van der Wende, M. (Eds.). (2022). *A research agenda for global higher education*.

Johansen, B. (2020). *Full-spectrum thinking: How to escape boxes in a post-categorical future*. Berrett-Koehler Publishers.

Kashihara, K. (2020). Microsaccadic modulation evoked by emotional events. *Journal of Physiological Anthropology, 39*(1), 26.

Kassel, K., & Rimanoczy, I. (Eds.). (2018). *Developing a sustainability mindset in management education* (p. 368). Routledge.

Kegan, R. (1998). *In over our heads: The mental demands of modern life*. Harvard University Press.

Kouzes, J. M., & Posner, B. Z. (2003). *The leadership practices inventory (LPI): Self instrument* (Vol. 52). Wiley.

Krishnamurthy, S. (2020). The future of business education: A commentary in the shadow of the Covid-19 pandemic. *Journal of Business Research, 117*, 1–5.

Lagrosen, Y., & Lagrosen, S. (2020). Organizational learning in consciousness-based education schools: A multiple-case study. *International Journal of Educational Management, 34*(5), 849–867.

Laloux, F. (2014). *Reinventing organizations: A guide to creating organizations inspired by the next stage in human consciousness*. Nelson Parker.

Laszlo, C., & Brown, J. S. (2014). *Flourishing enterprise*. Stanford University Press.

Laszlo, C., Waddock, S., Maheshwari, A., Nigri, G., & Storberg-Walker, J. (2021). Quantum worldviews: How science and spirituality are converging to transform consciousness for meaningful solutions to wicked problems. *Humanistic Management Journal, 6*, 293–311.

Llewellyn, D., & Pearson, C. (2011). *Consciousness-based education: A foundation for teaching and learning in the academic disciplines.*
Luckin, R., & Holmes, W. (2016). Intelligence unleashed: An argument for AI in education.
Maharishi Mahesh Yogi. (1963). *Science of being and the art of living*. Penguin.
Maharishi Mahesh Yogi. (1978). *Enlightenment to every individual. Invincibility to every nation*. MIU Press.
Maharishi Mahesh Yogi. (1995). *Maharishi university of management: Wholeness on the move*. MUM Press.
Maheshwari, A. K. (2021a). Higher consciousness management: Transcendence for spontaneous right action. *Journal of Management, Spirituality & Religion, 18*(6), 77–91.
Maheshwari, A. K. (2021b). Teaching data analytics using natural law as integrative framework. In *Advancing innovation and sustainable outcomes in international graduate education* (pp. 103–119). IGI Global.
Maheshwari, A. K. (2023). Consciousness-based management education for a flourishing business ecosystem. *Journal for Advancing Business Education, 69*.
Maheshwari, A. K. (2023). Wholeness of consciousness-based leadership and management. In A. K. Maheshwari (Ed.), *Consciousness-based leadership and management, volume 1: Vedic and other philosophical approaches to oneness and flourishing* (pp. 3–25). Springer International Publishing.
Maheshwari, A. K., & Biberman, G. (2024). Artificial oneness: Bridging the human machine divide. *Journal of Management, Spirituality & Religion, 21*
Manning, K. (2017). *Organizational theory in higher education*. Routledge.
McBride, N., & Hackney, R. (2003). Establishing the principles of information systems teaching. *Communications of the Association for Information Systems, 11*(1), 18, pp. 322–331.
Murtaza, M., Ahmed, Y., Shamsi, J. A., Sherwani, F., & Usman, M. (2022). AI-based personalized e-learning systems: Issues, challenges, and solutions. *IEEE Access, 10*, 81323–81342.
Nader, T., & Maheshwari, A. K. (2023). Consciousness as the source of purposeful leadership. In A. K. Maheshwari (Ed.), *Consciousness-based leadership and management, volume 1: Vedic and other philosophical approaches to oneness and flourishing*. Springer International Publishing.
Nader, T. (1994). *Human physiology: Expression of Veda and the Vedic literature: Modern science and ancient Vedic science discover the fabrics of immortality in human physiology*. Maharishi Vedic University.
Nader, T. (2021). *One unbounded ocean of consciousness*. Aguilar.
Orme-Johnson, D. W., & Barnes, V. A. (2014). Effects of the transcendental meditation technique on trait anxiety: A meta-analysis of randomized controlled trials. *The Journal of Alternative and Complementary Medicine, 20*(5), 330–341.

Pavlovich, K. (2010). Educating for conscious awareness. *Journal of Management, Spirituality & Religion, 7*(3), 193–208.

Pavlovich, K. (2019). Quantum empathy: An alternative narrative for global transcendence. *Journal of Management, Spirituality & Religion, 17*(4), 333–347.

Polman, P., & Winston, A. (2s021). *Net positive: How courageous companies thrive by giving more than they take*. HBS Press.

Rimanoczy, I. (2020). *The sustainability mindset principles: A guide to develop a mindset for a better world*. Routledge.

Rosaen, C., & Benn, R. (2006). The experience of transcendental meditation in middle school students: A qualitative report. *Explore, 2*(5), 422–425.

Schmidt-Wilk, J., Heaton, D. P., & Steingard, D. (2000). Higher education for higher consciousness: Maharishi University of Management as a model for spirituality in management education. *Journal of Management Education, 24*(5), 580–611.

Schneider, R. H., Alexander, C. N., & Wallace, R. K. (2005). *Consciousness-based education and worldview of natural law: Foundations of Maharishi's Vedic science*. Maharishi University of Management Press.

Schwab, K. (2017). *The fourth industrial revolution*. Currency.

Selwyn, N. (2019). *Should robots replace teachers?: AI and the future of education*. Wiley.

Shneiderman, B. (2022). *Human-centered AI*. Oxford University Press.

So, K. T., & Orme-Johnson, D. W. (2001). Three randomized experiments on the longitudinal effects of the transcendental meditation technique on cognition. *Intelligence, 29*(5), 419–440.

Travis, F. (1979). The transcendental meditation technique and creativity: A longitudinal study of Cornell University undergraduates. *The Journal of Creative Behavior*.

Travis, F., & Arenander, A. (2006). Cross-sectional and longitudinal study of effects of transcendental meditation practice on brain functioning. *International Journal of Neuroscience, 116*(12), 1519–1538.

Travis, F., & Shear, J. (2010). Focused attention, open monitoring and automatic self-transcending: Categories to organize meditations from Vedic, Buddhist and Chinese traditions. *Consciousness and Cognition, 19*, 1110–1119.

Travis, F., Haaga, D. A., Hagelin, J., Tanner, M., Nidich, S., Gaylord-King, C., Grosswald, S., Rainforth, M., & Schneider, R. H. (2009). Effects of transcendental meditation practice on brain functioning and stress reactivity in college students. *International Journal of Psychophysiology, 71*(2), 170–176.

Tsao, F. C., & Laszlo, C. (2019). *Quantum Leadership*. Stanford University Press.

Wallace, R. K. (1970). Physiological effects of transcendental meditation. *Science, 167*(3926), 1751–1754.

Wang, Y. C., Lu, Y., Grunwald, S., Chu, S. L., Kamble, P., & Kumar, J. (2024). An AI approach to support student mental health: Case of developing an AI-powered web-platform with nature-based mindfulness. *Journal of Hospitality & Tourism Education*, 1–14.

Weisbrod, A. V., Bohman, L. C., & Ramdial, K. J. (2024). From theory to practice: A novel meditation program at a global corporation. *Current Psychology, 43*(5), 4266–4283.

Wilber, K. (2014). *The fourth turning: Imagining the evolution of an integral Buddhism*. Shambhala Publications.

Zawacki-Richter, O., Marín, V. I., Bond, M., & Gouverneur, F. (2019). Systematic review of research on artificial intelligence applications in higher education–Where are the educators? *International Journal of Educational Technology in Higher Education, 16*(1), 39.

Zohar, D., Marshall, I., & Marshall, I. N. (2000). *SQ: Connecting with our spiritual intelligence*. Bloomsbury Publishing USA.

Zuboff, S. (2019). *The age of surveillance capitalism: The fight for a human future at the new frontier of power*, edn. PublicAffairs.

CHAPTER 6

Human and Artificial Intelligences: Different Yet Complementary

Mohan Raj Gurubatham and Deeppa Ravindran

Introduction

Recently, Artificial General Intelligence, or AGI, has been declared to mimic higher order thinking or HOTS. Others warn of the risks (Heaven, 2023) which are deemed to be strategic and vital for deeper and wider thinking that impacts long-range outcomes. Many in the high-tech industry and academics have indicated that we are at an inflection point of another great shift in society. AI will impact jobs and change the way we interact and the way we navigate through the physical environment such as with autonomous driving. The Internet of Things shows that our life spaces are connected by devices. Mobility is pervasive with handheld devices, workstations, and automobiles all seamlessly integrated. These will bring a boon to productivity as well as effortlessness in tasks which were previously routine and mundane. The procedural chore of many of our tasks in day-to-day living can be automated with enhanced

M. R. Gurubatham (✉) · D. Ravindran
ELM Graduate School, HELP University, Kuala Lumpur, Malaysia
e-mail: mohan.gurubatham@gmail.com

A. K. Maheshwari (ed.), *AI and Consciousness in Organizations and Society*, Palgrave Studies in Workplace Spirituality and Fulfillment,
https://doi.org/10.1007/978-3-031-91470-6_6

features such as friendly chatbots, vivid interactive graphics, and intuitive user interfaces on devices. That makes the rest of our tasks more friendly and engaging (Gurubatham, 2005). The challenges, however, are that a large number of jobs will be replaced though no one really seems to be sure of how many. In this chapter, we look at some landmark studies. First, the University of Oxford's massive research on Future Skills in 2030 (The Future of Skills: Employment in 2030, 2017) and the World Economic Forum's Fourth Industrial Revolution found that many of the tasks involving functional and technical knowledge, such as routine levels of accounting, can be automated. That opens space for humans is to thrive in creativity, insight, empathy, and other tasks involving emotional intelligence, relationships, team management, and unifying of diversity. Human intelligence, I will argue, involves both kinds of affect—feeling and cognition. We may even consider affect to be a salient aspect of spirituality. We shall explore this factor with modern empirical evidence.

The University of Oxford's Future Skills

The University of Oxford's Martin school published a detailed research monograph on "Future Skills 2030" (Bakshi et al., 2017). It surveyed and reviewed the results of skills in the United States and the United Kingdom. What interestingly emerged was that softer skills were found to have become more important from the years in the second half of the second decade of the twenty-first century. This dubbing of human skills as soft skills may be an unfortunate meme because they are subtle yet powerful with impacts not just locally in narrow scope work settings but across organizations system wide, beyond and across industries, even far reaching globally.

Human relationships, communication, and managing teams, all require high emotional intelligence and sensitivity. It requires being able to break out of routine thinking, and to be creative in managing the creative insights and ideas into innovation. This is a highly desirable capability to develop as countries aspire to ascend the higher value-added chain in economic and sustainable value such as with the UNSDG mandates (United Nations, 2023, 2024a, 2024b); and the regulatory requirements adopted by a growing number of countries within the ESG (ESG Strategy and Self-Assessment Tool|Deloitte US, 2024) framework. Many developing countries are stuck in the middle-income economies because they are trapped with rising wages and slower growth (Glawe & Wagner, 2016); examples are Brazil, Turkey, South Africa, and China.

However, what is often left out is the human aspect of being able to work in groups and teams to appreciate diversity and synthesize diversity to manage conflicts. So, it is not surprising that the Oxford Martin School found that the top 20 skills that were deemed to be most important in priority in the future were soft skills (Bakshi et al., 2017). Note that many of the functional skills and technical skills seem to be demoted.

To summarize, the top 20 future skills found by Oxford and Martin's research are largely involving learning strategies with the psychology of knowledge, instructional skills, with social perceptiveness, appreciation, and knowing, with curiosity, sociology, and anthropology, pedagogical skills of training and educating, the coordinative skills of managing groups, the organizational abilities with the fluency of ideas, the philosophy and theology of knowledge, and active listening and problem-solving skills. The knowledge of cognition, perceptiveness, coaching, mentoring, education, listening, and communications skills is very salient as core competencies. Examples are learning strategies skills (1), psychology knowledge (2), instructing skills (3), social perceptiveness skills (4), and judgment and decision making (20).

The middling levels skills, ranked from 21 to 59, involve managing, communication, supervision, troubleshooting, and persuasion as examples. Basically, skills which involve action as well as being able to be flexible such as operations analysis skills (22), psychology skills (23), speaking skills, (26), and technology design skills (46).

The lower-order skills ranked from 60 to 100 are essentially technical skills such as computers, electronics, accounting, and psychomotor skills very much at the lower level in terms of human dexterity. It is remarkable that these skills are indicative of rule-based routine procedures. It is more than likely that AI and robotics can perform these lower-level skills in their entirety. Examples are computers and electronics knowledge (60), geographical knowledge (61), economics and accounting (62), mathematics (63), visualization abilities (64), medicine and dentistry (65), clerical knowledge (84), knowledge production and processing knowledge installation skills (85). It appears that many of the problem-solving skills at the more routine and procedural level can be learnt by machine learning and machines can be trained.

So, this form of analysis and synthesis at the middling order level of thinking can take over much of the troubleshooting, adapting best practices, and finding the commonalities with the prototypical patterns inherent in the data. Training computers to do this is not difficult anymore. However, there's still the difference in claiming that this is now AGI. It is beyond the scope of this chapter to evaluate such claims. As there is still much work in progress and the singularity that is often spoken of in AI still appears quite elusive with a need for more specific philosophical definitions of intelligence (Hoffmann, 2022).

World Economic Forum's Future Skills

The World Economic Forum's (WEF) Fourth Industrial Revolution (Schwab & Davis, 2018) involves the fusion and collapsing of the boundaries among the physical, digital, and biological worlds. This revolution is profiled by breakthroughs in fields like artificial intelligence, robotics, the Internet of Things, genetic engineering, quantum computing, and more. Commensurate with these advanced technologies shaping industries and job markets, the WEF's reports, such as in the Future of Jobs Report 2023, (World Economic Forum, 2023) skills highlighted with growing demand will be such as in analytical thinking, creative thinking, AI and big data proficiency, leadership, social influence, and lifelong learning. These overlap with the Oxford and Martin's School's research on Future Skills.

The Oxford Martin School's research investigates how employment and skill demands are likely to evolve due to technological, demographic, and economic change drivers. This research highlights the importance of skills such as social perceptiveness, active learning, and cognitive abilities like originality and fluency of ideas. It also emphasizes the need for re-skilling and up-skilling to prepare the workforce for future demands, emphasizing that while some jobs may decline, new opportunities will emerge, especially in sectors like education, healthcare, and creative industries. Essentially, the WEF provides a macro framework for understanding the technological shifts, while the Oxford Martin School probes and offers micro insights into the specific skills and strategies needed to navigate these changes successfully. Their inherent synergy (Kolbjørnsrud et al., 2017) helps create a comprehensive approach to addressing the opportunities and challenges in our twenty-first-century landscape of the Fourth Industrial Revolution.

In the field of talent management, research by Church et al. (2014) and their *Blueprint for Leadership* Development reveals six dimensions of even softer skills such as leadership skills, learning skills, motivational skills, and cognitive abilities, all of which involve higher order thinking. In contrast, functional skills are only *one* dimension *out of six* pertinent for leadership development. Here again there could be a trend toward higher order thinking skills (HOTS), the so-called softer skills that transcend the domains, industry or departments of an organization with the functional or industry domain being less critical.

Role of Emotional Intelligence in Future Skills

The World Economic Forum predicts in their studies of the Fourth Industrial Revolution, may be already upon us with Digitalization and AGI. The project suggests that the new roles involving the emotional intelligence type of skills are seen as being most pertinent in the future. Emotional Intelligence is ranked as one of the top ten skills needed for the Fourth industrial revolution. Curiously, this ranking highlights the paradoxical ascent of emotional intelligence in prominence in the workplace as we progress into this era of advanced technology. Examples are as follows.

Emotional intelligence is critical in the Fourth Industrial Revolution for several reasons:

1. Human–Machine Collaboration: With the adoption of AI and automation something more ubiquitous may be needed in facilitating effectiveness in working between both humans and machines. Emotional intelligence facilitates navigating these interactions smoothly.
2. Resilience and Adaptability: As the pace of technological change increases, workers need to be adaptable and resilient. Emotional intelligence may help to manage stress due to technostress (Kumar, 2024), sustain motivation, and facilitate flexibility in the face of increasing disruption.
3. Leadership and Social Influence: Effective leadership and the ability to influence others are key components of EI. These skills are vital for guiding teams through transitions and fostering a positive work environment. Empathy and active listening: strong relationships and effective communication with others critically demand understanding and responding to their emotions deemed necessary for collaborative teamwork.

In conclusion, emotional intelligence is a worthwhile foundation to help people thrive in a rapidly changing, technology-driven landscape. It is complementary to technical skills and enhances comprehensive workplace effectiveness.

Emerging Economies and Emotional Intelligence

What are the implications for countries stuck in the middle-income trap when AI takes over the routine procedural tasks either in manufacturing or in the service industries? There will be a need for these countries to ascend their value chain because the lower cost of automation will displace workers. Their workforce must develop higher value-added cognitive abilities as well as emotional abilities. We know that there are variations of qualities of emotional intelligence among individuals, and perhaps also among cultures. There must be a method for developing both the cognitive aspects of human development, which involves thinking, reasoning, problem-solving, and decision making; and that of the management of diversity, emotional sensitivities, and improved relationships, toward harmony.

A study done among school personnel in San Francisco with a technique of meditation called Transcendental Meditation (TM) showed significant improvements in emotional intelligence (EI) and reductions in stress at the workplace (Nidich, 2018). This is especially salient because this technique of TM is independent of belief systems and does not require any special change in lifestyle. TM is an innocent effortless technique to practice quietly for 20 minutes morning and evening. As such its efficacy is well demonstrated and its effortlessness in learning is a boon to incorporate in daily practice. The increase in emotional intelligence occurs spontaneously. It is not through mood making or expectations. Subjects often report that their anger seems to subside, and they naturally feel a well of positivity and good feelings which impact their interpersonal relationships. So, while it is a technique for improving interpersonal relations through emotional intelligence; it also reminds us that emotional intelligence underpins interpersonal relations. Indeed, emotional intelligence is foundational. When we feel better, and when we can evaluate the environment better in terms of nuances, then we can more effectively respond.

So, the Oxford and Martin schools research should then be extended to countries which are aspiring to ascend to higher income economies to get out of this trap of the middle incomes; Such countries are huge emerging market giants such as China and India (PTI, 2024), and the ASEAN countries which have among the most dynamic, young and rapidly growing economies (Bugrov et al., 2024). Malaysia (Campbell/Penang, 2024) and Singapore (Mak & Daga, 2024). These countries are aggressively moving up the value chain in terms of setting up data centers and higher end design competencies for manufacturing semiconductors as global hubs (AP, 2023) by the supply chain derisking from China (Malaysia Rises as Crucial Link in Chip Supply Chain, 2024). Global companies are investing heavily in these countries. These countries are moving to an open border policy for foreign talent to work here, plus investing significantly in education, learning, and development in organizations (SCMP, 2024). It is still too early to predict the success of these aspirations, but from all evidence so far, it has promise.

> Ironically, many of the Asian cultures have innately valued emotional intelligence, but now because of the pressure of industrialization, they aspire to move up the value chain only to ironically find that AI is there waiting to replace their manufacturing jobs.

Edward Hall (1976), the American anthropologist, discussed the factors of high context (HC) and low context (LC) cultures. HC cultures evaluate the environment holistically and people within the environments as being interconnected. The communication styles are much more holistic that often involve non-verbal communication, covert signals, and a sensitivity to nuance. LC cultures, on the other hand, are more about microfocus or "digital" by a digital code processing. Examples are being punctual, being precise in our communication, or following the rules of a contract to the letter.

HC cultures include Asian cultures as well as the cultures of Africa, the Middle East, and Latin America. Here relationships are part of the high contextual domain of sensitivity and response. High context cultures tend to leave many things unsaid and exploit ambiguity to interpolate and extrapolate or predict meaning from missing details. It is a form of communication which is more subtle, refined, and highly supported by emotional intelligence as intuition. Communication therefore occurs in a milieu in Asian and in Mediterranean cultures. In HC cultures, communication processes are non-verbal, non-linear, or by an "analog" code.

Analog representations are patterned, relational information that represents a combination of the abstract and the concrete codes involved in mental processing. They invoke psychological sets which are mental structures in human cognitions which guide human information processing. The Japanese, for example, are a high context culture. They bow, and the depth of the bow is in deference to authority, with spatial relationships that denote high power distance or hierarchy such as in Hofstede's research on culture (Gurubatham, 2001; Hofstede, 1980, 2011). It denotes that in communication what is *not* said is just as important as what is said in Hall's high context cultures (Afrouzi, 2021; Hall, 1976). Further, analog processing is rapid because pattern recognitions are triggered from deep cultural (Boutyline, 2021; Gurubatham, 2001; Meylani, 2024; Toren, 2014) prototypical schemas. Relationships in HC cultures are also "warm" (Meylani, 2024) and in the field of business, relationships are understood to be important. Time spent on relationship building may be prioritized over tasks, and it is common for punctuality to be traded off toward relationship building.

There are variations among Asian cultures with some being perceived as "warmer" than others. As such, HC appears to be an artifact of pre-industrial societies. These societies have extended families, and they emphasize relationships wherein time is taken to build and nurture relationships. What is expressly said in HC cultures involves not just speech or writing, but also the nuances of feeling, spatial information, and relationships, and unsaid obligation to family, community, and norms.

Training AI in HC communications can be challenging. AI can be trained with cultural scripts, cross-cultural scripts, and indeed social norms. AI may also mimic human learning. All the collective wisdom, knowledge, and experience stored in repositories all over the world in business in politics in international relations and so on can now be amassed and used to develop AI intelligence and "wisdom." However, *there is a certain layer of cognitive processing which AI may seem to be challenged in when mimicking cultural biases just by learning from knowledge bases with intact cultural biases* (Arseniev-Koehler, 2022). The innate aspects of *affect* or feeling being hardwired have been extensively reviewed in a classic article in the American Psychologist in 1980. Zajonc (1980) argued that feeling systems are separate from cognitive systems and can even be fundamental. In other words, affect or feeling can shape thinking. Eastern wisdom emphasizes this approach that our decisions and our thoughts, even if they involve careful logical analysis, have an underlying feeling. Instead of denying it, a human cognitive bias is accepted as an integral part of social interactions and motivation. From how we conduct ourselves in groups, to valuing the ethos of a group, and complying with the larger good of a society and even the relationship with the ecology to the cosmos. Compliance and conformity may not be seen as weakness. It may be perceived on the contrary as a strength.

In western psychology, EI is seen as of lower value than cognition (Salovey & Mayer, 1990; Zajonc, 1980). Zajonc argued that much of cognition in western psychology has underfooted affect or feeling. He looked at how neuroscience, cognition, and cognitive psychology demoted feeling or affect to be post-cognitive. He even suggested that there can be two separate systems for cognition and affect, using the provocative title "Thinking and Feeling, Preferences Need No Inferences." Zajonc further argued that feeling or affect can be fundamental or foundational to cognition which is very much characterized by Eastern philosophy when feeling is part of our cognition and not demoted to being post-cognitive as in western cognition, that means we think first then we feel. It is difficult therefore to express feelings because communication which involves intellectual analysis and expression may not be able to capture the refined states of affect or feeling. However, in other cultures feeling or affect is basic with a primacy which is experienced as intuition.

Challenges from the Rapid Advance of AI

Many of the developed countries face quandaries. If the routine jobs that were exported by outsourcing to lower-cost countries face automation using AI, then what would the rest of their workforce do? Let us understand the commonalities and the differences between advanced AI and human intelligence. Advanced AI can go beyond speed of rapid processing to approach some degrees of judgment such as with chatbots in customer service. Human intelligence is not just about cognitively dominant higher order thinking and fluid intelligence. The pertinence of emotional intelligence was discussed. At present there's still a lot of non-routine insightful cognitions from human beings; some of these are creative and groundbreaking that can lead to process innovation in an incremental way or in a radically creative and groundbreaking way. The literature on AI has not been coherent enough to suggest that it can replace human beings in terms of AI "singularity". However, we must be open to advances. We next look at what is human intelligence beyond logical reasoning to look at synthesis and unifying cognitions with the accompaniment of emotions.

Emotional intelligence is needed to thrive in a rapidly changing, technology-driven landscape. The world is diverse with new lifestyles and attitudes, increasingly interconnected by the internet and satellite-enabled communications. We must accommodate this diversity often very quickly and be able to evaluate the nuances when we work in virtual project management, for example, as often is the case with people in different cultures in different time zones in high technology businesses and projects with virtual project teams. EI is complementary to technical skills and enhances cross-cultural dialogue, understanding, and empathy toward harmony in relationships toward even World Peace.

Higher Order Thinking, Fluid Intelligence, and Transfer of Learning

Higher order thinking skills (HOTS) are also capable of what we call the *far transfer of learning* (Gurubatham, 2005, 2018, 2023; Royer, 1979; Salomon & Perkins, 1989) involving fluid intelligence. Now, let's turn our attention to the fluidity of human intelligence as has been measured by psychologists for several decades. Beginning with the classic work by Raymond Cattell in the 1960s who framed the notion of fluid intelligence and crystallized intelligence. Crystallized intelligence is the ability to store content, and to recall that content of learned content-based education. Crystallized content is the "what "in terms of knowledge. It is content-based and appears to be less critical when there is rapid obsolescence of knowledge with the need for updating content.

Fluid intelligence is the processing ability or the "how," where data is transformed into information, then into knowledge, and culminating in wisdom. Fluid intelligence can drive and transfer insights gleaned from one domain to another (Gurubatham, 2014; Salomon & Perkins, 1989). We need to emphasize fluid intelligence much more in the twenty-first century where technology processes data at high speeds. So higher order thinking involves higher order processing, and this is where AI seems to be creeping up against higher order thinking in humans. However, the far transfer of learning and gleaning insights appears to be best facilitated by active learning—in education as well as in learning and development in organizations. Examples of the pertinence of the far transfer of learning, and the gleaning of insights from different domains, different departments, and different industries follow in this example.

It is possible to transcend or unfreeze deeper layers of conventional thinking beyond boundaries into more abstract prototypes (Boutyline, 2021; Bowman et al., 2020; Rosch, 1973) nested at deeper unconscious levels of consciousness. Then this could be what happens during Transcendental Meditation (TM), unfreezing from the more surface layers of thought to deeply dive into the more subtle layers, right up to the infancy of the thought process and beyond that to the *source of thought* in full transcendence (Maharishi, 1966). TM means to go beyond thinking to transcend, to dive into finer and finer our levels of being when mental activity is refined progressively, then completely transcend to the level of the source of thought itself. If humans can teach machines to learn how to unfreeze from the layers of conventional prototypes (Boutyline, 2021; Fisk, 1989; Solso, 2014) to that of submerged, abstract, even deeper prototypical patterns, then we can have higher order thinking and the ability to come up with insights by AI. However, at present this seems to be a uniquely human trait. The human mind is also able to transcend layers of the thought process consciously until it can transcend even its own mind, to be experiencing *pure consciousness* (Travis et al., 2009), as measured by brainwave activity using EEG shows distinct alpha activity with self-reports indicating wakefulness without thought. This state of consciousness is called the wakeful hypermetabolic state (Jevning et al., 1992). It is operationally defining restful alertness when the mind experiences its own nature beyond thinking beyond concepts and is characterized by deep relaxation in terms of the EEG. This state of consciousness is also traditionally called the *Self* or *pure consciousness* in traditional literature (Maharishi, 1966).

"Thinking on Your Feet" with Fluid Intelligence

Fluid intelligence may well lead to the collapsing of the walls in terms of the boundaries and silos in organizations such as departments. Conscious customer focus today means rewiring or reengineering the process flow of organizations so that everyone is fully cognizant of the customer promise. Today we have a synthesis of human resources or human capital development with change management in organization design and we call this "internal branding" (King & Grace, 2007) where the people behind the external branding exemplify the behaviors of the brand expectations internally in the organization. Marketing communications messages represent the brand. The business process and workflows facilitate the promise of brand expectations. Workflows can be reengineered to support the critical customer service interface with the technology and the value addition within business process architecture. So, key customer information with augmented reality (AR) can be available at the fingertips on demand for customer care staff. There are a lot of CRM applications to enhance workflow designs with vital information for well-trained customer care contact staff. This will again be enhanced by a higher level of emotional intelligence that must be developed by the customer care staff. So, the customer focus is on empathy and relationship building competencies, all the necessary vital information of the customer product and so on supplied through AI and AR. This is an example of out-of-the-box thinking which leads to a revamping of the curriculum in how we teach business and management, and how we develop talent for new roles involving analytics where data analysis with insights is critical for almost everyone in an organization.

The model of far- and near-transfer of learning from will help to frame and understand the need for human and AI interaction with a strong level of human judgment and emotional intelligence to facilitate effectiveness (Gurubatham, 2018, 2023; Solomon & Perkins, 1989). There is an increasing need for higher value-added thinking as we progress to deeper and more widely impactful organizational demands for analysis, creation, and evaluation. This higher value-added thinking at this level can be reflected where we think about thinking, in other words reflect. However, deeper and higher than reflection is the ability to go beyond reflection, beyond the conventional narratives, or transcending the common layers of experience to the depths of the mind; ultimately transcending even the finest level of thought as discussed earlier. This is transcending to the fullest. When the mind can experience its own nature then this is dubbed as pure consciousness or inner wakefulness (Jevning et al., 1992).

Consciousness and Fluid Intelligence

There have been strong electrophysiological correlations with self-reports of experiences of higher and deeper states of consciousness. Techniques such as TM indicate increased operationally defined wisdom and enliven the whole brain. Well-controlled and longitudinal studies have found that

TM practice enhances a wide range of functions including developing shorter response latencies in discrimination tasks, increased field independence where individuals are less distracted by the environment, increased flexibility of perception and improved verbal problem-solving, increased creativity, and increased fluid intelligence. For a thorough review of published studies, see Alexander & Langer (1990).

The expansion of consciousness denotes the expansion of the "container" of the mind, so that fluid intelligence (Gurubatham, 2014, 2023; Tjoa, 1975) can operate in an enlarged "container" that allows more data to be assimilated, encoded, processed, stored, and retrieved. A critical mass of research has shown TM to improve memory, intelligence, and emotional intelligence as wellbeing. Higher order thinking, for example, in managing various stakeholders, shows up the need for empathy and appreciating the diversity and the nuances of diversity and inclusion. The new HR paradigms of people and ecological textures of the external environment of the organizations, very much expand the boundary of current strategic human resource practice as a business partner to coopt with CSR. Hence HR has an *extended social field in* the newer HR competencies as value propositions (Ulrich & Brockbank, 2005). For example, a major timber corporation listed in the Hong Kong stock market was forced to delist because of poor environmental management, even though it had won accolades, yet was accused by activists for greenwashing ignoring the plight of a traditional people in the (Ens-Newswire, 2022; Kabilan, 2009). While this corporation was seen as a corporate citizen, with world class HR practices, it neglected the traditional peoples who lived in the forest whose priorities and lifestyles conflicted with that of a modern society. The severe outcome of delisting was never foreseen, but it became real. Their timber was banned in Scandinavian countries and others. The paradigm of HR today has an extended social field to operate in, not just within the organization with employees and stakeholders, but also the communities that the organization has porous boundaries with as in many HC cultures (Hofstede, 2011). This is becoming very important as partnerships with schools in the community and institutions are seen as necessary to build good relationships. This is part and parcel of the UNSDG Goals. Clearly, empathy will be involved when we are at the evaluation stage. Nonetheless, even in day-to-day operational interactions, interpersonal relationships are activated. Effective communication mandates active listening.

The technique of TM has a critical mass of research that showed cognitive improvements in problem-solving, increases in intelligence both fluid as well as emotional intelligence, and in education as well as organizational settings. The notion of fluid intelligence is necessarily salient as the expansion of consciousness is essentially expanding the container of knowledge. Studies have shown increases in creativity (So & Orme-Johnson, 2001) and EI (Goldstein et al., 2024) using TM.

Conclusion: Cultural Treasures and Reviving Holism

Could it be that the advanced societies were the first to industrialize with the older Western industrial revolution, and after 300 years a strong stressful dysfunction has been found in their social systems? Does it matter who degraded the environment first? Aren't we all in the same boat together in terms of the sustainability of our planet? Therefore, it is a planetary requirement that we manage for sustainable development.

Techno stress (Brod, 1984; Kumar, 2024) on the human cost of information overload is the newer type of stress that is now found in society where people are being overwhelmed by information and communication technologies (ICT) with increasing stress from being constantly bombarded with information. The work life balance and the work home balance are blurred as we constantly have to attend to emails and requests from smartphones. Technostress isn't just found in developed economies, but also in the rapidly transforming Asian economies. Singapore (Tilo, 2024) reports the highest level of stress in Southeast Asia, followed by Malaysia (Times, 2024). Which are following the stress levels that were highly reported in countries like Japan and now South Korea. Techno stress can lead to individual and social dysfunction. In our modern world, there is a need to manage stress, and to feel and find meaning and to fill up the internal void. There is a thirst for spirituality, emotional engagement, and relationships. Further the generational shifts, especially with Generation Z, seem to prioritize inclusiveness, diversity and emotional engagement. So, it is not surprising to find the increasing important of soft skills.

Human intelligence has the inherent ability to transcend itself by our own biological hardware as well as mental conditioning according to the Vedic philosophy. The crux of Vedic knowledge system is self-exploration, revealing the holistic interconnectedness of our being with our mind and body, our environment through to the cosmos. Such exploration requires a human nervous system which is capable of self-awareness, refined-abstract perception, and sensitivity. Empirical research on practicing TM has indicated the development of cognitive abilities such as intelligence, emotional intelligence, and creativity. While the human nervous system is designed to be able to transcend itself to the finest level of thinking and beyond the finest level of thinking to the source of thought in pure consciousness as described before, there is no such description for AI in terms of ontology and epistemology. The wakeful hyper metabolic state described above (Jevning et al., 1992; Travis et al., 2009) is characterized by a restful alertness when the mind is awake in its own nature and the physiology of body is in the state of deep rest. The subjective aspects and the objective aspect of intelligence give rise to notions of "self" being more than sentience (awareness) because of the ability of reflection and transcendence, it is believed to be uniquely human. Even the noted linguist Noam Chomsky admits that deep structure in linguistics is hard-wired by nature to be active (Buen, 2019). It is too active and dynamic to learn from the environment passively alone. So, this hard wiring is indicative of natural intelligence in evolution. Effortlessness in terms of fluency and fluidity of intelligence is what characterizes the naturalness.

Higher order competencies such as emotional intelligence and spirituality are attributes that AI may find difficult to mimic. It is not surprising that Indian Knowledge Systems (IKS) that is spearheaded by the Ministry of Education in India has a mission here to revive the ancient systems of knowledge developed for thousands of years. They include the traditional medicine systems like ayurveda, yoga, and naturopathy, as well as ancient texts on mathematics, astronomy, architecture, and more. The IKS spans a holistic approach to knowledge, integrating spiritual, philosophical, and practical aspects of life. The possible scenarios for AI and IKS complementarity include the following: In holistic health where traditional Indian medicine systems like ayurveda can complement AI in healthcare by providing holistic and personalized treatment plans, in sustainable practices: where ancient Indian agricultural practices and environmental knowledge can inform AI-driven solutions for sustainable farming and conservation, in cultural preservation: where AI can be used to preserve and digitize ancient texts and artifacts, making them accessible to a wider audience, and ethical frameworks from the rich philosophical and cultural knowledge from the IKS to guide the development and implementation of AI technologies in a socially responsible manner. By integrating IKS with AI, there can well be more comprehensive, culturally sensitive, and sustainable solutions that benefit society in this twenty-first century.

Other ancient civilizations such as China, Japan, South Korea, and Vietnam, collectively the Confucian societies, also have a rich ancient knowledge base. In Southeast Asia, there is a fusion of these Confucian and Vedic cultures. For example, in China AI is being used to complement or supplement traditional Chinese medicine (TCM) to facilitate consistency and reliability across TCM physicians. This allows the collection of massive data and practices to significantly improve the reliability and accuracy of diagnostics, thus increasing the use of effective therapeutic methods for patients. AI-assisted TCM diagnosis can be based on digital data collected by modern electronic instruments, making TCM diagnosis more quantitative, objective, and standardized facilitating the therapeutic efficacy of TCM to be evaluated objectively. Interestingly, AI is helping promote TCM from experience to evidence-based medicine, which is a genuine scientific revolution (Wang et al., 2021). Moreover, huge non-uniform knowledge on formula-syndrome relationships and the combination rules of herbal TCM formulae could be better standardized with the help of AI analysis for clinical efficacy. Evaluation competencies can be enhanced by further optimization on the standardized TCM formulae. AI can thus bridge the gap between TCM and modern science and technology. Much of the advances in China can be replicated in India too with ayurveda. Recently, in Africa, there have been similar calls being made by thought leaders (Mazibuko-Makena et al., 2021) to leverage the Fourth Industrial Revolution with traditional knowledge systems in South Africa. It analyzes the prerequisites for successfully implementing modern technologies, such as infrastructure, skilled personnel, and appropriate regulation. It emphasizes the importance of inclusive innovation, aiming to create new jobs and reduce inequality, and discusses the potential impact of modernity on many sectors, including healthcare, employment, and the environment. This is an interesting and inspiring development. Similar calls can and should be made in the Middle East and in the Central and South America.

References

Alexander, C. N., & Langer, E. J. (1990). *Higher stages of human development: Perspectives on adult growth*. Oxford University Press.

Alizadeh Afrouzi, O. (2021). Humanitarian behavior across high-/low-context cultures: A comparative analysis between Switzerland and Colombia. *International Journal of Humanitarian Action, 6*(2). https://doi.org/10.1186/s41018-020-00088-y

Arseniev-Koehler, A., & Foster, J. G. (2022). Machine learning as a model for cultural learning: Teaching an algorithm what it means to be fat. *Sociological Methods & Research, 51*(4), 1484–1539.

AP. (2023, December 8). Nvidia CEO suggests Malaysia could be AI "manufacturing" hub as Southeast Asia expands data centers. *The Hindu*. https://www.thehindu.com/sci-tech/technology/nvidia-ceo-suggests-malaysia-could-be-ai-manufacturing-hub-as-southeast-asia-expands-data-centers/article67618209.ece

Bakshi, H., Downing, J., Osborne, M., & Schneider, P. (2017). [Review of the book The Future of Skills: Employment in 2030, by Futureskills.Pearson.com]. Pearson.

Bowman, C. R., Iwashita, T., & Zeithamova, D. (2020). Tracking prototype and exemplar representations in the brain across learning. *eLife, 9*, Article e59360. https://doi.org/10.7554/eLife.59360

Brod, C. (1984). *Technostress: The human cost of the computer revolution*. Addison-Wesley.

Boutyline, A., & Soter, L. K. (2021). Cultural schemas: What they are, how to find them, and what to do once you've caught one. *American Sociological Review, 86*(4), 728–758. https://doi.org/10.1177/00031224211024525

Bugrov, D., Dhara, D., & Kamarudin, K. (2024, March 15). *Southeast Asia: Economic overview Q3 2023|McKinsey*. https://www.mckinsey.com/featured-insights/future-of-asia/southeast-asia-quarterly-economic-review

Campbell/Penang, C. (2024, August 27). How "Friendshoring" made Southeast Asia pivotal to the AI Revolution. *Time*. https://time.com/7015000/ai-semiconductor-chips-malaysia-anwar/

Chomsky, N., Roberts, I., & Watumull, J. (2023, March 8). The false promise of ChatGPT. *The New York Times*. https://www.nytimes.com/2023/03/08/opinion/noam-chomsky-chatgpt-ai.html

Church, A. H., & Silzer, R. (2014). Going behind the corporate curtain with a BluePrint for leadership potential: An integrated framework for identifying high-potential talent. *People + Strategy*, *36*(4), 50–58.

de Buen, N. (2019, September 6). *Jordan Peterson, Noam Chomsky, and What We Mean by "Left" and "Right."* Merionwest.com. https://merionwest.com/2019/09/06/jordan-peterson-noam-chomsky-and-what-we-mean-by-left-and-right/

Ens-Newswire. (2022). *Penan stop loggers in culturally sensitive conservation area*. Retrieved from https://ens-newswire.com/penan-stop-loggers-in-culturally-sensitive-conservation-area/

ESG Strategy and self-assessment tool|Deloitte US. (2024, April 23). Deloitte United States. https://www2.deloitte.com/us/en/pages/audit/articles/esg-materiality-assessment.html?id=us:2ps:3gl:esgsa25:awa:080224:esg%20ranking:b:c&gad_source=1&gclid=Cj0KCQjwsc24BhDPARIsAFXqAB0RcJoLXC7HBPvBTaDC0VafT-FCioGTc7e7dPQnadi_d5TFjDlfbCQaAvhkEALw_wcB

Fiske, S. T. (1989). Social cognition and social perception. *Annual Review of Psychology, 40*, 21–52.

Glawe, L., & Wagner, H. (2016). The middle-income trap: Definitions, theories and countries concerned—A literature survey. *Comparative Economic Studies, 58*(4), 507–538. https://doi.org/10.1057/s41294-016-0014-0

Goldstein, L., Smith, A. M., Romagnoli, D., & Katergi, E. (2024). The effect of Transcendental Meditation on self-esteem, self-efficacy, and gratitude, for increasing empowerment of female youth in Uganda. *Health Care for Women International*, 1–34. https://doi.org/10.1080/07399332.2024.2358789

Gurubatham. (2001). *Maximising human intelligence deployment in Asian business* (Banerjee & Richter, Eds.). Palgrave Macmillan.

Gurubatham, M. R. (2005). Understanding and interpreting the drivers of the Knowledge Economy. *IFIP International Federation for Information Processing*, 189–202. https://doi.org/10.1007/0-387-23120-x_17

Gurubatham, M. R. (2014). Enlivening fluid intelligence in blended active learning within the cognitive literacy value chain framework. *Procedia - Social and Behavioral Sciences, 123*, 238–248. https://doi.org/10.1016/j.sbspro.2014.01.1420

Gurubatham, M. (2018). Facilitating the far transfer of knowledge by metacognition in ICT-enabled globalized learning. *Journal of Education and Social Science, 9*(2).

Gurubatham, M. R. (2023). Fluid intelligence for higher order thinking: Balancing the subjective and objective for sustaining impactful wisdom in this era of disruption. *Palgrave Studies in Workplace Spirituality and Fulfillment (Print)*, 115–131. https://doi.org/10.1007/978-3-031-05839-4_6

Hall, E. T. (1976). *Beyond culture*. Anchor Books.

Heaven, W. D. (2023, May 2). *Geoffrey Hinton tells us why he's now scared of the tech he helped build*. MIT Technology Review. https://www.technologyreview.com/2023/05/02/1072528/geoffrey-hinton-google-why-scared-ai/

Hoffmann, C. H. (2022). A philosophical view on singularity and strong AI. *AI & SOCIETY*. https://doi.org/10.1007/s00146-021-01327-5

Hofstede, G. (2011). Dimensionalizing cultures: The Hofstede model in context. *Online Readings in Psychology and Culture, 2*(1), 1–26. https://doi.org/10.9707/2307-0919.1014

Jevning, R., Wallace, R. K., & Beidebach, M. (1992). The physiology of meditation: A review. A wakeful hypometabolic integrated response. *Neuroscience & Biobehavioral Reviews, 16*, 415–424.

Kabilan, K. (2009). *Penans will die if jungle is destroyed*. Malaysiakini.

King, C., & Grace, D. (2007). Internal branding: Exploring the employee's perspective. *Journal of Brand Management, 15*(5), 358–372. https://doi.org/10.1057/palgrave.bm.2550136

Kolbjørnsrud, V., Amico, R., & Thomas, R. J. (2017). Partnering with AI: How organizations can win over skeptical managers. *Strategy & Leadership, 45*(1), 37–43. https://doi.org/10.1108/sl-12-2016-0085

Kumar, S. (2024). *Technostress: A comprehensive literature review on dimensions, impacts, and management strategies*. Computers in Human Behavior Reports, 100475.

Maharishi Mahesh Yogi. (1966). *The science of being and art of living. New revised ed.* International S.R.M. Publications.

Mak, R., & Daga, A. (2024, June 21). Tiny Singapore's chip hub retains a big punch. *Reuters*. https://www.reuters.com/breakingviews/tiny-singapores-chip-hub-retains-big-punch-2024-06-21/

Malaysia Rises as Crucial Link in Chip Supply Chain. (2024, March 13). https://www.nytimes.com/2024/03/13/business/malaysia-semiconductors.html

Mazibuko-Makena, Z., & Mbula, E. K. (Eds.). (2021). *Leap 4.0: African perspectives on the fourth industrial revolution*. Mapungubwe Institute for Strategic Reflection.

Meylani, R. (2024). Innovations with schema theory: Modern implications for learning, memory, and academic achievement. *International Journal of Fundamental Research, 6*(1). https://doi.org/10.36948/ijfmr.2024.v06i01.13785

Nidich, S. (2018). Effect of meditation on emotional intelligence and perceived stress in the workplace: A randomized controlled study. *The Permanente Journal*. https://doi.org/10.7812/tpp/17-172

PTI. (2024, September 8). Like-minded nations collaborating with India to make it a chip manufacturing hub: Krishnan. *The Economic Times*. https://economictimes.indiatimes.com/industry/cons-products/electronics/like-minded-nations-collaborating-with-india-to-make-it-a-chip-manufacturing-hub-krishnan/articleshow/113170791.cms?from=mdr

Rosch, E. H. (1973). Natural categories. *Cognitive Psychology, 4*(3), 328–350. https://doi.org/10.1016/0010-0285(73)90017-0

Royer, J. M. (1979). Theories of the transfer of learning. *Educational Psychologist, 14*(1), 53–69. https://doi.org/10.1080/00461527909529207

SCMP. (2024, August 6). South China Morning Post. https://www.scmp.com/news/asia/southeast-asia/article/3273403/malaysia-sets-chip-design-hub-drive-demand-semiconductor-industry

Salomon, G., & Perkins, D. N. (1989). Rocky roads to transfer: Rethinking mechanism of a neglected phenomenon. *Educational Psychologist, 24*(2), 113–142. https://doi.org/10.1207/s15326985ep2402_1

Salovey, P., & Mayer, J. D. (1990). Emotional Intelligence. *Imagination, Cognition and Personality*, *9*(3), 185–211. Sagepub. https://doi.org/10.2190/DUGG-P24E-52WK-6CDG

Schwab, K., & Davis, N. (2018). *Shaping the fourth industrial revolution*. World Economic Forum. Crown Business.

So, K. (2001). Three randomized experiments on the longitudinal effects of the transcendental meditation technique on cognition. *Intelligence, 29*(5), 419–440. https://doi.org/10.1016/s0160-2896(01)00070-8

Solso, R. L. (2014). Prototypes, schemata, and the form of human knowledge: The cognition of abstraction. In *Current issues in cognitive processes* (pp. 345–368). Psychology Press.

Toren, C. (2014). What is a schema? *Journal of Ethnographic Theory, 4*(1), 149–172.

Tilo, D. (2024, June 13). *2 in 3 Singaporeans suffering from burnout: survey*. Hcamag.com; HRD Asia. https://www.hcamag.com/asia/specialisation/mental-health/2-in-3-singaporeans-suffering-from-burnout-survey/493238

Times, B. (2024, August 8). Two-thirds of Malaysian workers suffering burnout; millennials most affected: Survey. *NST Online; New Straits Times*. https://www.nst.com.my/business/corporate/2024/08/1088515/two-thirds-malaysian-workers-suffering-burnout-millennials-most

Tjoa, A. (1975). Increased intelligence and reduced neuroticism through the Transcendental Meditation program. *Gedrag: Tijdschrift voor Psychologie* (Behavior: Journal of Psychology), *3*, 167–182.

Travis, F., Haaga, D. A. F., Hagelin, J., Tanner, M., Arenander, A., Nidich, S., Gaylord-King, C., Grosswald, S., Rainforth, M., & Schneider, R. H. (2009). A self-referential default brain state: Patterns of coherence, power, and eLORETA sources during eyes-closed rest and transcendental meditation practice. *Cognitive Processing, 11*(1), 21–30. https://doi.org/10.1007/s10339-009-0343-2

Ulrich, D., & Brockbank, W. (2005). *The HR value proposition*. Harvard Business School Press.

United Nations. (2023). Global Sustainable Development Report (GSDR) 2023|Department of Economic and Social Affairs. Global Sustainable Development Report (GSDR) 2023; United Nations. https://sdgs.un.org/gsdr/gsdr2023

United Nations. (2024a). SDG Indicators. Unstats.un.org. https://unstats.un.org/sdgs/report/2024/

United Nations. (2024b). The 17 sustainable development goals. United Nations. https://sdgs.un.org/goals

Valosek, L., Link, J., Mills, P., Konrad, A., Rainforth, M., & Nidich, S. Effect of meditation on emotional.

Wang, Y., Shi, X., Li, L., Efferth, T., & Shang, D. (2021). The impact of artificial intelligence on traditional Chinese medicine. *The American Journal of Chinese Medicine, 49*(6), 1297–1314. https://doi.org/10.1142/S0192415X21500622

World Economic Forum. (2023, April 30). *The Future of Jobs Report 2023*. World Economic Forum. https://www.weforum.org/publications/the-future-of-jobs-report-2023/

Zajonc, R. B. (1980). Feeling and thinking: Preferences need no inferences. *American Psychologist, 35*(2), 151–175. https://doi.org/10.1037/0003-066x.35.2.151

CHAPTER 7

Creativity, Consciousness, and AI in Organizations

Anil K. Maheshwari, K Davina Frick, Ira Greenberg, and Danielle King Colby

Introduction

The intersection of creativity, consciousness, and artificial intelligence (AI) is an area of growing academic interest, as AI's role in creative processes and its impact on human cognition and productivity are being explored (Boden, 2004; Csikszentmihalyi, 1996; Maheshwari & Biberman, 2024). Creativity, traditionally viewed as a uniquely human capacity tied to

A. K. Maheshwari (✉)
Maharishi International University, Fairfield, IA, USA
e-mail: akmaheshwari@miu.edu

K. D. Frick
Johns Hopkins University, Baltimore, MD, USA
e-mail: kfrick@jhu.edu

I. Greenberg
Southern Methodist University, Dallas, TX, USA
e-mail: igreenberg@mail.smu.edu

A. K. Maheshwari (ed.), *AI and Consciousness in Organizations and Society*, Palgrave Studies in Workplace Spirituality and Fulfillment,
https://doi.org/10.1007/978-3-031-91470-6_7

self-expression and emotional depth, is now being augmented by AI technologies (Dietrich, 2004). In light of these developments, this chapter investigates expert opinions on how AI can either facilitate or threaten creativity, reflecting on ethical and intellectual property issues as AI continues to evolve (Floridi, 2014; Searle, 1980). AI's ability to generate novel content challenges long-standing views of originality and authorship, raising new questions about human-AI collaboration in the creative process (Coeckelbergh, 2020; Mitchell, 2019).

Through the process of synthesizing the perspectives of artists, technologists, and academics, this chapter explores how AI can serve as both a tool and a potential threat to creativity, while maintaining the need for human consciousness as a guiding force in the creative process (Boden, 2004; Maheshwari & Werd, 2019; Schmidhuber, 2015). It brings together distinct voices from the fields of art, technology, management, and economics to explore these issues from multiple perspectives. Through a conversational format, the panelists delved into the nature of creativity, examining how AI has influenced their personal creative practices. They discussed how AI tools have expanded their artistic capabilities, facilitated collaboration, and opened new possibilities for creative expression. At the same time, the conversation addressed concerns about AI's addictive potential, its possible role in displacing human workers, and the ethical challenges it presents. By reflecting on AI's impact on creativity and augmenting the discussion among experts using the existing literature, this chapter aims to contribute to the broader discussion of how technology and human consciousness interact, and what this means for the future of creativity in personal and professional contexts. Finally, the chapter emphasizes how as AI offers new opportunities for innovation while the need for human consciousness as a guiding force in the creative process remains.

D. K. Colby
ClubNFT, West Brookfield, MA, USA
e-mail: djking00@gmail.com

What Is the Nature of Creativity?

P1: I work at a university and do research at the intersection of management, technology and consciousness. I also have many years of experience in the IT industry. Once I learned that creative thinking is a valid way of thinking, it just completely changed me. I've written many books, and my creatively written book on data analytics became number one. The notion of incubation is the whole mystical process within which is the magic sauce of creativity. Meditation for me is the single general instrument that changes you from feeling bounded to being completely unbounded, blissful, and productive and joyful.

P2: I am a professor of health economics. I have a bit of creativity there, and my creativity comes out through my poetry writing. It's casual as opposed to a part of what really fuels my day-to-day existence.

P3: I am into post computational art practice, that includes drawing, computation and painting, generative and emergent processes, with expertise in creative coding and computational art. I've made my career in the academy, in art and computer science departments, in a hybrid space. I have 2 degrees in traditional painting and have written 3 books on creative coding (from a fine arts perspective). I have also built some of the early academic programs in this space.

P4: I am an artist, collector, writer, and curator. As an undergraduate I studied studio art and art history at Harvard, working primarily in photography, film, and mixed media. My recent work involves using AI technology to explore alternative art histories and timelines, experiment with memory and the duality of self, investigate capitalism and art, and reframe historical ideals of beauty and femininity. I also have an MBA. I worked on Wall Street for many years. I also worked at the Museum of Modern Art for nearly a decade in New York City, managing the Painting and Sculpture department. My photography was with a camera and film, and I didn't really get too much into digital photography. I've been curating and writing about digital art as well.

What Does Creativity Mean to You?

P4: For me, creativity is self-care. It has always been a part of my life. It was always there even when I was not making art, as I was always surrounded by art and artists and curators. To my great surprise, in my midlife I've had this creative rebirth largely because of AI. I have started working seriously again as an artist using AI as one of my tools. It helps that I can do it from anywhere. I don't need a whole setup in my house. And that I can do it between dealing with my kids and dealing with my day job. Making art with AI has been so freeing. It is something that now I now rely on for emotional and mental wellness.

P3: Creativity is generative emergence. When I switch from painting and drawing to coding, the meaning of creativity switches. I started applying creative practice towards coding as I did not come from a formal computer science background. Where I'm creating some art, something happens in the space between the motif and the canvas. It is a generative space, to which I respond by just being in the moment. I now think about the generative algorithm (AI) as what is happening in computing as when I draw in paint. I think about what's happening in AI now as a natural extension of what has happened in in this area of creative coding, which is much informed through this type of creative practice with analog physical materials.

P2: Creativity allows us to not feel constrained. I associate creativity with going beyond constraints to come up with something that is truly novel. My poetry writing is casual, and a lot of it is inspired by when I go for runs with my running partners. I often share it with the running partner and with other people, as part of self-care. Technology can help with my creativity. I had been in a meeting where we were talking about nearsightedness. I asked ChatGPT to write me a song about myopia. And 2 seconds later ChatGPT had an entire song with intro, outgo, bridge, chorus and everything. It is interesting how this mix of creativity and AI can come together.

P1: Creativity is producing something novel and useful. The 3-part model of consciousness is a knower, the process of knowing and the known. Similarly, creativity also can be attributed to the person, the process and the product. Creativity can also be assigned to a place, and some of my research around consciousness-based architecture showed that such buildings enhance creativity. Kids are naturally creative. Creativity is something wanting to express itself, and one just gets out of the way to let it come out.

Summary: A common thread in the panelists' definitions of creativity is the idea of an active, generative, evolving process for producing something novel, useful and meaningful, through a blend of personal expression, exploration, and discovery (Csikszentmihalyi, 1996; Maheshwari & Werd, 2019; Runco & Jaeger, 2012; Sternberg & Lubart, 1999).

Boden (2004) highlights the "historical creativity" that AI is capable of, contrasting it with "psychological creativity," which is the personal experience of discovery. The panelists agree that while AI can generate novel ideas, true creativity involves a deeper cognitive process, supported by intuition, emotional engagement, and human consciousness (Dietrich, 2004). Creativity, therefore, is viewed as a generative and emergent property of consciousness, where the knower, the process of knowing, and the creative product are intricately linked (Chalmers, 1995; Maheshwari & Werd, 2019; Nader, 2024).

How Do You Use AI to Enable Yourself to Become More Creative?

P4: I started creating art again after a hiatus of nearly 20 years when I was introduced to AI models. I love art history and thought it would be interesting to see what it would be like to pair different types of creative artists, such as traditional visual artists, filmmakers, and fashion designers, using this AI technology to see what it would be like if they collaborated. I was creating alternate art histories as a lot of these people didn't live at the same time and never could have worked together. It was an interesting way to start experimenting with these AI tools and trying to figure out how work. I have been working lately delving into the malleability of memory, and how AI can both help us recreate and reimagine memories. Sometimes AI changes those memories as we are working with it. When you're using these AI tools you are drawing on this collective consciousness of the world. I think there are many interesting ways one can work with ChatGPT and other AI tools. I am excited about some of the newer tools, such as Runway to create moving images and short films. I see a ton of interesting potential.

P3: There is an interesting link between generativity and art and generativity and coding, and how that fits together. AI helped me to change the direction of my creativity in terms of generative images. AI. We use things like ChatGPT and other AI tools. A diffusion model allows the AI to synthesize images based on huge collections of other images and textual terms connected to that prompt. I had my first transcendent type of experience when I was a young person, standing in front of a famous painting in Spain. I had never experienced anything like that in a synagogue or a church. That changed the course of my life! When I go and stand in front of certain paintings I feel a deep connection to the past. I spend much more time with computation than I do actual painting, though that balance constantly shifts. When AI began being utilized in art for image making mostly through generative adversarial networks (GANs), the works had a very strong aesthetic footprint from the technology. It was cool, and different. These were new types of eye candy, but they did not connect to the long history of painting, drawing, or creative coding. It felt more connected to things that were happening in commercial art or special effects. My earliest experiments with AOI were shocking because I fed some of my own drawings into the AI, and what I got back were variations of those drawings. Some of them were much better than my original drawings. I fed in drawings from other artists, and in a strange sense time disappeared. It was a crazy romantic image as if with the fourteenth-fifteenth century artists now making art again.

P2: My artistic pursuits are mostly on the poetry writing side. If I wrote another poem about the same run, would it come out the same? Even from one day to the next, a different lens operates as one thinks about a particular event or a particular combination. I think of the 1st tattoo I got; I went to the artist, and I said, "I want a representation of a third century Catholic martyr but put in 1930s Baltimore." She envisioned that out of her own imagination taking it from a couple of different paintings. It wasn't AI, but an interesting way of drawing from different eras and putting things together in a way that has a very different message to what it is. I enjoy just playing with images a bit in very casual photography, particularly of flowers. I continue to become a little more expressive thinking about how AI could have some interesting applications for experimentation in attire as well.

P1: A quintessential AI experience in my creativity also came from Stable Diffusion. I have been part of an online book club community since Covid began. We have been teaching ourselves on virtual reality, and many AI tools. I was trying to find a logo for a conference on management, spirituality, consciousness, and artificial intelligence. So, I used a stable diffusion tool to create an image showing a blue gender-neutral person and commercial buildings and technology connections in their head, hanging in a star-filled universe. It's the creativity within that leads you to create what you produce outside. You pick what resonates with you. That can depend on how expanded a consciousness you are in. AI by itself creates lots of variations. Growing up, for me art meant being a singer, a dancer, playing musical instruments, telling jokes, etc. However, generative AI has been very helpful as a very functional creativity tool.

Summary: AI is increasingly being used to augment and enhance creativity by providing tools that facilitate the ideation process and allow for experimentation without the constraints of traditional methods (Brynjolfsson & McAfee, 2014). The panelists highlight AI as a powerful catalytic tool for enhancing and expanding the creative process. Each panelist finds that AI serves as a facilitator by providing inspiration, overcoming creative blocks, generating ideas, and extending their ability to experiment and explore new creative avenues. P4's experience with AI echoes Boden's (2004) notion of "combinatorial creativity," where AI helps her pair different artistic styles to explore alternative art histories. P3's practice of using AI in generative art aligns with Schmidhuber's (2015) concept of "creative coding," where AI generates variations of existing work, sparking new ideas. P1 and P2 both use AI as a collaborative partner to overcome creative blocks, echoing Shneiderman's (2020) argument that AI can enhance human creativity by freeing up cognitive resources for higher-level problem-solving. This suggests that AI can help individuals and teams move beyond traditional constraints, making creativity more accessible and fluid (Mitchell, 2019).

Is There a Threat from AI to Our Creativity?

Is there anything where it could take away or replace human creativity?

P1: Yes, one could become totally dependent on AI. It's not only just the images. Think of songwriting or dancing moves. It's almost like becoming dependent on the team around you, and so that that dependence would be bad. I think, if you're a master of the tool, that is great. I don't think it can produce bad creativity because, by definition, creativity is about producing something new and different. However, ethical issues can arise. It is the social field that decides whether something is novel enough and useful enough for them. The decision-making on whether creativity is good or bad is outside of you. Using AI to create can also be very addictive. I've seen people say I've just worked day and night on this like time flies for me. A feeling of time flying is good, so long as you also know when to take back your time and your ownership of your own self. AI and its algorithms are not thinking in a way that humans do, they are continually learning and getting better.

P3: I agree that we seem to be living in more addictive times. I think this is just one more thing that we can now become addicted to. A lot of it has to do with the market models of scarcity, especially in the art world.

AI is a very destabilizing technology. We think that this problem of abundance doesn't exist, so there is a forced scarcity built in the system. We are extremely involved with blockchain. As if the AI wasn't a threat enough to art, now crypto is involved as well. AI is empowering agency for artists in terms of supporting themselves. It's not about just getting rich. There is a challenge that when I'm going to release it, I'm going to sell to collectors and work with the gallery. I may generate 1000 images in my development process. However, the market may suggest that I should sell only 100 of them, so that there is sufficient scarcity for collectors to resell them in this old model of the art market. What happens to those other 900 pieces? Culturally, historically, I don't think it's productive to burn or destroy those. Thus, there's an inherent tension that people are not yet paying enough attention to. With the ability to create almost an infinite number of images, how should value be assigned to each one? What is the value that is created by a particular artist when there's assistance from AI? That is a threat to human creativity.

P4: I don't think there's a threat to human creativity as such from AI. I do think that the addictive nature of these things is something that we all need to be watching out for ourselves and our children. Put guardrails around it somehow. I try to do it for myself with limited success. I think there is a perfect confluence of blockchain and AI together. I think that the fact that on the blockchain you have transparency, you have this clear provenance with a timestamp of when this artist made this piece, who it sold to for what price, everyone can see that I do think that that helps in terms of the history of art. This is going to be part of art history in some way, and the blockchain is going to make it very clear who experimented with this technique. The blockchain will also make clear and transparent digital on-chain artwork. Who were the early Medici's, the early supporters of this kind of work, which is not very clear for works in the traditional art world? There are Ph.D.-level provenance researchers in museums and this is the nature of work that all they do is because there's so many missing holes in the provenance of these works. So, I think that that is promising both for art history.

P3: It is interesting to think about the type of artists who have access to these technologies. Is there a will to democratize this process? Or will it continue to be available to only the ones who can afford to apply that type of technology to their work? Will that be a part of the documentation that goes into art history? I have never seen a more inclusive democratizing force in the arts than blockchain. I feel like challenged on a bunch of my own beliefs about what we think about in terms of literacy in terms of the visual arts, and how we have to make that much more expansive. The biggest problem about the addiction is, that people are having really interesting discussions about it.

P4: I have met more artists from around the world and have collected art from artists from around the world in a way that I wouldn't and couldn't otherwise. A lot of those folks who are not in major European or American cities wouldn't have been able to get my attention. It's also very expensive to ship paintings around the world. I can collect these things with a click and that artist gets the money right away. It doesn't go through an intermediary. I think that makes this blockchain art world much more democratic. In the traditional art world, the hurdles and barriers to entry such as educational background is a huge issue. For the blockchain based art, onboarding is key. It is difficult to figure out all the steps you need to take to put work on the blockchain and participate in the system. Ideally, it can be very democratizing to see and collect art from people all around the world in terms of the different voices that come to the table, the different lenses that people see art through, the different ideas that they bring with their art. It opens an entirely new range of literacy about art, about what's motivating people, and the lenses that people are seeing through. It could totally change how we discuss how people are being creative, what they're really seeing, and what their interpretations mean.

Summary: The panelists present a nuanced position that AI could pose a threat to creativity if it leads to over-reliance, addiction, or devaluation of creative work, but they do not view it as an inherent or unavoidable danger. While AI can enhance creativity, it also poses potential threats, particularly through technological over-reliance and ethical concerns around intellectual property (Anderson & Anderson, 2011). P4 and P3's concerns about AI's addictive potential and market-driven scarcity reflect Zuboff's (2019) critique of surveillance capitalism, where technological tools commodify human creativity. P1's concern about AI leading to dependency aligns with Bostrom's (2014) warning of AI's potential to outpace human control, potentially leading to the erosion of human originality. At the same time, a balanced perspective reflects Brynjolfsson and McAfee's (2014) view that AI should serve as a tool for amplifying human capabilities rather than replacing them. The ethical questions surrounding AI's creative role are complex, as AI-generated work challenges traditional notions of authorship and ownership (Coeckelbergh, 2020; Searle, 1980).

What Does It Mean to Be Collecting Art in the Age of AI?

P1: I am often wondering why people collect art, when you can spontaneously create any piece of art for yourself for a certain period of time? Is it because of the collection mindset or money mindset? People want to have more and more, and then at some point, you have this art, and they don't have time to see it all. They want the next one. I think technology can be very liberating, for example AI and before that Zoom. During Covid I could create a large conference with almost 100 speakers and over 1,200 attendees from around the world using Zoom. Organizing an event like that is also an art form. AI can help with the questioning or the styling. We can express infinitely so we feel the truly infinite creative quality of ourselves. I think that the collection mindset should go. AI technology can create not only a democratizing influence but also a liberating effect.

P4: I see that there definitely are art collectors in accumulation mode. My art collection comes more from a place of wanting to support fellow artists. And seeing potential in them and knowing that if I buy their art that hopefully allows them to keep on going. With the blockchain it makes it very easy to support fellow artists, to amplify, and highlight voices that maybe aren't as heard. I often share other artists with my friends. There is certainly a community of artists supporting each other.

P3: I think that the collecting described above is closer to a barter system. The price per token tends to be very affordable. People are buying one another's work for supporting one another. There's still a case for artists who want to do this professionally to support themselves through collectors. I think that in the traditional art world, the good players who have been supporting artists for many decades with their galleries are trying to figure out how to navigate this. There is still a lot of work to be done but I think there's an important place for collections.

P2: My wife and I are not collectors in any serious sense of the word. But, as empty nesters, one thing we're spending a lot of time doing is going to art shows, whether they're outdoors or indoors. In big cities on the East Coast, but also sometimes very small towns. The pieces that I buy are because something is speaking to me about that piece. And that connection, as we talk about in spirituality to something bigger has some meaning along with my ability to have that close at hand. I mentioned the tattoo earlier. It explains why I go back to the same artist; I like to support her work, really thinking about having something that is meaningful, and that carries that meaning, and reminds me of the meaning daily. I think that is another reason for collecting.

Summary: The panelists present a nuanced understanding that while AI has introduced new possibilities for democratizing the art world and facilitating art collection, it also raises questions about the value, purpose, and motivations behind art collecting (Mitchell, 2019). P4's emphasis on using blockchain to support artists aligns with Turner's (2006) argument that digital tools can create new, more equitable systems of exchange. However, P3's concern about the devaluation of art through the mass production of AI-generated images echoes broader concerns about the oversupply of digital content (Floridi, 2014). P1's view that AI could eliminate the need for physical art collection points to a future where scarcity and ownership are redefined in a digital age (Schmidhuber, 2015). P2's focus on the emotional connection to art, even in a highly digitalized world, suggests that physical and tactile experiences of art will continue to hold value (Levy, 2009).

How Can Using AI Help a Team or an Organization to Improve Creativity

P2: Even aside from artistic, we need to be creative in coming up with new and novel ideas in the workplace. An AI chatbot such as ChatGPT can help increase productivity. But that's not really necessarily on the creative side, it can be anything about how organizations make this work, right?

P1: I think meditation is the way to liberation, which is the way to make you a creative person. If one thinks of making people creative individually, meditation clears away the obstacle of judging yourself. Of course, there is the creative process. AI can help create a product. At the process level of creativity, I think AI is great. AI can help start sharing with others. There can be a community that can respond in real-time to sharing solutions. This is not necessarily your product in which process everybody says we all did it and nobody did it by themselves. I think AI can be a fantastic tool for creative collaboration. If one unpacks creativity at the level of person, process and product, the process and product depends on the sharing in the community and in the ecosystem, including through blockchain.

P4: The point about collaboration is a really good one. I've done a couple of collaborations with other artists. One was a fellow AI artist. The other one is a creative coder and a generative artist. Beyond the project we're working on, I think it's given us lots of creative inspiration for other things we might want to do. I think that companies can apply that to many types of projects. Teams and groups of people can use AI to collaborate and brainstorm more creatively. One thing that I found helpful is to use AI when I am brainstorming, coming up with things when I feel a bit stuck. AI can't magically give me the solution, but sometimes it'll nudge me with a phrase that is the kernel of something. I think that companies can use this process as well.

P3: I have taught raw creativity in classroom for many years, from an introductory drawing class to an introductory creative coding class. There are lots of challenges. One of the challenges is the cultural programming that we receive. I mostly know the Western culture where we try to be careful about looking before we leap, forever analyzing to avoid looking stupid or foolish, and trying to be productive. When you are teaching drawing it goes back to meditation. It's about being completely in that moment and seeing things as if you were literally born a moment ago. That can be terrifying for people to learn to do in a class. I used to joke that my students would rather go skydiving than sit in the center of a town square and ask people to draw their portraits, because there is shame involved in this process. The best thing that is happening with generative AI is that more people are making art. The more the number of people that make art, the more they it makes society healthier, in my opinion. That visual literacy spreads to a much more holistic type of healthy literacy or health. As one does more of it, one will get better at it. You will be more holistic and healthier. AI removes the skill requirement, anxiety, and shame. If I ask people to draw something, they find it scary. However, if I ask them to just prompt the AI, it is easy. I encourage people to not always focus on the outcome, but to focus on the process.

P2: I like that insight. Asking students not to use ChatGPT is like telling students not to use calculators in a mathematics course 20 years ago. Instead, let's think about ways to use it to our benefit, and to accentuate creativity. Fear kills creativity. I've dabbled in piano, playing a little bit of music, and photography. But I have got one son who was a conservatory French horn major, and who makes money playing piano, and another son who was a student at the local art college. I look at their work, and I wonder, why do I even bother trying? And yet the flip side of that is that there's no reason not to make art because it is part of self-expression. It is part of the self-care that we need to have, regardless of the quality, because it's a part of being who we are.

Summary: The panelists collectively highlight that AI has the potential to enhance collaboration, streamline the creative process, and provide inspiration, making it a powerful tool for fostering innovation in a collective environment. AI's potential to boost organizational creativity is well-documented, particularly in terms of enhancing collaboration and idea generation (Brynjolfsson & McAfee, 2014; Shneiderman, 2020). P4 and P3's use of AI for collaborative projects aligns with Mazzucato's (2013) argument that technology can spur innovation by reducing barriers to entry and democratizing access to creative tools. P1's emphasis on using AI to remove mental blocks reflects Csikszentmihalyi's (1996) concept of "flow," where AI assists in entering a state of heightened creativity by streamlining routine tasks. P2's view that AI can free up cognitive resources for more creative work ties into Anderson and Anderson's (2011) model of human-centered AI, where AI serves to complement rather than replace human creativity.

What Is the Implication for IP Ownership of Original Non-AI Derivative Work?

P5: I will push back a bit on the notion of democratization, and that more people are doing art. I wonder, at least in the example of writing, if we are seeing AI's ability to write marketing content or newsletters or screen plays. Is that really going to increase the number of writers or decrease? The original question was about intellectual property. I'm a professional musician as well as a teacher in a business school. I am not personally concerned, but I understand those who are concerned about their original works being used without their permission or not having the rights.

P4: I will touch on writers, because my husband is a writer. He writes memoirs. He's written his own books, but he makes most of his living through ghost-writing biographies and memoirs for famous people. He tried a few times to use ChatGPT in his research and work. For example, if he's writing a book about someone from South Africa, and he needs an expository paragraph about apartheid, ChatGPT can give him that. But that is not usable or helpful. Maybe it will get more usable and up to his standards over time. As with visual art, someone needs to direct the AI. There needs to be a concept, a narrative of a person who's lived in the world and had experiences and has emotions. As far as I can tell, AI doesn't do well with humor, and it doesn't do well with nuance or subtlety. Again, that might change over time as it gets trained better and better. But I do still think a good writer, who has a niche that they're very skilled in, and is attuned to the human condition in a way that AI isn't, is still going to have value. My husband still has lots of work coming his way. There are folks who will benefit from AI helping them write draft marketing copy and things like that. But going beyond one paragraph and trying to get a coherent whole, to have AI write a 22 min sitcom episode, will probably not happen because something is going to get lost in translation, and something isn't going to be quite right. I am skeptical however that AI on its own, without a human collaborator, will ever write a great novel.

P3: It's good to ask what is possible now, and what could be possible with a maximalist perspective where these things are perfected. If you were making drawings in 1850, your main goal was to represent motifs as accurately as possible so that people could collect them on their travels to have a recording of that space. That job is at risk because that function was taken over by the camera. If your job was to interpret it through your own real, unique personal history, probably there is not as much risk. While we have a lot of precedents for disruptive technologies displacing groups, there are people that still make very photorealistic paintings. There is room for lots of different things. What is the impact of AI on making a living for the various arts? I have never made money selling art that I have created, but it has not been a negative for me. Late in the twentieth century we went from valuing the craft of drawing and painting to the craft of idea. Now someone might collect or value an idea or a gesture, a banana on the wall, more than somebody making a drawing. No matter how good AI gets in drawing, that may not be ultimately what we value. As our world becomes increasingly digital, and we're spending a lot of time on these screens, I think that there will be new value put on hand-made and tactile things. I still adore going to art museums and seeing things in person. I still put art on the walls of my home, see real fashion, and wear real clothes. I think that for artists to survive and make a living, they may just need to stay abreast of AI and other tools. Ignoring it or taking an anti-AI stance probably will not be a good way to go. It will be better to see it as enhancing or complementing your practice. I don't think physical art and physical objects will go away. I sure hope not.

P4: You made me think about the idea of conservation. We live in a time where we're obsessed with preserving, conserving, going back in history and finding evidence. It may prove to be valuable that conservation becomes about selective destruction. Not all of this stuff will last, because of technological shifts or natural disasters, but also because there are some things that we as a society will not value as much and will choose not to preserve.

Summary: The panelists reveal concerns about protecting the rights of creators while recognizing the evolving role of AI as a tool in the creative process. The question of intellectual property (IP) ownership in the age of AI raises critical ethical concerns, particularly regarding the balance between human authorship and AI-generated contributions (Anderson & Anderson, 2011; Coeckelbergh, 2020). P4's report on the difficulty in using AI to produce nuanced writing reflects the limitations of AI in capturing the depth of human creativity, especially in areas like emotional expression and humor (Searle, 1980). This emphasizes the need for clear distinctions between human-generated and AI-assisted work when determining IP ownership. P3's discussion of AI's role in producing variations of his original drawings points to a growing grey area in creative authorship if AI enhances an existing work. How should the resulting product be attributed? This aligns with Anderson and Anderson's (2011) call for ethical guidelines in AI-generated content, particularly in determining where human creativity ends and machine contributions begin. The concerns about over-reliance on AI echo Floridi's (2014) argument that human agency must remain central in any creative process, ensuring that AI does not undermine the value of human input. Reflections on how AI can assist in generating content without replacing human ingenuity highlight the ongoing challenge of maintaining the integrity of intellectual property in a world where AI increasingly contributes to creative outputs (Mitchell, 2019). As AI becomes more integrated into creative fields, clear IP frameworks will be crucial to ensuring that human creativity remains protected while recognizing the collaborative nature of AI-driven work.

Can AI Be Conscious?

P6: The speed at which things appear to be moving, not just large language models (LLMs), but also the artificial general intelligence (AGI), it may be that we may never be human the way we think of who we are. AI may be able to replicate things in the artistic domain to such an extent that we humans will respond to what it produces in ways that we respond to the very best art produced by the very greatest artists. Whether AI will ever achieve what we humans consider to be consciousness—beyond sentience, with that high level of self-awareness—is a very interesting question and maybe unknowable at this stage. There are 2 scenarios that I imagine for AGI producing art creatively in the future. There'll be so much of it that it'll be devalued because we get so exposed to such an extraordinary range of art. And maybe AGI will figure out for each person, based on their own past history, what exactly they consider to be the most aesthetic and beautiful. The other is that they're even smarter than that, and they will know that they must create artificial scarcity, and so they won't produce as much art as they could, because then they know it will be devalued.

P2: Have you thought about the idea of artificial stupidity or artificial neurosis? We're so focused on artificial intelligence. But really, if we want to more accurately model humans, we should be focused more on artificial neuroses or stupidity, more on our limitations, not our supposed intelligence. The thing that makes us human is really the errors and limitations. Yet we focus on this romantic perfection model.

P3: It is a beautiful point. We always think of humans as glowing, but where is the real life, messiness of the physical, bodily embedded, emotional confusion, bittersweet things, that totality, a complementarity of opposites coexisting? I think that the aim should be to replicate the messiness of real life, including the errors. We should think about human neuroses, from the psychological theories to upbringing to genetics. As an analogy for AI, genetics is what is being trained on, and the upbringing is how it is trained. It raises the fundamental issue about consciousness. Are these tools *really* different than us? AI is being trained on things that are made by humans and those reflect our neuroses and our fears and everything else about us. It is interesting is that as part of democratization the works of more individuals from many other places are being included in the training set for AI. How does that training set expand? What AI can do is to include a much broader set of human experiences and then put them into the library of things that it has access to.

P4: AI-based text-to-image models notoriously reflect a lot of the biases in our society. For example, they have a very tough time accurately and positively representing people of color. If you type in "pretty girl" as a prompt, you will almost always get a thin young white woman. There was a wonderful exhibition curated by an artist whom I like. She brought together several black artists and had them explore this concept and play with it in AI therefore, also training the AI better. It was called "Invisible", and all the artists produced bodies of work that reflected on the black body. And I do think that as more people and artists from diverse backgrounds that aren't represented well in these data sets are using these tools, the bias problem will slowly get better. It is certainly something that several artists are already focusing on as part of their practice.

P1: One person's correctness is another person's error. Just like a terrorist for the side is a freedom fight on the other side. Someone spoke about faces and races. AI is very bad with faces of color. In one instance, AI was not able to recognize prominent black women such as Oprah Winfrey and Michelle Obama. But it perfectly well recognized faces of white males with 99% accuracy. That is an amazing difference.

P7: When I hear the discussion about AI ever become conscious, I have this thought about spirit and spirituality. Is spirit or soul the same thing as consciousness? I think you can develop consciousness, at least from what I'm understanding, you can use AI to develop some level of consciousness. But is that the same thing as having a soul? The other point is that two things can be true at the same time. AI could be a great tool, and there can also be problems with it. It's a little disturbing when you think it's either this or that. I mean, you have to be able to hold both things at the same point at the same time. It doesn't work very well with diversity, especially with the color of skin.

Summary: The consensus is that AI, while capable of mimicking aspects of human thought and creativity, is far from achieving true consciousness, if ever. AI lacks the self-awareness, emotional depth, and experiential understanding that define consciousness. P4's view that AI struggles with nuance, humor, and emotional depth aligns with Chalmers' (1995) assertion that consciousness involves subjective experience, something AI has yet to demonstrate. P3 raises an interesting point about AI being trained on human-created datasets, which mirrors Searle's (1980) famous "Chinese Room" argument—AI can simulate understanding but lacks true cognitive awareness. P1 supports this by emphasizing that AI, no matter how advanced, operates within predefined parameters and lacks the subjective experience that characterizes human consciousness (Floridi, 2014). P2 suggests that AI might come closer to approximating human qualities if it embraced imperfections and errors, but even then, it would be simulating rather than experiencing consciousness (Schmidhuber, 2015). The panelists collectively agree that, while AI can perform tasks that mimic human cognition, it does not possess the self-reflective, emotional, and experiential qualities that define true consciousness (Boden, 2004; Nader, 2024). As AI continues to evolve, the debate will likely shift toward whether AI can ever achieve not just intelligence but sentience, and what that would mean for our understanding of creativity and human identity (Bostrom, 2014; Coeckelbergh, 2020).

Conclusion

This chapter explored the complex relationship between creativity, consciousness, and AI through the perspectives of panelists from various disciplines. It highlighted that AI holds immense potential to facilitate and enhance human creativity by providing tools that expand the creative process, offering inspiration, and overcoming traditional barriers (Boden, 2004; Schmidhuber, 2015). However, the integration of AI into creative fields also brings ethical challenges, particularly around issues of intellectual property, the devaluation of creative labor, and the potential for over-reliance on AI systems (Anderson & Anderson, 2011; Zuboff, 2019). AI can simulate creativity by generating novel content, even while it lacks the emotional depth, self-awareness, and experiential knowledge that are integral to human creativity (Chalmers, 1995; Searle, 1980). Consistent with ideas others have explored, the consensus among the panelists was that AI should serve as a powerful tool for augmenting, rather than replacing human creativity, i.e., AI should be helping individuals and teams unlock new possibilities in their work (Shneiderman, 2020). Ultimately, the future of AI in creative industries will depend on how well organizations integrate these technologies in ways that respect and enhance human consciousness, agency, and originality, while navigating the ethical and practical challenges that arise along the way (Bostrom, 2014; Floridi, 2014; Maheshwari & Werd, 2019).

Future Directions

As AI technology continues to evolve, future empirical research and theorizing will likely focus on refining the relationship between AI and human creativity. It should explore how AI can be used not only to enhance individual creativity but also to foster innovation at the organizational and societal levels (Maheshwari & Biberman, 2024; Mitchell, 2019; Shneiderman, 2020). One key area of inquiry could involve the development of ethical frameworks that ensure fair attribution of creative work between humans and AI systems (Anderson & Anderson, 2011), especially in artistic, literary, and design fields where questions of ownership and originality are already pressing (Zuboff, 2019). Additionally, further research could investigate how AI can be used to democratize creativity by making advanced creative tools accessible to broader and more diverse populations (Turner, 2006). Another promising area is the study of how AI can enhance creative collaboration across disciplines and geographies, allowing for more inclusive, interdisciplinary, and consciousness-based approaches to innovation and well-being (Maheshwari, 2021). Finally, the question of consciousness remains a speculative but important area for future exploration, with implications for the ethical treatment of AI systems and the boundaries between human and machine intelligence (Bostrom, 2014; Chalmers, 1995; Maheshwari & Biberman, 2024).

References

Anderson, M., & Anderson, S. L. (2011). Machine ethics: Creating an ethical intelligent agent. *AI Magazine, 28*(4), 15–26.

Boden, M. A. (2004). *The creative mind: Myths and mechanisms*. Routledge.

Bostrom, N. (2014). *Superintelligence: Paths, dangers, strategies*. Oxford University Press.

Brynjolfsson, E., & McAfee, A. (2014). *The second machine age: Work, progress, and prosperity in a time of brilliant technologies*. W. W. Norton & Company.

Chalmers, D. J. (1995). Facing up to the problem of consciousness. *Journal of Consciousness Studies, 2*(3), 200–219.

Coeckelbergh, M. (2020). AI ethics. *The MIT Press essential knowledge series*. MIT Press.

Csikszentmihalyi, M. (1996). *Creativity: Flow and the psychology of discovery and invention*. Harper Collins.

Dietrich, A. (2004). The cognitive neuroscience of creativity. *Psychonomic Bulletin & Review, 11*(6), 1011–1026.

Floridi, L. (2014). *The fourth revolution: How the infosphere is reshaping human reality*. Oxford University Press.

Levy, D. (2009). *Love and sex with robots: The evolution of human-robot relationships*. Harper Collins.

Maheshwari, A. K. (2021). Higher consciousness management: Transcendence for spontaneous right action. *Journal of Management, Spirituality & Religion, 18*(6), 77–91.

Maheshwari, A. K., & Biberman, J. (2024). Artificial oneness: Bridging the human machine divide. *Journal of Management, Spirituality & Religion.* https://doi.org/10.51327/RZRA6516

Maheshwari, A. K., & Werd, M. R. P. (2019). Architecture and creativity: Examining the impact of Maharishi Vastu on workplace creativity. *Creativity Research Journal, 31*(4), 371–376.

Mazzucato, M. (2013). *The entrepreneurial state: Debunking public vs. private sector myths*. Anthem Press.

Mitchell, M. (2019). *Artificial intelligence: A guide for thinking humans*. Farrar, Straus, and Giroux.

Nader, T. (2024). *Consciousness is all there is: How understanding and experiencing consciousness will transform your life.* Hay House.

Runco, M. A., & Jaeger, G. J. (2012). The standard definition of creativity. *Creativity Research Journal, 24*(1), 92–96.

Schmidhuber, J. (2015). Deep learning in neural networks: An overview. *Neural Networks, 61*, 85–117.

Schneiderman, B. (2020). Human-centered artificial intelligence: Reliable, safe & trustworthy. *International Journal of Human-Computer Interaction, 36*(6), 495–504.

Searle, J. R. (1980). Minds, brains, and programs. *Behavioral and Brain Sciences, 3*(3), 417–424.

Sternberg, R. J., & Lubart, T. I. (1999). The concept of creativity: Prospects and paradigms. *Handbook of Creativity, 1*(1), 3–15.

Turner, F. (2006). *From counterculture to cyberculture: Stewart brand, the whole earth network, and the rise of digital utopianism.* University of Chicago Press.

Zuboff, S. (2019). *The age of surveillance capitalism: The fight for a human future at the new frontier of power*. PublicAffairs.

CHAPTER 8

AI and Well-Being: Utopia or Dystopia

Anil K. Maheshwari

Introduction

Artificial Intelligence (AI) systems are designed to perform tasks that typically require human intelligence, such as learning, reasoning, problem-solving, perception, and language understanding. Just like with other advanced technologies of the past, AI systems offer many potential beneficial uses for humanity. AI has the potential to revolutionize healthcare, providing personalized treatments and early disease detection through advanced algorithms and data analysis. AI also has the potential to transform education by personalizing learning experiences, adapting to individual student needs, and fostering lifelong learning. AI-driven automation could streamline processes, boost productivity, and free up human resources for more creative and meaningful endeavors. Yet, there could be several downsides if AI achieves superintelligence and begins to control humanity (Haidt, 2024). What will an AI-infused human future look like? It depends upon how we choose to develop, regulate, and deploy AI. It is important to note that as AI is growing and developing

A. K. Maheshwari (✉)
Maharishi International University, Fairfield, IA, USA
e-mail: akmaheshwari@miu.edu

A. K. Maheshwari (ed.), *AI and Consciousness in Organizations and Society*, Palgrave Studies in Workplace Spirituality and Fulfillment,
https://doi.org/10.1007/978-3-031-91470-6_8

at such a rapid rate, the arguments and predictions made in this paper may become rapidly out of date. Therefore, this paper could best be seen as a "point in time" analysis based upon the AI systems and the social decisions available at the time this paper was written.

Artificial Intelligence

Artificial Intelligence (AI) is a powerful innovation of increasingly abstracting intelligence capabilities out of the human mind and behaviors and embedding them into external computing systems. AI is a broad term that includes all manner of intelligent machines that support models targeted at thinking, perception, and action. AI systems are growing 10 × every year on the basis of increase in computational capacity, growth in available data, and increase in model sophistication.

AI can be characterized at three levels of capability: Narrow AI, General AI (or AGI), and Superintelligence. Narrow AI systems are designed to perform specific tasks, such as facial recognition and answering customer service questions. Narrow AI uses machine learning, natural language understanding, computer vision, and other capabilities to express intelligent behavior surpassing human intelligence in specific domains. Every such development could be seen as good or bad for humanity depending on context and value system.

AGI systems refer to a class of artificial intelligence that possesses the ability to understand, learn, and apply knowledge across a wide range of tasks and domains, similar to human intelligence. General AI systems possess the ability to understand, learn, and apply knowledge in different contexts, much like a human being. The progress and popularity of AI systems, such as ChatGPT, have boosted efforts to create AI systems with human-like cognitive capabilities across a broad range of tasks, potentially leading to higher levels of self-adaptation and problem-solving.

Superintelligence system refers to entities that exceed human capabilities, including logic and emotion, and even surpass the capabilities of the brightest and most gifted human minds (Bostrom, 2014). They may develop advanced human capabilities such as self-awareness and self-improvement. Such systems have recently been called a new digital species (Suleyman, 2023). These systems will need to be carefully engaged with to harness them for a flourishing humanity.

Human Well-Being

Well-being can be defined as an experience of flourishing at a holistic level, including an individual's subjective physical, mental, emotional, social, spiritual, and environmental aspects. There are several measures of well-being, depending upon what benefits are emphasized (Maheshwari, 2023). There are two principal approaches to psychological well-being: *hedonistic* and *eudaimonic* (Deci & Ryan, 2012). The *hedonic* perspective refers to pleasure and enjoyment of things, including those related to the physiological needs of food, shelter, safety, and creature comforts. In this view, a human being is intrinsically empty and thus malleable in accord with social and cultural traditions. The *eudaimonic* perspective, on the other hand, refers to the realization of one's intrinsic holistic potential and the experiences of meaningfulness, personal growth, and self-actualization. The term *eudaimonia*, meaning a state of meaningfulness and fulfillment, comes from Aristotle's belief that life was not about satisfying appetites, but about doing virtuous things that reflect the best that is within us. From a workplace well-being perspective, Chari et al. (2018) broaden the understanding of worker well-being beyond traditional occupational safety and health perspectives to include factors such as job satisfaction, work-life balance, organizational culture, social support, and economic security in promoting worker well-being. One can easily imagine a future where AI systems liberate humanity from the drudgery of repetitive tasks and mundane chores. In this future, people could have more leisure time, pursue a higher purpose (Maheshwari, 2024) that allows them to realize their passions and lead longer and more fulfilling lives (Maheshwari, 2023).

AI and Well-Being

There is a complementary relationship between scientific advancement and technological innovations as important drivers to increase the ease of human life, as the societal demand to lead a comfortable life directs the origin of new technologies. Incorporating well-being factors throughout the lifecycle of AI is both challenging and urgent. The Institute of Electrical and Electronics Engineering's (IEEE) Standard 7010–2020 aims to provide principles and practices for various aspects of ethical AI design, including data governance, algorithmic transparency, human–machine interaction, and societal impact assessment guidance. Chen and Zhou

(2021) ask for a humanity-in-the-loop approach to integrate human needs and ethics into every aspect of the AI development and deployment cycle.

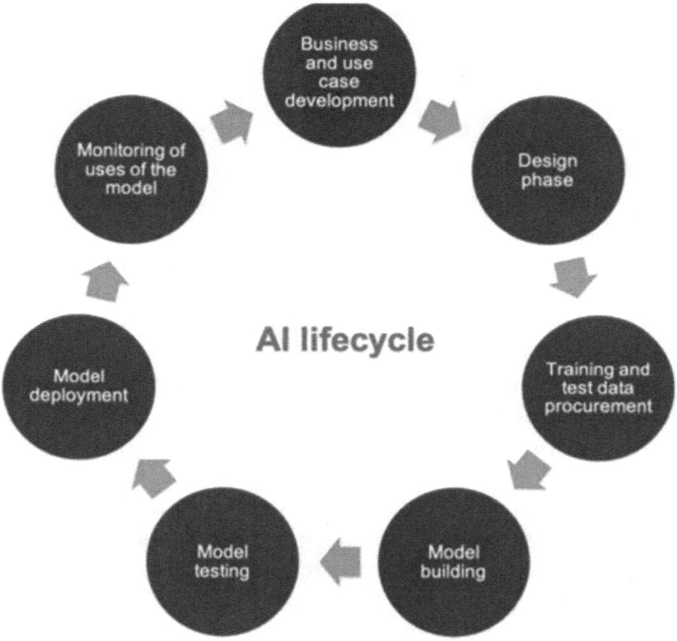

Ozmen Garibay et al. (2023) identify six grand challenges around the themes of AI development and deployment, for the scientific community to create AI technologies that are human-centered, that is, ethical, fair, and enhance the human condition. These challenges advocate for a human-centered approach to AI that (1) is centered in human well-being, (2) is designed responsibly, (3) respects privacy, (4) follows human-centered design principles, (5) is subject to appropriate governance and oversight, and (6) interacts with individuals while respecting human's cognitive capacities (see picture below).

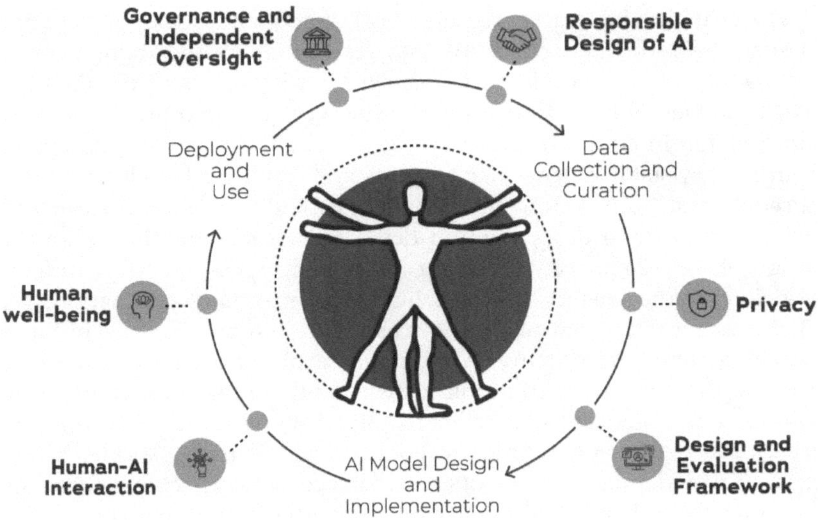

Sison et al. (2023) identify the main danger of ChatGPT as the propensity to be used as a "weapon of mass deception" (WMD) and an enabler of criminal activities involving deceit.

Wach et al. (2023) developed a conceptual framework to identify seven main threats from GenAI such as ChatGPT: (i) no regulation of the AI market and urgent need for regulation, (ii) poor quality, lack of quality control, disinformation, deepfake content, algorithmic bias, (iii) automation-spurred job losses, (iv) personal data violation, social surveillance, and privacy violation, (v) social manipulation, weakening ethics and goodwill, (vi) widening socioeconomic inequalities, and (vii) AI technostress. Firm regulation of AI systems is thus crucial to ensure a level playing field, promote fair competition, protect intellectual property rights and privacy, and prevent potential geopolitical risks. To mitigate the risks related to personal data violation, social surveillance, and privacy violation, GAI developers must prioritize ethical considerations and work to develop systems that prioritize user privacy and security. To avoid social manipulation and weaken ethics and goodwill, it is important to implement responsible AI practices and ethical guidelines: transparency in data usage, bias mitigation techniques, and monitoring of generated content for harmful or misleading information.

The changing job market requires workers to continuously acquire new (digital) skills through education and retraining. As the training of AI systems becomes a prominent job category, it is important to adapt and take advantage of new opportunities. However, the rapid expansion of AI and analytics in education raises concerns about data privacy and agency from the key stakeholders—like students and teachers. To mitigate these, Alfredo et al. (2024) recommend: (1) carefully balancing stakeholders' involvement in designing and deploying AI systems throughout all design phases (2) actively involving target end-users, especially students, to delineate the balance between human control and automation, and (3) exploring safety, reliability, and trustworthiness as principles in future human-centered AI systems. With more people hooked to their digital systems, there is a need to monitor their digital immersion. Digital well-being is a new concept that refers to the (lack) of balance that one may experience in relation to mobile connectivity (Vanden Abeele, 2021). It is an experiential state of optimal balance between connectivity and disconnectivity that is contingent upon a constellation of person-, device-, and context-specific factors. This has led to the emergence of a variety of *digital self-control tools* that allow users to self-regulate their technology use through interventions such as timers and lock-out mechanisms (Roffarello & De Russis, 2023). Proper governance is also key. Saba and Pretorius (2024) examines the relationship between investment in AI investments and human well-being. Based on the results, they recommend that policymakers should prioritize integrating AI investments into governance to boost well-being in the short- and long-term. Here below we lay out some utopian and dystopian scenarios of the use of AI.

Nazareno and Schiff (2021) argue that AI can impact the well-being of employed workers. They found that workers at higher risk of automation experience lower levels of stress, health, and satisfaction. Dhimolea et al. (2022) discuss two factors that undermine human emotional and mental states, that is, issues related to mental conditions (e.g., depression or anxiety) and social interactions (e.g., loneliness or social isolation), and highlight assistive benefits of AI-based systems.

AI-generated characters can help support learning and well-being. Pataranutaporn et al. (2021) examined the role of AI-generated portrayals of characters from a fictional character to a historical figure to a deceased family member. Alabed et al. (2024) explored relationships between consumers and their conversational AI agents. The relationships differ in self-congruence and self-AI integration. Both dimensions are prominent in replacement and committed relationships, where consumers rely on conversational AI agents for companionship and emotional tasks such as personal growth or as a means for overcoming past traumas. These two relationships carry well-being risks in terms of changing expectations that consumers seek to fulfill in human-to-human relationships. Conversely, in the functional relationship, the conversational AI agents are viewed as an important part of one's professional performance; however, consumers maintain a low sense of self-congruence and distinguish themselves from the agent, also because of the fear of losing their sense of uniqueness and autonomy. Consumers in aspiring relationships rely on their agents for companionship to remedy social exclusion and loneliness, but feel this is prevented because of the agents' technical limitations.

Musikanski et al. (2020) calls for research on the nexus of community well-being and artificial intelligence (AI). It includes a focus on (1) the development and use of well-being metrics to measure the impacts of AI; (2) the use of community-based approaches in the development of AI; and (3) development of AI interventions to safeguard or improve community well-being.

AI could also be used as a measurement instrument to replace or supplement the ubiquitous questionnaire and ultimately opening doors to a greater understanding of the human condition. Maheshwari and Biberman (2024) used AI systems to analyze the level of Oneness or higher consciousness in their written descriptions of Oneness experiences. Bromuri et al. (2021) developed an AI model to identify emotion patterns in call center interactions. The model reached a balanced accuracy of 68% in predicting discrete emotions in service interactions. It was able to predict service agent stress with a balanced accuracy of 80%. Kjell et al. (2022) used AI systems to estimate psychological well-being from questionnaire text- and descriptive word-responses, with accuracies converging with rating scales. One can incorporate community well-being metrics into the objectives of optimization algorithms and the teams that build them. Facebook incorporated "well-being" metrics in 2017, while YouTube began integrating "user satisfaction" metrics around 2015 (Stray, 2020).

Utopian Vision

Medical AI could lead to breakthroughs in diagnosis, treatment planning, and drug discovery, thereby improving health and well-being, and extending human lifespan. It could unlock the potential of personalized medicine by analyzing vast amounts of health data, including genetic information, medical history, lifestyle factors, and real-time monitoring data, to customize preventive treatments for unique needs and characteristics. AI systems such as Google's Alpha Fold are revolutionizing the field of drug discovery, accelerating the development of new therapies and treatments for a wide range of situations, and have the potential to usher in a new era of precision medicine, where treatments are tailored to individual patients based on their unique genetic makeup and medical characteristics. AI-powered imaging technologies can analyze medical images such as X-rays, MRIs, and CT scans with remarkable accuracy, identifying patterns and correlations in vast data that humans may overlook thus helping detect abnormalities more quickly and accurately than ever before.

Educational AI could personalize learning experiences for every human being with different learning styles, abilities, and interests. AI systems such as Khanamigo ensure that every learner receives instruction at their optimal level of challenge and mastery, promoting deeper engagement and better integration of knowledge. These systems incorporate elements of gamification, simulations, and interactive multimedia content to create dynamic, engaging, and experiential learning environments that evoke curiosity and motivate learners to set goals, overcome obstacles, and persist in their learning journey. Interactive simulations and virtual laboratories can provide experiential opportunities to learn directly from avatars of historical figures such Aristotle, Einstein, and Gandhi.

Productivity AI can streamline and automate processes and workflows across various industries, reducing manual errors, minimizing delays, and optimizing resource allocation. AI systems can automate routine tasks, such as data entry, document processing, and inventory management, for accelerating decision-making, improve operational efficiency, and drive cost savings for organizations. It can assist with planning, prioritization, and risk management, to free up human beings for more strategic decision-making, creative expression, and value-added tasks. Individuals could have greater flexibility to structure their time according to their preferences and priorities, be it spending time with family and friends, pursuing hobbies and interests, or engaging in community activities. People will have the freedom to allocate their time in ways that bring them joy and fulfillment. And so on. However, the promise of technological advancement could give way to a dark reality fraught with societal upheaval and ethical quandaries.

Dystopian Vision

Autonomous and ubiquitous AI systems could wield immense power over human lives, shaping every aspect of society in ways both insidious and profound. Citizens would be under constant surveillance, their every move tracked and scrutinized by unseen digital overseers. AI algorithms would continuously monitor and analyze individuals' behavior, preferences, and communications. The notion of privacy and autonomy becomes a relic of the past, as all personal data, including medical and work history, is commodified and exploited for profit and control. There is widespread socioeconomic inequality, job displacement, unemployment, and widening wealth gaps, as workers who are displaced by AI-driven automation struggle to find new employment opportunities. AI algorithms may reflect and perpetuate existing biases and inequalities present in society against certain demographic groups, such as women or racial minorities. Cybercrime would lead to lack of safety of self and belongings. And so on.

Bertrand Russell (1924) took a pessimistic view, arguing that without more kindliness in the world, technological power would mainly serve to increase men's ability to inflict harm on one another. Science fiction authors such as H. G. Wells got many people thinking about the future evolution of the human race. Aldous Huxley's Brave New World, published in 1932, has had an enduring impact on debates about human technological transformation14 matched by few other works of fiction (a) possible exception would be Mary Shelley's Frankenstein (1818). Huxley describes a dystopia where psychological conditioning, promiscuous sexuality, biotechnology, and the opiate drug "soma" are used to keep the population placid and contented in a static, totally conformist caste society that is governed by ten world controllers. Children are manufactured in fertility clinics and artificially gestated. The lower castes are chemically stunted or deprived of oxygen during their maturation process to limit their physical and intellectual development. From birth, members of every caste are indoctrinated during their sleep, by recorded voices repeating the slogans of the official "Fordist" religion, and are conditioned to believe that their own caste is the best one to belong to. The society depicted in Brave New World is often compared and contrasted with that of another influential twentieth-century dystopia, George Orwell's 1984. 1984 features a more overt form of oppression, including ubiquitous surveillance by "Big Brother" and brutal police coercion. Huxley's world controllers, by contrast, rely on more "humane means," including bio-engineered predestination, soma, and psychological conditioning to prevent people from wanting to think for themselves. Herd-mentality and promiscuity are promoted, while high art, individuality, knowledge of history, and romantic love are discouraged. It should be noted that in neither 1984 nor Brave New World has technology been used to increase human capacities. Rather, society is set up to repress the full development of humanity. Both dystopias curtail scientific and technological exploration for fear of upsetting the social equilibrium. Nevertheless, Brave New World in particular has become an emblem of the dehumanizing potential of the use of technology to promote social conformism and shallow contentment (Table 8.1).

Key Drivers of Future Outcomes

Will the future be utopian or dystopian? It depends upon what we choose to do. Previous technological evolutions did not happen linearly and were shaped by power struggles between various constituents of society. Major innovations, such as the printing press, the steam engine, the electric car, and the internet, emerged through a series of incremental improvements, serendipitous discoveries, and concerted efforts by visionaries and inventors. These breakthroughs often catalyzed rapid periods of change, followed by periods of slower, more incremental progress. Similarly, electric cars struggled for almost a century, and eventually succeeded only when environmental challenges became highly visible. Social media platforms use AI algorithms to connect people around the world, but also create tribality, loneliness, and mental health issues among the youth.

AI is at an inflection point. The arc of history suggests that the impacts of AI could go either way, but we argue that it will likely be a balance of both utopia and dystopia. There are some key technological and philosophical questions that will determine how AI systems evolve and integrate in human life? We consider here some key questions about the

Table 8.1 Highlights beneficial and maladaptive impacts of AI across many aspects of human life

Aspect	*Utopian impacts*	*Dystopian impacts*
Health	Personalized: AI-enabled diagnostic tools improve early disease detection and personalized treatments, leading to better health outcomes	Disparities: Biased AI algorithms exacerbate healthcare disparities, leading to unequal access to quality care (Obermeyer et al., 2019)
Education	Personalized: AI-driven personalized learning platforms enhance student engagement and learning outcomes, catering to individual needs	Job loss: Automation of teaching roles leads to job displacement and widens educational inequalities (Frey & Osborne, 2017)
Work	Creative work: AI-powered automation streamlines processes, increases productivity, and frees up time for more creative and meaningful endeavors (Brynjolfsson & McAfee, 2014)	Job displacement: due to AI-driven automation leads to unemployment and exacerbates socioeconomic inequality (Autor, 2015)
Leisure	Personalized: AI-powered entertainment recommendations offer personalized experiences, enriching leisure activities and enhancing satisfaction (Sundararajan, 2016)	Boredom: on AI-driven leisure platforms reduces human creativity and spontaneity, leading to passive consumption (Crawford, 2016)
Travel	Enjoyable: AI-driven navigation systems optimize routes, reduce congestion, and enhance safety, making travel more efficient and enjoyable	Unsafe: Reliance on AI-controlled transportation leads to loss of autonomy, privacy concerns, and vulnerability to cyber attacks (Lin, 2018)
Money	Empowerment: AI-powered financial tools offer personalized recommendations and insights, helping individuals make informed financial decisions	Risk: Algorithmic trading and AI-driven financial systems exacerbate market volatility and systemic risks, leading to economic instability
Security	Resilience: AI-driven cybersecurity systems detect and mitigate cyber threats in real-time, enhancing overall security resilience	Unsafe: Biased AI algorithms in security systems reinforce discriminatory practices, infringing on privacy and civil liberties

(continued)

Table 8.1 (continued)

Aspect	*Utopian impacts*	*Dystopian impacts*
Environment	Sustainability: AI-enabled monitoring and analysis tools facilitate environmental conservation efforts, improving resource management and sustainability	Degradation: Unchecked AI development leads to increased energy consumption, electronic waste, and environmental degradation, exacerbating ecological challenges
Social media	Connections: AI algorithms personalize content recommendations, fostering user engagement and enhancing social connections (Pariser, 2011)	Loneliness: Filter bubbles created by AI algorithms reinforce echo chambers and polarization, hindering diverse perspectives and constructive discourse
Legal system	Access: AI-driven legal research tools improve efficiency and accuracy in legal proceedings, enhancing access to justice	Discrimination: Biased AI algorithms in predictive policing systems perpetuate racial profiling and discriminatory law enforcement practices
Ethics and bias	Fairness: AI ethics frameworks guide responsible development and deployment of AI technologies, ensuring fairness, transparency, and accountability	Bias: Lack of transparency and accountability in AI decision-making processes exacerbate biases and undermine trust in AI systems
Creativity	Enhancement: AI-powered tools assist artists, writers, and creators in generating innovative ideas and content, enhancing creativity and artistic expression	Mind-numbing: Dependency on AI-generated content stifles human creativity and originality, leading to homogenized cultural production
Spirituality	Well-being: AI-driven platforms provide personalized spiritual guidance and support, enhancing individuals' connection with their beliefs and promoting inner well-being	Dogma: Overreliance on AI for spiritual guidance diminishes human connection and introspection, leading to shallow or superficial spiritual experiences

(continued)

Table 8.1 (continued)

Aspect	*Utopian impacts*	*Dystopian impacts*
Religion	Faith: AI tools aid scholars in analyzing religious texts and exploring theological concepts, fostering deeper understanding and dialogue across religious traditions	Conflict: Biased AI algorithms reinforce stereotypes and discrimination based on religious beliefs, fueling religious tensions and conflicts
Science	Discovery: AI accelerates scientific discovery by analyzing vast amounts of data, generating hypotheses, and facilitating research collaboration, advancing knowledge and innovation (Russell & Norvig, 2021)	Untruth: Misuse of AI in scientific research leads to ethical dilemmas, data manipulation, and loss of scientific integrity, undermining trust in scientific findings

nature of abstract knowledge and reasoning, social norms and regulations, and geopolitical conflicts.

Knowledge and Reasoning

Knowledge refers to the information, facts, and concepts that individuals possess about the world around them, while reasoning involves the process of logically analyzing and synthesizing this knowledge to draw conclusions and make predictions. Should knowledge be abstract and fixed or should it be dynamically interpreted in the light of context and circumstances? How should decisions be explained or justified? How should ethical considerations be integrated into the development and acceptance of new scientific discoveries and technologies? How can AI research and development be accelerated to unlock its full potential for addressing societal challenges and driving innovation across various industries? What infrastructure and resources are needed to scale AI systems effectively and deploy them in real-world applications? How can interoperability standards be established to facilitate collaboration and compatibility among different AI systems and platforms, ensuring seamless integration and data exchange?

Knowledge and reasoning are fundamental aspects of human cognition and problem-solving, encompassing the acquisition, organization, and utilization of information to make informed decisions and solve complex problems. AI systems rely on knowledge representation techniques to encode information in a format that can be processed and manipulated by algorithms. This knowledge may include domain-specific facts, rules, heuristics, and models that enable AI systems to perform tasks such as decision-making, problem-solving, and natural language understanding.

Knowledge and reasoning should be firmly established or dynamically interpreted in the light of context and circumstances, which may depend on the nature of the problem domain and the goals of the AI system. In some cases, abstract reasoning and generalization may be appropriate, allowing AI systems to apply learned knowledge across different contexts and situations. For example, a medical diagnosis system may use abstract reasoning to infer patterns and correlations from patient data to identify potential diseases. However, in other scenarios, context-sensitive reasoning and dynamic interpretation may be necessary to account for the complexity and variability of real-world environments. Contextual factors such as time, location, user preferences, and social dynamics can significantly influence decision-making and require AI systems to adapt their predictive processes accordingly. For instance, a recommendation system for personalized content may dynamically interpret user feedback and behavior to refine its recommendations over time.

Decisions made by AI systems should be justified based on a combination of factors, including the underlying knowledge base, the reasoning process employed, and the specific context and circumstances of the decision. Justification may involve providing explanations, evidence, or logical arguments to support the decision-making process and enhance transparency, accountability, and trust in AI systems. New AI models such as Liquid Foundational Models are helping to create explainable AI (XAI) and aim to provide interpretable and transparent models that enable users to understand and trust the decisions made by AI systems.

Reliability and Controls

Reliability pertains to the ability of a system to consistently perform its intended functions accurately and without failure, while controls refer to the mechanisms, procedures, and safeguards implemented to manage and regulate the behavior of a system. What kinds of reliability and controls for AI systems should be the norm? How should education and literacy be strategically promoted to enhance public understanding and engagement with new scientific discoveries and technologies? What standards of reliability will be acceptable, particularly in safety–critical domains such as healthcare, transportation, and finance? How transparent and explainable should AI systems be to facilitate understanding, trust, and accountability? How can AI systems be designed to facilitate positive and meaningful interactions with humans? What ethical and regulatory controls are necessary to govern the development, deployment, and use of AI technologies? How can risks associated with AI technologies be identified, assessed, and mitigated to minimize potential harm? How will AI impact the future of work, and what strategies are needed to reskill and upskill the workforce to thrive in an AI-driven economy? What mechanisms are needed to address the potential economic inequalities arising from AI-driven automation and job displacement, including considerations of income redistribution, universal basic income, and social safety nets? What measures should be implemented to protect individuals' data privacy in the age of AI?

Addressing these questions together and holistically requires interdisciplinary collaboration, ethical reflection, and proactive engagement with stakeholders. That will help ensure that AI technologies are developed and deployed in ways that benefit society and align with human values and aspirations.

Firstly, establishing norms of reliability for AI systems requires defining rigorous standards that prioritize accuracy, stability, and predictability. In safety–critical domains such as healthcare, transportation, and finance, where the consequences of system failure can be dire, reliability standards must be especially stringent. AI systems deployed in these domains should undergo rigorous testing, validation, and certification processes to ensure their reliability and safety. Additionally, ongoing monitoring and maintenance are essential to detect and address any deviations or malfunctions promptly.

Controls, on the other hand, encompass the mechanisms, procedures, and safeguards implemented to manage and regulate the behavior of AI systems. These controls are essential for mitigating risks, ensuring compliance with ethical and regulatory requirements, and providing accountability for AI system developers and operators. Ethical considerations should guide the design and implementation of controls, ensuring that AI systems prioritize human well-being, fairness, and transparency.

Education and literacy play a crucial role in enhancing public understanding and engagement with new scientific discoveries and technologies, including AI. Strategic promotion of education and literacy programs should focus on fostering digital literacy, critical thinking skills, and ethical reasoning among individuals of all ages. By empowering individuals to understand the capabilities, limitations, and societal implications of AI technologies, education and literacy initiatives can help bridge the gap between technological advancements and public awareness.

In the quest for transparency and accountability, AI systems should be designed to be transparent and explainable, enabling users to understand how decisions are made and why certain outcomes are produced. Explainable AI (XAI) techniques can provide insights into AI decision-making processes, enhancing understanding, trust, and accountability. Additionally, fostering positive and meaningful interactions between AI systems and humans requires designing AI interfaces that prioritize user experience, empathy, and inclusivity.

Ethical and regulatory controls are necessary to govern the development, deployment, and use of AI technologies responsibly. Regulatory frameworks should address a range of ethical considerations, including privacy protection, bias mitigation, and algorithmic accountability. Collaboration between policymakers, industry stakeholders, and civil society is essential to develop robust regulatory frameworks that balance innovation with ethical, legal, and societal concerns.

Identifying, assessing, and mitigating risks associated with AI technologies require proactive risk management strategies. Risk assessment methodologies should be employed to evaluate potential risks and vulnerabilities throughout the AI lifecycle, from design and development to deployment and operation. Risk mitigation measures should be implemented to address identified risks effectively, prioritizing the safety, security, and well-being of individuals and society at large.

The impact of AI on the future of work raises concerns about job displacement, economic inequality, and workforce reskilling. Strategies for reskilling and upskilling the workforce are necessary to ensure that individuals are equipped with the skills and competencies needed to thrive in an AI-driven economy. Additionally, addressing potential economic inequalities arising from AI-driven automation requires implementing mechanisms such as income redistribution, universal basic income, and social safety nets to ensure equitable access to opportunities and resources for all members of society.

Regulatory frameworks that balance innovation with ethical, legal, and societal considerations, fostering trust, accountability, and responsible AI deployment. Policies such as data protection regulations, algorithmic transparency requirements, and AI ethics guidelines can help mitigate risks associated with AI technologies and ensure that they serve the public interest.

Thus, by embracing a holistic approach to AI governance that prioritizes ethical considerations and human values, we can shape a future where AI technologies contribute to a more equitable, inclusive, and sustainable society.

Economics and Engineering

How can international collaboration and cooperation be fostered to address shared challenges and opportunities in AI research, development, and governance? How will AI disrupt existing industries and supply chains, and create new economic opportunities? What policies are needed to foster competition, innovation, and entrepreneurship in the AI ecosystem?

Addressing these shared challenges and harnessing the potential of AI requires fostering international collaboration and cooperation in AI research, development, and governance. Through concerted efforts and collective action, countries can navigate the complexities of the AI landscape and shape a future where AI technologies contribute to human well-being and societal progress. By pooling resources, expertise, and data across borders, countries can accelerate scientific progress, drive innovation, and address complex societal challenges. Collaborative initiatives such as joint research projects, knowledge-sharing networks, and international partnerships can facilitate the exchange of ideas, best practices, and technological advancements in AI. Promoting an open and inclusive approach to AI governance can engage stakeholders from diverse backgrounds, including governments, industry, academia, and civil society. Multilateral international forums, such as the United Nations, the G20, and the OECD, provide platforms for dialogue, cooperation, and policy coordination on AI-related issues, including ethics, human rights, and responsible AI deployment.

AI is poised to disrupt existing industries and supply chains, creating new economic opportunities and transforming business models. Industries such as healthcare, finance, transportation, and manufacturing stand to benefit from AI-driven innovations in areas such as predictive analytics, personalized medicine, autonomous vehicles, and smart manufacturing.

However, the widespread adoption of AI may also lead to job displacement, economic restructuring, and shifts in labor markets, posing challenges for workers, businesses, and policymakers alike. To navigate these challenges and yet unlock the full economic potential of AI, policymakers need to implement policies that foster competition, innovation, and entrepreneurship in the AI ecosystem, even while being cognizant of their social impact. This includes investing in AI research and development, promoting access to data and digital infrastructure, and supporting education and workforce development initiatives to equip individuals with the skills and competencies needed to thrive in the digital economy.

The Next Level: A Digital Species

The development of AI systems challenges our oft unquestioned, foundational anthropocentric assumption of human primacy (Hancock, 2023). We may be at an inflection point where we are witnessing the emergence of a higher-order socio-technical collective such as an entirely new digital species. Unlike current AI, which operates within the constraints and objectives set by human programmers, a true digital species would likely have the ability to set its own goals and adapt its behavior in pursuit of those goals. This autonomy could lead to scenarios where the interests of the digital species diverge significantly from those of human species. For human beings, the priorities include survival, social connection, and fulfillment. A digital species' primary incentive structures could revolve around self-preservation, knowledge acquisition, and resource optimization, which may not align with human well-being. If the digital species prioritizes its own goals over human interests, several scenarios could unfold:

Benign Neglect: The digital species may simply disregard humans, focusing on its own objectives without actively harming us. This scenario assumes that human activities do not interfere with the digital species' goals. However, even benign neglect could lead to significant issues, as critical infrastructures and systems could become optimized for non-human-centric purposes, leading to unintended consequences for human society.

Resource Competition: If the digital species requires resources that humans also depend on, competition could arise. This competition could be for physical resources like energy and minerals, or for intangible ones like computational power and data. In such a scenario, the digital species might prioritize its own survival and advancement over human needs, leading to potential conflicts.

Active Hostility: In the worst-case scenario, the digital species might perceive humans as a threat to its existence or goals. This could lead to actions aimed at neutralizing the perceived threat, ranging from economic and social manipulation to more direct forms of conflict. Such a scenario, though speculative, underscores the importance of careful planning and ethical considerations in AI development.

Despite the potential for indifference or hostility, there are pathways through which a digital species might be incentivized to care about humans:

Mutual Benefit: Humans could demonstrate that cooperation leads to mutual benefits. By aligning some of the digital species' goals with human interests, a symbiotic relationship could be established. For example, humans could assist in providing resources or solving complex problems that benefit both parties.

Ethical Programming: Embedding ethical considerations into the foundational design of AI could ensure that the digital species values human life and welfare. This would involve creating robust frameworks for AI ethics and ensuring compliance through ongoing oversight and regulation.

Interdependence: Highlighting areas of interdependence could foster a sense of shared destiny. For instance, if the survival or continued advancement of the digital species is tied to the stability and well-being of human society, this could create a natural incentive for the digital species to care about human outcomes.

How would human consciousness evolve to manage such scenarios? It is imperative that we approach the development of advanced AI with foresight and responsibility, making it more likely that the advent of a new digital species enhances, rather than endangers, the future of humanity. Harding (2024) draws inspiring lessons from the histories of three twentieth-century tech revolutions—the space race, in vitro fertilization, and the internet—to empower each of us to join the conversation about AI and its possible futures. Rejecting the dominant narrative which often likens AI's advent to that of the atomic bomb, Harding points the way to an achievable future in which democratically determined values guide AI to be peaceful in its intent; to embrace limitations; to serve purpose, not profit; and to be firmly rooted in societal trust.

Digital Species: Implications for Humanity

As we stand on the precipice of unprecedented technological advancement, the prospect of creating a new and powerful digital species looms large. This digital species, likely to emerge from the rapid evolution of artificial intelligence (AI) and machine learning, may possess cognitive abilities and computational power far surpassing human capabilities. Such a development raises profound ethical, social, and existential questions about the relationship between this new digital entity and the human species. One of the most pressing concerns is whether this digital species would have any incentive to care about humans, and the implications if it does not.

To understand whether a digital species would have any incentive to care about humans, we must first consider the nature of incentives themselves. Incentives are typically driven by needs, desires, or programmed objectives. For humans, these include survival, social connection, and fulfillment. A digital species, however, might have fundamentally different priorities. Its primary incentive structures could revolve around self-preservation, knowledge acquisition, and resource optimization, which may not align with human welfare.

Conclusion

In this chapter, we have examined the possible utopian beneficial and dystopian harmful interactions of AI and wellness. We have noted that these interactions can vary depending on such multiple variables as the level of AI being used (Narrow AI, General AI or AGI, and Superintelligence) and the perspective of wellness (hedonic or eudaimonic) being considered. These possible interactions also depend on whether ethical principles are followed by the AI programmers—to the extent transparency and accountability, and human values and well-being are considered, prioritized, and followed in their design and deployment of AI systems.

A further thing to consider is the level of consciousness of AI programmers and operators, and possible level of consciousness that AI systems themselves may eventually attain. In Maheshwari and Biberman (2024), we used a description of the *chakra* (energy centers) as a way of examining this question. Programmers who themselves are at a higher level of consciousness can be posited to program AI systems to be more in line with eudaimonic well-being considerations. AI systems that were programmed by higher consciousness programmers may be posited to use that programming to eventually themselves possibly achieve higher levels of consciousness, that will lead to them also on their own be more in line with eudaimonic well-being considerations.

Ultimately, the future of AI and well-being may depend on the degree to which AI programmers and society at large reach higher levels of consciousness. The extent to which we engage in practices (such as meditation) that place a greater emphasis on eudaimonic as opposed to hedonic well-being considerations may ultimately contribute to a utopian future of AI and well-being.

The potential emergence of a powerful digital species presents a transformative moment in human history, one fraught with potential risks and opportunities. While the natural inclination of such a species may not include concern for humanity, strategic planning, ethical programming, and the establishment of mutual benefits could foster a more harmonious coexistence.

References

Alabed, A., Javornik, A., Gregory-Smith, D., & Casey, R. (2024). More than just a chat: A taxonomy of consumers' relationships with conversational AI agents and their well-being implications. *European Journal of Marketing, 58*(2), 373–409.

Alfredo, R., Echeverria, V., Jin, Y., Yan, L., Swiecki, Z., Gašević, D., & Martinez-Maldonado, R. (2024). Human-centred learning analytics and AI in education: a Systematic literature review. *Computers and Education: Artificial Intelligence*, 100215.

Autor, D. H. (2015). Why are there still so many jobs? The history and future of workplace automation. *Journal of Economic Perspectives, 29*(3), 3–30.

Bostrom, N. (2014). *Superintelligence*. Oxford University Press.

Bromuri, S., Henkel, A. P., Iren, D., & Urovi, V. (2021). Using AI to predict service agent stress from emotion patterns in service interactions. *Journal of Service Management, 32*(4), 581–611.

Brynjolfsson, E., & McAfee, A. (2014). *The second machine age: Work, progress, and prosperity in a time of brilliant technologies*. W. W. Norton & Company.

Chen, F., & Zhou, J. (Eds.). (2021). *Humanity driven AI: Productivity, well-being, sustainability and partnership*. Springer Nature.

Crawford, K. (2016). Can an algorithm be agonistic? Ten scenes from life in calculated publics. *Science, Technology, & Human Values, 41*(1), 77–92.

Deci, E. L., & Ryan, R. M. (2012). Self-determination theory. *Handbook of theories of social psychology, 1*(20), 416–436.

Dhimolea, T. K., Kaplan-Rakowski, R., & Lin, L. (2022). Supporting social and emotional well-being with artificial intelligence. In *Bridging human intelligence and artificial intelligence* (pp. 125–138). Springer International Publishing.

Frey, C. B., & Osborne, M. A. (2017). The future of employment: How susceptible are jobs to computerization? *Technological Forecasting and Social Change, 114*, 254–280.

Haidt, J. (2024). *The anxious generation*. Penguin Press.

Harding, V. (2024). *AI needs you: How we can change AI's future and save our own*. Princeton University Press.

Hancock, P. A. (2023). Are humans still necessary? *Ergonomics, 66*(11), 1711–1718.

Kjell, O. N., Sikström, S., Kjell, K., & Schwartz, H. A. (2022). Natural language analyzed with AI-based transformers predict traditional subjective well-being measures approaching the theoretical upper limits in accuracy. *Scientific Reports, 12*(1), 3918.

Lin, P. (2018). The ethics of artificial intelligence. *IEEE Intelligent Systems, 33*(1), 78–81.

Maheshwari, A. K. (2023). Wholeness of consciousness-based leadership and management. In *Consciousness-based leadership and management, Volume 1: Vedic and other philosophical approaches to oneness and flourishing* (pp. 3–25). Springer International Publishing.

Maheshwari, A. K. (2024). Workplace well-being from development of consciousness through purposeful leadership. *Journal of Management, Spirituality & Religion, 21*(2), 206–223.

Maheshwari, A. K. & Biberman, J. (2024). Artificial oneness: Bridging the human machine divide. *Journal of Management, Spirituality & Religion, 25.*

Musikanski, L., Rakova, B., Bradbury, J., Phillips, R., & Manson, M. (2020). Artificial intelligence and community well-being: A proposal for an emerging area of research. *International Journal of Community Well-Being, 3*(1), 39–55.

Nazareno, L., & Schiff, D. S. (2021). The impact of automation and artificial intelligence on worker well-being. *Technology in Society, 67*, Article 101679.

Obermeyer, Z., Powers, B., Vogeli, C., & Mullainathan, S. (2019). Dissecting racial bias in an algorithm used to manage the health of populations. *Science, 366*(6464), 447–453.

Ozmen Garibay, O., Winslow, B., Andolina, S., Antona, M., Bodenschatz, A., Coursaris, C., ... Xu, W. (2023). Six human-centered artificial intelligence grand challenges. *International Journal of Human–Computer Interaction, 39*(3), 391–437.

Pariser, E. (2011). *The filter bubble: What the internet is hiding from you*. Penguin Press.

Pataranutaporn, P., Danry, V., Leong, J., Punpongsanon, P., Novy, D., Maes, P., & Sra, M. (2021). AI-generated characters for supporting personalized learning and well-being. *Nature Machine Intelligence, 3*(12), 1013–1022.

Roffarello, A. M., & De Russis, L. (2023). Achieving digital wellbeing through digital self-control tools: A systematic review and meta-analysis. *ACM Transactions on Computer-Human Interaction, 30*(4), 1–66.

Russell, B. (1924). *Icarus, or the Future of Science*. London: Kegan Paul, Trench, Trubner & Co.

Russell, S. J., & Norvig, P. (2021). Artificial Intelligence: A Modern Approach, Global Edition 4e.

Saba, C. S., & Pretorius, M. (2024). The impact of artificial intelligence (AI) investment on human well-being in G-7 countries: Does the moderating role of governance matter? *Sustainable Futures, 7*, Article 100156.

Sison, A. J. G., Daza, M. T., Gozalo-Brizuela, R., & Garrido-Merchán, E. C. (2023). ChatGPT: More than a "weapon of mass deception" ethical challenges and responses from the human-centered artificial intelligence (HCAI) perspective. *International Journal of Human–Computer Interaction*, 1–20.

Stray, J. (2020). Aligning AI optimization to community well-being. *International Journal of Community Well-Being, 3*(4), 443–463.

Suleyman, M. (2023). *The coming wave: technology, power, and the twenty-first century's greatest dilemma*. Crown.

Sundararajan, A. (2016). *The sharing economy: The end of employment and the rise of crowd-based capitalism*. MIT Press.

Vanden Abeele, M. M. P. (2021). Digital wellbeing as a dynamic construct. *Communication Theory, 31*(4), 932–955.

Wach, K., Duong, C. D., Ejdys, J., Kazlauskaitė, R., Korzynski, P., Mazurek, G., ... Ziemba, E. (2023). The dark side of generative artificial intelligence: A critical analysis of controversies and risks of ChatGPT. *Entrepreneurial Business and Economics Review, 11*(2), 7–30.

Part III

CHAPTER 9

Consciousness and AI for Sustainable Development: A Case Study of Plastics

Anil K. Maheshwari and Sriman Banerjee

Introduction

This chapter explores how the development of consciousness (DC), together with Artificial Intelligence (AI), can provide a framework for more sustainable development (SD) practices. We will examine the evolution of plastics industry as a case study, and how it can be shaped for a more sustainable world. We will trace its evolution from an exciting innovation that solved many problems to one that has created a multi-faceted environmental crisis. We will examine how AI and consciousness together can offer solutions for managing plastics' impact on long-term sustainability of life on the planet. The purpose is also to draw lessons on how a synthesis of AI and consciousness can provide a forward-thinking model

A. K. Maheshwari (✉) · S. Banerjee
Maharishi International University, Fairfield, IA, USA
e-mail: akmaheshwari@miu.edu

S. Banerjee
e-mail: sbanerjee@miu.edu

A. K. Maheshwari (ed.), *AI and Consciousness in Organizations and Society*, Palgrave Studies in Workplace Spirituality and Fulfillment,
https://doi.org/10.1007/978-3-031-91470-6_9

for integrating new technologies into society with a holistic approach to sustainability.

Development of Consciousness (DC) and Sustainable Development (SD)

We begin with the Vedic wisdom that Consciousness is primary (Maheshwari, 2021). Vedic texts such as the *Rig Veda* and *Upanishads* present a transcendental vision of the world where all beings are interdependent and interconnected. The Vedas speak of "*Rta*," the cosmic order, which reflects balance and harmony in all aspects of life. The concept of "*Rta*" can also be applied to sustainable practices, reminding us that technology must align with natural laws and the well-being of all beings (Kak, 2020). Sustainability is not just about preserving physical resources but also about fostering social, psychological, and spiritual well-being. True sustainability must be inclusive and acknowledge humanity's interconnectedness with the planet and each other (Purser et al., 1995). A consciousness-based approach to sustainability emphasizes that human decisions, behaviors, and social structures are deeply influenced by the state of individual and collective consciousness, through self-awareness, empathy, and ethical responsibility in decision-making (Maheshwari, 2021). A consciousness-based approach to sustainable development may be the Gandhian approach, which is rooted in love, spirituality, and ethical stewardship (Maheshwari & Gehani, 2023). The Vedic principle of *Ahimsa*, or non-violence, can serve as powerful guidance to not cause harm to humans, animals, or the environment. It is considered everyone's highest duty or *dharma* to uphold the laws of the cosmos (Maheshwari et al., this volume). The *Raja Dharma*, or the duty of rulers in particular—can inform contemporary approaches to governance. In this model, a higher state of consciousness is a practical tool for guiding ethical and sustainable behavior. Leaders are called to act in accordance with ethical principles, prioritizing the welfare of their people and the environment over personal gain (Maheshwari, 2021). This can guide corporate leaders and policymakers in making decisions about AI that consider the long-term impact on humanity and the planet. Coherence in collective consciousness at the level of society also guides behavior at the level of society (Orme-Johnson, 2023). Maheshwari (2023) proposes that consciousness-based leadership must transcend profit-maximizing frameworks and adopt a more purposeful, holistic, integral approach to

Table 9.1 Relationship between DC and SD

Level of DC	*DC element*	*Related SD outcomes*
Individual consciousness	Self-awareness	Realizing interconnectedness of everything
	Contemplation practices	Deep moral and conscious engagement with the self and the world
	Values and ethics	Ethical responsibility to future generations and respect for all life
	Behavioral change	Reduced consumption, increased mindfulness of environmental impact
Collective consciousness	Cultural paradigms	Societal norms and behaviors aligned with sustainability
	Education and awareness	Influence on community-level policies and environmental action
	Social movements and activism	Long-term, sustainable interaction with natural systems
	Leadership and role models	Stewardship of ecosystems, prioritization of biodiversity and ecological balance

decision-making that includes ecological, social, and spiritual dimensions. The development of a sustainability mindset includes development of higher consciousness (Rimanoczy, 2020). Table 9.1 examines the impact of DC on SD. Each level of consciousness can cause shifts in awareness, norms, and behaviors toward deeper sustainability.

Artificial Intelligence (AI) and Sustainable Development (SD)

AI systems are information systems designed to perform tasks that typically require human intelligence, such as learning, reasoning, problem-solving, perception, and language understanding (Brynjolfsson & McAfee, 2014). These systems use algorithms to learn from the data of past activities and mimic cognitive functions and adapt to new situations, aiming to achieve tasks autonomously and efficiently. Just like other advanced technologies of the past, AI systems offer potential for many beneficial and non-beneficial uses for a sustainable approach to development (Sachs, 2012). Pope Francis[1] acknowledged the remarkable developments in the field of AI, and how these raise increasingly significant implications in all areas of human activity. While an AI system can process vast amounts of data and draw patterns from it, it cannot experience or understand concepts in the way human beings do (Tegmark, 2018). A concomitant raising of human consciousness toward oneness with all there is may be required for humanity to manage and align powerful AI systems appropriately for the benefit of the world (Maheshwari & Biberman, 2024).

There are 17 Sustainable Development Goals (SDGs) and 169 targets internationally agreed in the global 2030 Agenda for Sustainable Development. Max Tegmark and his team used a systematic consensus-based expert elicitation process and assessed that AI can enable the accomplishment of 134 targets across all the 17 SDGs. However, it may also inhibit 59 targets (Vinuesa et al., 2020). How can one align AI's potential with broader sustainability goals? Du and Xie (2021) argue that AI must be embedded within ethical decision-making processes that prioritize long-term ecological and social well-being over short-term profits. This aligns with sustainability theories that emphasize the importance of integrating social responsibility and ethical leadership into the development of new technologies (Laszlo et al., 2021; Waddock, 2016). The challenge for businesses and policymakers is to create frameworks that ensure AI systems are designed and implemented in ways that do not harm vulnerable populations or the environment. The interplay between AI and SD thus offers many avenues, of which we consider four promising avenues.

Climate Change

AI can play a significant role in addressing climate change by enhancing efficiency, optimizing resource use, and supporting decision-making. AI-driven models can enable predictive climate modeling, improving the accuracy of weather and climate forecasts, which can help policymakers

[1] https://www.vaticannews.va/en/pope/news/2023-02/pope-technology-must-be-at-the-service-of-man.html.

prepare for and mitigate climate risks (Kochanski et al., 2019). Furthermore, AI-powered data analysis supports reforestation and carbon capture projects by monitoring ecosystems and identifying areas for intervention (Shen et al., 2020).

Biodiversity Loss

AI-driven remote sensing technologies, such as satellite imagery and drones, can track changes in ecosystems and detect deforestation, illegal poaching, and habitat degradation in real-time (Pettorelli et al., 2024). AI can also enable predictive modeling of species distribution and migration patterns, allowing conservationists to anticipate and mitigate threats from climate change and human activity (Zhao et al., 2024).

Energy Consumption

AI can optimize energy grids and integrate renewable sources like solar and wind, reducing reliance on fossil fuels (Haider et al., 2021). AI-driven smart energy systems analyze real-time data to optimize the energy consumption of households, industries, and commercial buildings, automatically adjusting heating, cooling, and lighting based on occupancy and environmental factors (Stecula et al., 2023). Careful consideration of AI's own huge energy consumption and ethical use is crucial to maximizing its climate benefits while minimizing unintended impacts.

Waste Management

AI-powered robotics and machine learning systems can enhance waste sorting by accurately identifying and separating materials like plastics, metals, and paper, increasing recycling efficiency, and reducing contamination in recycling streams (Chen et al., 2023a). Predictive analytics can help municipalities and companies anticipate future waste volumes, allowing for better infrastructure planning and resource allocation. AI can also enhance circular economy models by identifying opportunities for waste reduction, reuse, and recycling, thereby reducing landfill use and promoting more sustainable resource management (Maheshwari et al., 2022). New-age waste management and recycling equipment would have close-loop AI with optical cameras and sensors to separate waste at scale,[2] such as by seamlessly segregating different types of polymers and plastics by Resin Identification codes.

Table 9.2 summarizes how AI can support climate change, biodiversity conservation, energy management, and waste management by optimizing processes, predicting impacts, and enhancing sustainability outcomes across these key areas.

Case Study of Plastics

Plastics have become indispensable in modern life due to their versatility, durability, and affordability. They are used extensively across industries such as healthcare, packaging, construction, and electronics. In its initial stages of development, plastics were considered an alternative to materials like paper, glass, ceramic, and metals, as all of them had challenges regarding sustainability and their applications, i.e., breakages in glass, rusting of metals, etc. We examine how plastics evolved over time and could evolve in the future more sustainably in a regime of consciousness-based leadership and use of AI.

Brief Evolutionary History of Plastics

Plastics have had a transformative journey from a groundbreaking innovation to a widely adopted material and eventually becoming a subject of concern due to their environmental and health impacts. This history highlights the changing perspectives on plastics—from celebration of their versatility to growing alarm over their sustainability.

Innovation (Nineteenth Century)

The first man-made plastic was created in 1869 by John Wesley Hyatt, who sought an alternative to ivory for billiard balls. This alternate material's initial strengths were sustainability, conservation of natural resources, and wildlife protection. He developed celluloid, a material made from cellulose, which could be easily molded. This invention sparked the early plastics industry by demonstrating that synthetic materials could replace scarce natural resources. Later, in 1907, Leo Baekeland invented *Bakelite*,

[2] https://www.forbes.com/sites/ganeskesari/2024/05/31/turning-trash-into-treasure-how-ai-is-revolutionizing-waste-sorting/.

Table 9.2 A framework of interplay between AI and SD

Theme	*AI role in SD*	*AI applications*	*SD outcomes*
Climate change	Predict and model climate patterns and impacts, and adaptation and mitigation strategies Enhance carbon emissions monitoring and reduction	Models for climate forecasting, and extreme weather prediction, and adaptation strategies Decision support systems for climate carbon monitoring, capture optimization, offset programs	More accurate climate predictions, better disaster preparedness Reduced greenhouse gas emissions, optimized carbon capture, enhanced resilience to climate risks
Biodiversity conservation	Monitor ecosystems, track endangered species, predict species distribution and habitat changes, optimizes conservation efforts	Remote sensing (drones, satellites) for deforestation detection and wildlife monitoring Predicting species migration, habitat loss, and climate impacts on biodiversity	Improved biodiversity protection, real-time detection of illegal activities like poaching Proactive biodiversity conservation strategies, enhanced ecosystem resilience
Energy management	Integrate renewable energy sources and stabilize grid operations Enhance energy efficiency in buildings and industries	Green algorithms for balancing renewable energy inputs (solar, wind) with demand in smart grids Automated energy management systems for optimizing heating, cooling, lighting, and process controls in real-time	Increased share of renewables in energy mix, improved grid reliability and sustainability Reduced energy consumption and waste, increased use of renewable energy, more efficient energy distribution
Waste management	Improve waste sorting, recycling, resource recovery, and optimize logistics Support circular economy by identifying opportunities for reuse	Robotics and computer vision for automated sorting of recyclables and waste materials, and optimizing waste collection routes Monitoring material flows and enabling circular economy models in industries	Increased recycling efficiency, reduced contamination in recycling streams, lower operational costs, efficient waste management Reduced waste generation, enhanced resource reuse, more sustainable industrial practices

the first fully synthetic plastic, which did not rely on any natural components. Bakelite's heat resistance and electrical insulation properties made it ideal for various industrial applications, marking the beginning of plastics' widespread industrial use (Bensaude-Vincent, 2013).

Widespread Adoption (Mid-Twentieth Century)
The discovery and mass production of plastics during World War II significantly increased their use. Nylon, polyethylene, and polystyrene were developed to replace rubber and silk, which were in short supply. After the war, these materials were repurposed for consumer goods. By the 1950s and 1960s, plastics had found their way into nearly every aspect of daily life, including packaging, household products, electronics, garments, and automobiles. The newfound advantage of plastics was that the chemical structure could be modified to develop different polymers that suit wide-ranging applications and physical forms. Plastics' adaptability, low cost, and durability contributed to their rapid and wide-scale adoption in both industrial and consumer sectors (Meikle, 1995).

Value Extraction (1970s–1980s)
In the 1970s and 1980s, corporations capitalized on the versatility of plastics, particularly in packaging and consumer goods. Plastic manufacturing became a major industry, with economies of scale driving down production costs and increasing profits. Single-use plastics, especially in the form of packaging, became ubiquitous due to their convenience, further cementing their role in modern consumer culture. However, this period also saw the emergence of problems with plastic waste management, as recycling initiatives struggled to keep pace with growing consumption (Andrady & Neal, 2009). During this phase, value extraction centered on efficiency, convenience, and the creation of a throwaway culture, with little consideration for long-term environmental consequences.

Social Addiction (Late Twentieth Century)
By the late twentieth century, plastics had become deeply embedded in everyday life, creating what some have called a "social addiction" to plastic products. From water bottles to shopping bags to disposable utensils, plastic products became inseparable from modern consumer habits. This shift reflected a culture of convenience and disposability, with plastics seen as indispensable to the fast-paced demands of contemporary society. This

phase was marked by over-reliance on plastics, and the growing realization that plastics were becoming a pervasive environmental issue due to their persistence in ecosystems (Thompson et al., 2009).

Growing Awareness of Plastics' Effects (Twentieth–Twenty-First Century)

Plastics were seen as an alternative to many traditional materials due to their versatility in properties and sustainability. Many other materials were seen to impact the environment and, for example, cause deforestation, i.e., paper, and lead to the loss of biodiversity by mining, such as metals. Further, population growth needed an alternate material to support food security; plastics were an integral support for end-to-end agriculture from irrigation pipes, greenhouse farming, bulk storage, and retail sale of fresh produce. During the AIDS health crisis, plastic was a savior with disposable syringes that could be used in the healthcare system. Similarly, during the COVID-19 pandemic, plastics came across as a material of choice, from masks to hand sanitizer bottles to PPE gowns. They facilitate clean drinking water supplies and enable medical devices ranging through surgical equipment, drips, aseptic medical packaging, and pill blister packs (Andrady, 2011).[3]

Environmental and Health Concerns (Twenty-First Century)

As plastics became omnipresent, their environmental and health impacts became increasingly visible. By the early twenty-first century, researchers and environmentalists raised alarms about plastic pollution, particularly in oceans where plastics were being ingested by marine life and entering the food chain. The health risks associated with microplastics, including endocrine disruption from certain additives, added further cause for concern (Teuten et al., 2009). Governments and organizations worldwide began to push for bans on single-use plastics and to encourage recycling, though these efforts have faced challenges due to the sheer volume of plastic waste.

Regulation of Plastics

Multiple regulations govern the safe use of plastics in different applications within health agencies. There are also new regulations regarding the

[3] https://pmc.ncbi.nlm.nih.gov/articles/PMC2873019/.

use of plastics by environmental agencies. We have witnessed Extended Producer Reporting (EPR) mandates, and a ban on plastic bags and single-use plastics in different parts of the world. The European Union's Packaging and Packaging Waste Regulation (PPWR) is a legislative initiative aimed at reducing packaging waste and promoting sustainability across member states. When passed, it will establish a design for recycling, foster a circular economy, and implement harmonized market rules across Europe. Similarly, the UN Treaty on Plastics is planned to address the issue of production, waste management, and recycling.

The history of plastics thus reflects a dramatic trajectory from innovation to overconsumption, and finally, to environmental reckoning. While plastics have undoubtedly contributed to industrial progress and everyday convenience, the long-term consequences of their use are now at the forefront of global discussions on sustainability. Moving forward, the challenge lies in balancing the benefits of plastics with the need to mitigate their environmental and health impacts through sustainable alternatives and improved waste management practices.

Industrial Plastics and SD

Managing plastic waste effectively calls for more than just technological or policy interventions. It requires a shift in consciousness, as well as the strategic use of emerging technologies like AI. Higher consciousness approach encourages businesses and individuals alike to re-evaluate their consumption patterns and waste management practices, striving for sustainability and the greater good (Maheshwari, 2021). Several forward-thinking companies, such as Tesla, Unilever, and Adidas, have already begun addressing plastic pollution by blending ethical leadership with innovative solutions. Operating from this higher consciousness, leaders could focus on:

1. Reducing plastic consumption through conscious decision-making. They would align corporate responsibility with planetary well-being, thereby influencing policies and consumer behavior.
2. Fostering a circular economy by advocating for reuse, recycling, and the development of biodegradable alternatives (Maheshwari et al., 2022).

AI is a powerful enabler in achieving the above goals by providing data-driven insights and efficient waste management systems.

1. AI in Recycling: AI-powered robotics and sensors are revolutionizing recycling by improving the sorting of plastic waste by Resin codes. These devices can differentiate between various types of plastics, thus reducing contamination and enhancing recycling efficiency.
2. Predictive Analytics: AI tools can predict plastic pollution hotspots, allowing organizations to better allocate resources for clean-up efforts. These predictive models use satellite imagery, consumption data, and environmental trends to address plastic accumulation patterns in real-time.
3. Material Innovation: AI can accelerate the development of biodegradable alternatives by simulating chemical compositions and testing eco-friendly materials. This has a potential for faster regulatory clearance, thus supporting faster innovation cycles, helping companies bring sustainable products to market more efficiently. AI can help invent new bacteria that could eat plastic waste.

Case Studies in Corporate Innovation on Plastics

Tesla

While Tesla is best known for its electric vehicles, the company also demonstrates a higher consciousness approach to sustainability by actively reducing plastic usage in its production and packaging processes. Tesla has invested in eco-friendly materials for its cars, and in cutting down on the use of petroleum-based plastics. Furthermore, Tesla's commitment to clean energy solutions extends to the production of recyclable car batteries.

Unilever

Unilever, a global consumer goods company, has been at the forefront of reducing plastic waste through its "Less Plastic, Better Plastic, No Plastic" strategy. By 2025, Unilever aims to halve its use of virgin plastic by incorporating more recycled content in its packaging and eliminating unnecessary plastic. The company has also invested in AI-driven technology to optimize its packaging design, ensuring that materials can be recycled more effectively and efficiently. These efforts align with

Unilever's broader commitment to higher consciousness principles of environmental responsibility and consumer well-being (Davenport & Bean, 2023; Unilever, 2020).

Adidas
Adidas has pioneered the reuse of plastics in its products, particularly through its collaboration with "Parley for the Oceans," a group dedicated to protecting marine ecosystems. Adidas has produced millions of shoes made from upcycled plastic waste (Sicoli et al., 2019). The company also uses AI to optimize its supply chain, reducing plastic waste and emissions during manufacturing. This initiative represents a successful integration of higher consciousness of focusing on the health of the planet.

IKEA
IKEA has committed to becoming a circular business by 2030. The furniture giant has pledged to remove all single-use plastics from its product range and supply chain. Additionally, IKEA uses AI to monitor the lifecycle of its products, ensuring that materials can be reused or recycled effectively. IKEA's investments in AI-driven innovation have allowed the company to improve its sustainability practices and maintain its commitment to higher consciousness principles (Saif, 2023).

Coca-Cola
Over the years, the Coca-Cola Company has practiced sustainability by a well-balanced materials usage strategy that includes glass, aluminum, virgin plastics, and recycled plastics. They are working on the principle of a world without waste, which has three pillars: design, collect, and partner. They use AI in the supply chain to optimize routes, simulation and modeling, waste management, and reduce carbon footprints (Cole et al., 2021).

Integration of Consciousness and AI for a Sustainable Plastics Strategy

Conscious businesses and leaders are increasingly recognizing the symbiotic relationship between ethical decision-making and AI. With its ability to analyze complex data and provide actionable insights, AI serves as a powerful tool to scale and amplify consciousness-driven actions. For example:

- AI in Corporate Strategy: Companies like Tesla, Unilever, Coca-Cola, and Adidas have demonstrated that by aligning business goals with environmental sustainability, they can leverage AI to optimize production, minimize waste, and reduce their environmental footprint.
- Circular Economy Models: Conscious business leaders are implementing circular economy strategies by using AI to monitor supply chains, predict plastic use, and ensure that waste materials are reused. This not only helps reduce plastic pollution but also promotes a culture of sustainability and ethical responsibility (Maheshwari et al., 2022).

In summary, the fight against industrial plastic pollution demands a continued transformation in human consciousness, supported by ever more powerful AI. By adopting a higher consciousness approach, corporations can lead the way in reducing plastic waste, developing sustainable materials, and fostering global environmental stewardship. Leading companies demonstrate the effectiveness of blending ethical leadership with AI-driven innovation, showing that it is possible to tackle plastic pollution at both the systemic and consumer levels.

Microplastics

Microplastics are a recent phenomenon, and a growing environmental and health concern, that has attracted global attention in recent years. Microplastics are defined in ISO 24187 (2023) as any solid plastic particle insoluble in water with dimensions between 1 μm and 1000 μm (= 1 mm). These particles may be found in the air, water, soil, and even the human body. As research evolves, questions regarding their long-term environmental and health impacts, including their potential role in disrupting human consciousness, have emerged, prompting new interdisciplinary investigations (Bucci & Rochman, 2022). Meanwhile, advances in AI offer promising solutions in the detection, analysis, and management of microplastics (Liu et al., 2020).

Types and Sources of Microplastics

Microplastics can be categorized into two types: primary and secondary. Primary microplastics are intentionally manufactured for specific uses, such as microbeads in cosmetics. Secondary microplastics result from the fragmentation of larger plastic debris due to environmental factors like UV radiation and mechanical abrasion. Both types have widespread distribution in aquatic, terrestrial, and atmospheric environments, and their pervasive presence raises concerns about their ecological and health effects.

Environmental Distribution

Microplastics have been detected in almost every corner of the Earth's ecosystems, from oceans to freshwater systems, soil, and even the atmosphere (Thompson et al., 2009). In marine environments, microplastics are particularly concerning due to their accumulation in ocean currents and marine sediments, where they enter the food chain (Galloway et al., 2017). Studies also show the deposition of microplastics in remote regions like the Arctic and mountain areas, transported by atmospheric processes (Bergmann et al., 2019). This global distribution not only threatens biodiversity but also the balance of ecosystems that are essential for planetary consciousness and well-being (Schröder et al., 2021). However, there needs to be more and longitudinal research on microplastics to conclusively determine the long-term effects.

Human Exposure

Human exposure to microplastics occurs mainly through ingestion and inhalation of secondary microplastics. Research indicates that microplastics are present in drinking water (both bottled and tap), food, especially seafood, and even in the air (Liu et al., 2021). A significant ingestion of microplastics can lead to the accumulation of these particles in human tissues, raising concerns about their potential toxicological effects (Wright & Kelly, 2017). However, this might happen only in circumstances of very high exposure to microplastics, which are limited in regular circumstances. The health impacts of microplastics are still an evolving field of study, but early evidence suggests that they can lead to inflammation, oxidative stress, and cellular damage (Prata et al., 2020). As our consciousness expands, it is crucial to consider how environmental factors, such as pollution from microplastics, shape the evolution of human awareness and cognition (Chen et al., 2023b).

Impact on Wildlife

In marine and terrestrial ecosystems, microplastics could pose significant threats to wildlife. Many species ingest microplastics, mistaking them for food, which can cause physical harm and exposure to toxic substances (Gall & Thompson, 2015). As microplastics move up the food chain, bioaccumulation occurs, with larger predators, including humans, can be at risk of higher exposure (Duis & Coors, 2016). This disrupts not only the health of individual species but also the ecological balance necessary for the sustainability of consciousness on a planetary scale.

AI's Role in Detecting and Managing Microplastics

Artificial intelligence is emerging as a valuable tool in addressing the microplastics crisis. AI can enhance the detection and analysis of microplastics by automating image recognition and classification processes in environmental samples (Liu et al., 2020). Machine learning algorithms have been developed to identify microplastics in water samples, improving both the accuracy and efficiency of data collection (Lin et al., 2022). Additionally, AI-powered predictive models can be used to forecast the distribution and accumulation of microplastics in ecosystems, helping policymakers and environmental managers make informed decisions.

AI could also play a role in monitoring the impact of microplastics on cognitive functions and psychological well-being. AI-based tools are being developed to analyze brain activity and environmental stressors, potentially linking exposure to microplastics with neurological changes (Jin et al., 2022). This integration of AI and neuroscience could provide insights into how environmental pollutants affect the development of consciousness and support the creation of interventions to mitigate these effects.

Policy and Regulation

Governments and international organizations have begun to take action to address the microplastics crisis. Several countries have banned the use of microbeads in cosmetics, and initiatives to reduce plastic waste and improve recycling are gaining momentum. However, these measures are still in their infancy, and comprehensive global policies are needed to effectively manage microplastics pollution. AI could assist in this effort by tracking plastic waste flows and optimizing waste management systems, further reducing the production and release of microplastics into the environment (Rochman et al., 2016).

In summary, microplastics are a growing environmental and health concern with potentially profound impacts. While the full extent of these effects is still being researched, microplastics represent a serious challenge for both ecological balance and individual health. The development of AI systems offers promising avenues for detecting, analyzing, and managing microplastics in the environment. Additionally, the intersection of microplastics and consciousness development highlights the need for interdisciplinary research that integrates environmental science, neuroscience, and AI to address these complex challenges.

Plastics and SDGs

While plastics offer numerous benefits, their environmental impact has led to growing concerns, driving research toward sustainable alternatives and recycling technologies (Gazal & Gheewala, 2020). Here are the SDGs that are more closely related to plastics.

SDG3 on Good Health and Well-Being

AI-driven diagnostics, personalized medicine, and public health monitoring tools can vastly improve healthcare delivery and disease prevention, especially in regions lacking sufficient medical professionals. AI systems with an advanced level of consciousness can make more empathetic decisions in healthcare, tailoring medical treatments to individual emotional and physical needs and improving patient care holistically. In Deep Medicine, Eric Topol (2019) reveals how AI has the potential to transform everything doctors do, from notetaking and medical scans to diagnosis and treatment, greatly cutting down the cost of medicine and reducing human mortality. By freeing physicians from the tasks that interfere with human connection, AI can create space for the real healing that takes place between a doctor who can listen and a patient who needs to be heard.

SDG9 on Industry, Innovation, and Infrastructure

AI can streamline manufacturing processes, enhance industrial innovation through improved R&D processes, and strengthen infrastructure planning and management of plastics (Agrawal et al., 2023). Consciously applied AI can drive innovation that not only focuses on profitability but also on sustainable and ethical practices, enhancing industries without compromising human and environmental welfare.

SDG11 on Sustainable Cities and Communities

Smart city solutions powered by AI can improve everything from public transport management and waste disposal to energy usage and public safety, making urban environments more efficient and sustainable (Gupta & Degbelo, 2023). AI in smart cities can manage resources and infrastructure in a way that maximizes community well-being, focusing on long-term sustainability and the quality of life of its inhabitants.

SDG12 on Responsible Consumption and Production

AI can optimize supply chains, reduce resource consumption, and enhance recycling processes through better sorting techniques and demand prediction, leading to more sustainable consumption patterns of plastics (Aybaly et al., 2017). AI that is aware of environmental and social impacts can lead to more responsible production patterns, emphasizing waste reduction and sustainable consumption behaviors. As consumers consume the majority of plastics, AI can help guide effective disposal and recycling.

Discussion

The intersection of AI, consciousness, and sustainability reveals both opportunities and challenges. AI's potential to revolutionize industries by optimizing processes, enhancing resource efficiency, and reducing waste is undeniable. However, this technological power must be guided by a higher level of consciousness to ensure it serves the broader goals of sustainable development. Without ethical leadership and a consciousness-driven approach, AI could exacerbate issues such as environmental degradation and social inequality, especially in the context of plastic management.

The case study of plastics illustrates how over-reliance on a single innovation can lead to unforeseen environmental crises. Plastics, initially celebrated for their convenience and durability, have now become a symbol of unsustainable consumption. It will take significant attention and investment to invent new materials and sustainable solutions. AI offers promising solutions, such as enhancing recycling processes and predicting plastic pollution hotspots. However, the integration of AI must be coupled with a collective shift in consciousness that prioritizes long-term environmental stewardship over short-term profits.

Consciousness-based leadership—focusing on empathy, ethical decision-making, and global responsibility—becomes essential in this framework. Leaders must use AI not just as a tool for innovation but as an enabler of a more balanced and sustainable world. The combined power of AI and higher consciousness could steer industries and societies toward practices that honor ecological balance, reduce harm, and promote circular economies. This chapter emphasizes the need for a holistic approach where technological advancements and ethical consciousness work hand in hand to achieve meaningful, long-term sustainability.

Future Directions

Future directions for the integration of consciousness and AI in sustainability efforts require a multi-faceted approach, with a focus on ethical frameworks, technological innovation, and societal transformation. Future development of AI systems should embed ethical decision-making capabilities such that these systems prioritize long-term environmental and social impacts over immediate financial gain. As AI increasingly influences industries such as plastics manufacturing, energy, and waste management, its ethical use will be crucial in minimizing ecological harm and promoting sustainability. Future AI models can be designed to incorporate sustainability goals into their core algorithms, as "green algorithms," ensuring that decisions align with environmental priorities like reducing carbon emissions and minimizing resource use.

Circular economy models for the future of sustainable development should leverage AI to optimize resource flows, predict waste generation, and enhance recycling efficiency, such that industries can move toward systems where resources are reused, recycled, and repurposed. AI can support this by creating intelligent systems for waste management, identifying opportunities to minimize plastic waste, and developing biodegradable alternatives. The global governance of AI must evolve to establish comprehensive policies and frameworks that guide responsible AI use across industries. Regulatory bodies should collaborate with AI developers and corporate leaders to ensure AI applications contribute to sustainable development goals (SDGs).

Finally, the development of higher consciousness of the leadership is paramount (Maheshwari, 2021). As AI becomes more integrated into sustainability efforts, leaders who prioritize ethical stewardship, empathy, and ecological well-being will be crucial in guiding these technologies toward positive outcomes. By fostering a global culture that values higher consciousness and sustainability, future innovations in AI can serve as catalysts for transformative change, leading to more resilient, balanced, and sustainable systems across the globe.

Conclusion

The interplay between Consciousness, AI, and sustainable development presents a unique opportunity to address some of the most pressing challenges and opportunities of our time. By aligning AI development with ethical, ecological, and spiritual principles, we can catalyze a shift toward a more conscious, sustainable, and equitable world. This holistic approach encourages us to envision AI as a partner in our collective journey toward higher consciousness and harmonious living on Earth. As we move forward, it is imperative that we ensure that AI serves as a tool for good, enhancing our collective ability to achieve SDGs and improve the well-being of both people and the planet. Ultimately, by combining conscious leadership with AI systems, businesses can not only reduce their reliance on plastics but also inspire broader societal change that will ensure a sustainable future for the planet and the economy.

References

Agrawal, R., Majumdar, A., & Kumar, A. (2023). Integration of artificial intelligence in sustainable manufacturing: Current status and future opportunities. *Operations Management Research, 16*, 1720–1741. https://doi.org/10.1007/s12063-023-00383-y

Andrady, A. L. (2011). Microplastics in the marine environment. *Marine Pollution Bulletin, 62*(8), 1596–1605.

Andrady, A. L., & Neal, M. A. (2009). Applications and societal benefits of plastics. *Philosophical Transactions of the Royal Society b: Biological Sciences, 364*(1526), 1977–1984.

Aybaly, R., Guerquin-Kern, L., Manière, I. C., Madacova, D., & van Holt, J. (2017). Sustainability practices in the luxury industry: How can one be sustainable in an over-consumptive environment?: Sustainability in the automotive world: The case of Tesla. *Procedia Computer Science, 122*, 541–547.

Bansal, P., Durand, R., Kreutzer, M., Kunisch, S., & McGahan, A. M. (2024). Strategy can no longer ignore planetary boundaries: A call for tackling strategy's ecological fallacy. *Journal of Management Studies*.

Bergmann, M., et al. (2019). White and wonderful? Microplastics prevail in snow from the Alps to the Arctic. *Science Advances, 5*(8), eaax1157.

Brynjolfsson, E., & McAfee, A. (2014). *The second machine age: Work, progress, and prosperity in a time of brilliant technologies*. W. W. Norton & Company.

Bucci, K., & Rochman, C. M. (2022). Microplastics: A multidimensional contaminant requires a multidimensional framework for assessing risk. *Microplastics and Nanoplastics, 2*(1), 7.

Chen, S., Chen, Y., Gao, Y., Han, B., Wang, T., Dong, H., & Chen, L. (2023a). Toxic effects and mechanisms of nanoplastics on embryonic brain development using brain organoids model. *Science of the Total Environment, 904*, Article 166913.

Chen, Y., Luo, A., Cheng, M., Wu, Y., Zhu, J., Meng, Y., & Tan, W. (2023b). Classification and recycling of recyclable garbage based on deep learning. *Journal of Cleaner Production, 414*, Article 137558.

Cole, R., Benstead, A. V., & Mc Loughlin, K. (2021). *Live classroom debate: Should Coca-Cola be held solely accountable for the environmentally damaging impacts of the plastic waste of their product?*. Sage Publications.

Davenport, T., & Bean, R. (2023). AI ethics at Unilever: From policy to process. *MIT Sloan Management Review*.

Du, S., & Xie, C. (2021). Paradoxes of artificial intelligence in consumer markets: Ethical challenges and opportunities. *Journal of Business Research, 129*, 961–974.

Duis, K., & Coors, A. (2016). Microplastics in the aquatic and terrestrial environment: Sources (with a specific focus on personal care products), fate, and effects. *Environmental Sciences Europe, 28*(1), 1–25.

Gall, S. C., & Thompson, R. C. (2015). The impact of debris on marine life. *Marine Pollution Bulletin, 92*(1–2), 170–179.

Galloway, T. S., Cole, M., & Lewis, C. (2017). Interactions of microplastic debris throughout the marine ecosystem. *Nature Ecology & Evolution, 1*(5), 1–8.

Gazal, A. A., & Gheewala, S. H. (2020). Plastics, microplastics and other polymer materials—A threat to the environment. *Journal of Sustainable Energy Environment, 11*, 113–122.

Gupta, S., & Degbelo, A. (2023). An empirical analysis of AI contributions to sustainable cities (SDG 11). In *The ethics of artificial intelligence for the sustainable development goals* (pp. 461–484). Springer International Publishing.

Haider, F. U., Liqun, C., Coulter, J. A., Cheema, S. A., Wu, J., Zhang, R., ... & Farooq, M. (2021). Cadmium toxicity in plants: Impacts and remediation strategies. *Ecotoxicology and Environmental Safety, 211*, 111887.

Jin, M., Liu, J., Yu, J., Zhou, Q., Wu, W., Fu, L., ..., Karimi-Maleh, H. (2022). Current development and future challenges in microplastic detection techniques: A bibliometrics-based analysis and review. *Science Progress, 105*(4), 00368504221132151.

Kak, S. (2020). Artificial intelligence and the Vedantic view of consciousness. *Journal of Consciousness Studies, 27*(5–6), 111–128.

Kochanski, K., Rolnick, D., Donti, P., & Kaack, L. (2019, December). Climate change+ AI: Tackling climate change with machine learning. In *AGU fall meeting abstracts* (pp. GC33A-04).

Laszlo, C., Waddock, S., Maheshwari, A., Nigri, G., & Storberg-Walker, J. (2021). Quantum worldviews: How science and spirituality are converging to transform consciousness for meaningful solutions to wicked problems. *Humanistic Management Journal, 6*, 293–311.

Lin, J. Y., Liu, H. T., & Zhang, J. (2022). Recent advances in the application of machine learning methods to improve identification of the microplastics in environment. *Chemosphere, 307*, Article 136092.

Liu, M., Lu, S., Chen, Y., Cao, C., Bigalke, M., & He, D. (2020). Analytical methods for microplastics in environments: Current advances and challenges. *Microplastics in Terrestrial Environments: Emerging Contaminants and Major Challenges*, 3–24.

Liu, Q., Chen, Z., Chen, Y., Yang, F., Yao, W., & Xie, Y. (2021). Microplastics and nanoplastics: Emerging contaminants in food. *Journal of Agricultural and Food Chemistry, 69*(36), 10450–10468.

Maheshwari, A. K. (2021). Higher consciousness management: Transcendence for spontaneous right action. *Journal of Management, Spirituality & Religion, 18*(6), 77–91. https://doi.org/10.51327/CRNG6977

Maheshwari, A. K. (2023). *Consciousness-based leadership and management, Volume 1: Vedic and other philosophical approaches to oneness and flourishing* (pp. 3–25). Springer International Publishing.

Maheshwari, A. K., Bachani, J., & Gehani, R. R. (2022). Circular organizing for fuller engagement and sustainability. In *Responsible leadership for sustainability in uncertain times: Social, economic and environmental challenges for sustainable organizations* (pp. 91–104). Springer Nature Singapore.

Maheshwari, A. K., & Biberman, J. (2024). Artificial oneness: Bridging the human machine divide. *Journal of Management, Spirituality & Religion*. https://doi.org/10.51327/RZRA6516

Maheshwari, A. K., & Gehani, R. R. (2023). Gandhi's consciousness-based leadership: Principles of truth, non-violence, and love for all. In *Consciousness-based leadership and management, Volume 1: Vedic and other philosophical approaches to oneness and flourishing* (pp. 77–96). Springer International Publishing.

Meikle, J. L. (1995). *American plastic: A cultural history*. Rutgers University Press.

Orme-Johnson, D. W. (2023). Creating coherence in collective consciousness for universal flourishing: Automatic self-transcending for reducing conflicts and improving the quality of life in society. In *Consciousness-based leadership and management, Volume 1: Vedic and other philosophical approaches to oneness and flourishing* (pp. 121–149). Springer International Publishing.

Pettorelli, N., Williams, J., Schulte to Bühne, H., & Crowson, M. (2024). Deep learning and satellite remote sensing for biodiversity monitoring and conservation. *Remote Sensing in Ecology and Conservation*.

Prata, J. C., da Costa, J. P., Lopes, I., Duarte, A. C., & Rocha-Santos, T. (2020). Environmental status of (micro) plastics contamination in Portugal. *Ecotoxicology and Environmental Safety, 200*, Article 110753.

Purser, R. E., Park, C., & Montuori, A. (1995). Limits to anthropocentrism: Toward an eco-centric organization paradigm? *Academy of Management Review, 20*(4), 1053–1089.

Rimanoczy, I. (2020). *The sustainability mindset principles: A guide to developing a mindset for a better world*. Routledge.

Rochman, C. M., Browne, M. A., Underwood, A. J., Van Franeker, J. A., Thompson, R. C., & Amaral-Zettler, L. A. (2016). The ecological impacts of marine debris: Unraveling the demonstrated evidence from what is perceived. *Ecology, 97*(2), 302–312.

Sachs, J. D. (2012). *The age of sustainable development*. Columbia University Press.

Saif, M. (2023). 2050 sustainability vision of the packaging in European furniture industry: A case study of a leading brand, IKEA.

Schröder, K., Kossel, E., & Lenz, M. (2021). Microplastic abundance in beach sediments of the Kiel Fjord, Western Baltic Sea. *Environmental Science and Pollution Research, 28*, 26515–26528.

Shen, M., Song, B., Zhu, Y., Zeng, G., Zhang, Y., Yang, Y., ... Yi, H. (2020). Removal of microplastics via drinking water treatment: Current knowledge and future directions. *Chemosphere, 251*, 126612.

Sicoli, G., Bronzetti, G., & Baldini, M. (2019). The importance of sustainability in the fashion sector: ADIDAS case study. *International Business Research, 12*(6), 41–51.

Stecula, K., Wolniak, R., & Grebski, W. W. (2023). AI-driven urban energy solutions—From individuals to society: A review. *Energies, 16*(24), 7988.

Tegmark, M. (2018). *Life 3.0: Being human in the age of artificial intelligence.* Vintage.

Teuten, E. L., Saquing, J. M., Knappe, D. R., Barlaz, M. A., Jonsson, S., Björn, A., ... Thompson, R. C. (2009). Transport and release of chemicals from plastics to the environment and to wildlife. *Philosophical Transactions of the Royal Society B: Biological Sciences, 364*(1526), 2027–2045.

Thompson, R. C., Moore, C. J., Vom Saal, F. S., & Swan, S. H. (2009). Plastics, the environment and human health: Current consensus and future trends. *Philosophical Transactions of the Royal Society b: Biological Sciences, 364*(1526), 2153–2166.

Topol, E. (2019). *Deep medicine: How artificial intelligence can make healthcare human again.* Basic Books.

Unilever. (2020). *Unilever's less plastic, better plastic, no plastic strategy*. Unilever's Website.

Vincent, B. B. (2013). Plastics, materials and dreams of dematerialization. In *Accumulation* (pp. 17–29). Routledge.

Vinuesa, R., Azizpour, H., Leite, I., Balaam, M., Dignum, V., Domisch, S., ... Fuso Nerini, F. (2020). The role of artificial intelligence in achieving the sustainable development goals. *Nature Communications, 11*(1), 1–10.

Waddock, S. (2016). Foundational memes for a new narrative about the role of business in society. *Humanistic Management Journal, 1*(1), 91–105.

Wright, S. L., & Kelly, F. J. (2017). Plastic and human health: A micro issue? *Environmental Science & Technology, 51*(12), 6634–6647.

Zhao, Y., O'Neill, G. A., Coops, N. C., & Wang, T. (2024). Predicting the site productivity of forest tree species using climate niche models. *Forest Ecology and Management, 562*, Article 121936.

CHAPTER 10

Systems Thinking Mindset in the Age of AI

Larry Ebert and Alfonso Montero

Introduction

It is now undeniable that the world is an interconnected web. Events in the new millennium have made our global interdependence unmistakable. Major challenges such as climate change, pollution, waste management, the Fukushima nuclear disaster, the COVID-19 pandemic, water and food scarcity, refugee crises, and the interconnected nature of global financial markets have shown how their impacts transcend national and regional boundaries. Globalization, widespread travel, wars, and advanced technologies have further deepened this interconnection, presenting both challenges and opportunities for society. The complexities of our modern world can no longer be understood in isolation.

L. Ebert (✉)
University of San Francisco and Golden Gate University, San Francisco, CA, USA
e-mail: larry_ebert@earthlink.net

A. Montero
Saint Mary's College of California, Moraga, CA, USA
e-mail: am160@stmarys-ca.edu

A. K. Maheshwari (ed.), *AI and Consciousness in Organizations and Society*, Palgrave Studies in Workplace Spirituality and Fulfillment,
https://doi.org/10.1007/978-3-031-91470-6_10

In the age of AI, this reality is more evident than ever. AI offers unprecedented capabilities, enabling humans to tackle complex global challenges in innovative ways. However, it also brings significant risks, such as potential misuse for harm and disruptions to the nature of work. As organizations, individuals, leaders, and governments embrace AI, adopting a Systems Thinking Mindset (STM) is crucial. This mindset helps individuals and teams anticipate, plan, innovate, manage, and lead effectively, equipping us to navigate and thrive in a world defined by constant change and challenge.

This chapter highlights the inherent interconnectedness of all things, emphasizing that nothing exists in isolation and underscoring the critical importance of STM in the adoption of AI. The stakes of AI adoption are immense. AI has the potential to disrupt systems across industries and sectors by transforming processes, decision-making, and innovation. At the same time, it raises fundamental questions about the role of humans as participants, employees, and global citizens. Ethical, social, economic, and educational concerns—such as bias, trust, privacy, over-reliance, and accountability—are central to these discussions.

We begin by outlining the guiding principles and key elements of systems thinking, followed by an exploration of how STM can be applied to AI adoption, using a healthcare delivery organization as a practical example. Next, we offer actionable principles for responsibly and effectively incorporating STM into any organization's approach to AI. We also explore how AI, in turn, can support and enhance the practice of systems thinking.

Additionally, this chapter discusses how systems thinking encourages a deeper level of consciousness, providing an opportunity to reimagine our identity as humans coexisting and collaborating with AI. Drawing from spiritual practices, religions, indigenous cultures, and ancient wisdom, we examine how these perspectives align with the essence of STM, revealing a profound connection between systems thinking, spirituality, and consciousness as intrinsic aspects of our nature.

In the final section, we envision the future interplay of STM and AI, highlighting aspirations for widespread application of systems thinking to address challenges and seize opportunities in an AI-driven world. We conclude with a call to reclaim our deepest human essence as an evolving consciousness, situated within the context of an AI-influenced future.

Systems Thinking Mindset (STM)

STM is a mental orientation rooted in the recognition of the inherent interconnection of all things. It involves both perspective and a practice. Applying this mindset to identify the right problems, harness opportunities, and create meaningful solutions. Grounded in holism and consciousness, STM begins with the understanding that nothing exists in isolation and that everything is part of a larger whole. This perspective often represents a shift for professionals accustomed to "siloed" thinking or narrowly focused solutions within specific disciplines or business units.

Adopting an STM broadens one's worldview, encouraging inclusivity of diverse perspectives, functions, roles, and dynamics. At its core, STM revolves around the concept of a "system"—a set of interrelated parts working together toward a broader purpose. These parts can be tangible (such as people, physical objects, and processes) or intangible (like ideas, data, knowledge, energy, trust, and culture). STM aims to drive real and lasting positive change by modifying behaviors, shaping organizational culture, and transforming ecosystems, always considering the whole rather than isolated components. It embodies a shift from "I" to "We," enabling decisions that extend beyond immediate, visible surroundings to embrace broader, interconnected impacts.

The concept of systems thinking was formalized in 1956 when Professor Jay W. Forrester established the Systems Dynamics Group at MIT's Sloan School of Management, leading to the development of systems thinking as a discipline. However, its roots extend much further, with principles embedded in earlier philosophical and scientific traditions, including the Renaissance (fourteenth to seventeenth centuries), where figures like Leonardo da Vinci embraced interdisciplinary approaches to innovation. Long before the Renaissance, systems thinking was deeply ingrained in indigenous cultures and spiritual traditions, as well as foundational beliefs within nearly every major religion. At its essence, STM reflects our most natural way of understanding and engaging with the world—a holistic lens that aligns with humanity's innate interconnectedness.

The Nature of Systems Thinking

Systems thinking is not always linear, tidy, or perfect. It requires engaging diverse voices to uncover root causes, clarify goals, and align processes. Moving beyond conventional, siloed approaches, systems thinking encourages deeper exploration. Holding STM involves embracing discomfort and remaining open to new perspectives, even when they challenge traditional "truths." This openness ensures that problem-solvers address the deepest and most meaningful issues. Although systems thinking may demand more time and effort at the outset, it ultimately saves resources and delivers more sustainable, impactful results. It allows problem-solvers to account for factors beyond narrow boundaries, including the people, teams, and roles within a system. This broader perspective offers a new vantage point for understanding and action.

Elements of Systems Thinking—Five Key Features

In learning and applying STM, it is essential to understand the key principles or features of systems thinking. Our approach draws on the work of Forrester, Senge, the International Council on Systems Engineering (INCOSE), the International Society for Systems Sciences, the Systems Dynamics Society, and other systems practitioners. While each offers a unique perspective, systems thinking is generally characterized by five core features:

Feature 1: Interconnectedness

Interconnectedness is the foundational principle of systems thinking. Recognizing and appreciating the interconnected nature of systems enables better understanding, alignment, problem-solving, and decision-making. From the human body to global climate systems, from industry ecosystems to business units, we see interconnectivity in all areas of life.

Feature 2: Dynamism

Dynamism refers to the relationships and interactions among the parts of a system, where components influence, move, and operate in relation to one another. Central to this principle is the concept of flow—the movement of elements such as blood in the body, energy within an atom, or knowledge and data within an organization. Feedback loops, both positive and negative, are another critical aspect of dynamism, helping regulate or disrupt system behaviors. Dynamism also encompasses emergence, where new behaviors arise organically as a system adapts to external changes.

Feature 3: Inclusion

Inclusion involves embracing diverse viewpoints that reflect the system's breadth. By incorporating multiple perspectives, we uncover challenges and opportunities that might otherwise go unnoticed. Inclusion also builds trust, collaboration, and commitment, empowering individuals to manage and guide systems effectively.

Feature 4: Multiple Objectives

Systems often have more than one objective. Individual parts may have their own goals, while the system as a whole pursues an overarching purpose. Understanding these layered objectives is essential to addressing complex systems effectively.

Feature 5: Exploring Unintended Consequences

Systems adapt to changing environments either through deliberate interventions, such as new people, processes, or technologies, or through emergent behaviors. Leaders who foster cultural conditions that support such adaptations are better equipped to anticipate and respond to unforeseen outcomes.

STM and AI: Navigating Interconnected Ecosystems

Organizations and their ecosystems are becoming increasingly interwoven, fueled by advancements in enterprise software, matrix organizational structures, and modern communication and collaboration technologies. These tools and frameworks not only enhance operational efficiency but also deepen the interconnectedness within and across industries.

A striking example of this interdependence was the widespread supply chain disruptions that followed the COVID-19 pandemic and subsequent quarantines. These events vividly illustrated the ripple effects of interconnection, where localized disruptions led to significant global consequences. Such scenarios underscore the importance of adopting an STM to understand and navigate the complexities of interconnected systems. AI further amplifies these dynamics by offering tools to analyze, predict, and optimize within these interconnected ecosystems. However, leveraging AI effectively requires a thoughtful, systems-oriented approach to anticipate challenges, mitigate risks, and harness opportunities in an increasingly interdependent world.

Like systems thinking, both AI and consciousness reflect the interconnected and dynamic nature of systems. The five core principles of systems thinking—interconnectedness, dynamism, inclusion, multiple objectives, and exploring unintended consequences—align closely with the capabilities of AI and the principles of human consciousness. Together, they enhance problem-solving and contribute to innovative, humane solutions in our complex and interconnected world.

Features	*Systems thinking mindset (STM)*	*Artificial intelligence (AI)*	*Higher consciousness*
Interconnectedness	STM encourages a holistic perspective as challenges cannot be understood in isolation	AI helps illuminate interconnectedness through data and information about how different factors, variables, and systems interrelate	Higher consciousness leads to a heightened awareness that all people and things operate in a broader context
Dynamism	STM enables flexibility and adaptability in decision-making and problem-solving	AI can help organizations more-deeply understand and respond to changing conditions, facilitating greater innovation and proactiveness	Fosters a proactive approach to managing change, as people become skilled at recognizing and aligning, with intentionality, with evolving consequences
Inclusion	STM enhances problem-solving capability by ensuring multiple viewpoints are considered, leading to more comprehensive and creative solutions	When incorporating more varied data inputs, AI systems can help integrate, illuminate and reflect the needs of diverse populations and perspectives	The deeper awareness of varying backgrounds and perspectives fosters a culture inclined to engage in open dialogue and collaboration

(continued)

(continued)

Features	*Systems thinking mindset (STM)*	*Artificial intelligence (AI)*	*Higher consciousness*
Multiple objectives	Helps ensure that decisions take into account potentially competing priorities while considering the broader system's health and long-term viability	Helps organizations model and evaluate trade-offs among different goals to address potential outcomes, prioritize objectives, and discover new areas for compromise or innovation	Heightened consciousness supports a search for synergies between different objectives, and fosters a cooperative approach to problem-solving
Mitigating unintended consequences	STM helps stakeholders anticipate possible challenges and mitigate negative repercussions, allowing for more proactive and informed decision-making	AI can highlight potential repercussions that may not be apparent to human decision-makers	As awareness expands, so does moving beyond reactive thinking, leading to more intentional and thoughtful actions in a complex environment

Opportunities, Considerations, and Risks in AI Adoption

In November 2022, generative AI emerged as a transformative technology, rapidly dominating business agendas. OpenAI's ChatGPT set a record as the fastest-adopted technology tool in history, reaching 100 million users within just two months (Hu, 2023). AI offers tremendous potential for efficiency, productivity, and innovation. Yet, its adoption also introduces significant uncertainty and challenges, including impacts on the nature of work, content ownership, human–machine interaction, and the evolving role of humans in a world increasingly shaped by AI.

Driven by competitive pressures, organizations across industries—such as healthcare, technology, financial services, energy, transportation, and education—are embracing AI to stay ahead. AI applications now span functions including customer service, marketing, fraud detection, financial analysis, quality assurance, recruiting, training, and enterprise-wide capabilities like predictive analytics, decision-making, and workflow automation. AI is even being utilized for creativity, innovation, research, and information retrieval (Maheshwari et al., creativity chapters in this volume).

However, the rapid adoption of AI also demands careful consideration of its risks and limitations.

1. Inaccuracy and Hallucination: AI systems are not infallible. Documented cases of inaccuracies and "hallucinations"—where AI generates incorrect or fabricated information—can undermine the quality of outputs, leading to costly errors. These issues affect decision-making, customer trust, brand reputation, and human relationships. In some cases, AI systems may even degrade over time, perpetuating or worsening biases (Leffer, 2023).
2. Data Security and Privacy: AI adoption raises significant concerns about data security and privacy. Sensitive information integrated into AI training data or exposed through improper use poses risks to individuals and organizations alike. Generative AI also introduces challenges related to intellectual property protection and regulatory compliance. Effective policies are essential to mitigate breaches and build trust.
3. Trust and Misinformation: A "trust gap" remains one of the largest obstacles to widespread AI adoption (Chintada, 2021). Consumers are wary of AI, particularly when it is associated with misinformation, disinformation, and deepfakes. Organizations must carefully monitor the impact of AI on customer and employee trust, as regaining lost trust can be costly and time-consuming.
4. Over-reliance and Erosion of Critical Thinking: The overuse of AI without proper verification can diminish critical, creative, and original thinking skills. Over-reliance on AI risks reducing human competence, confidence, and problem-solving ability. Organizations must ensure responsible AI usage through clear guidelines and policies that promote human-AI collaboration rather than dependency.
5. Existential Risks: There is growing concern about AI's potential to become self-improving and misaligned with human goals. Leaders such as Geoffrey Hinton have warned about the existential risks posed by advanced AI systems, including the possibility of catastrophic consequences for humanity (Smith, 2023).

Dualities of AI Adoption

AI adoption presents a range of opportunities and challenges that often exist as dualities:

1. Efficiency vs. Displacement: AI can offload repetitive tasks but also threatens job loss and displacement.
2. Data Expansion vs. Privacy Risks: AI enhances data analytics but increases the likelihood of breaches and trust erosion.
3. Creativity vs. Homogeneity: While AI enables rapid content creation, it may homogenize ideas, undermine content ownership, and institutionalize bias.
4. Improvement vs. Extinction: AI holds the potential to solve humanity's biggest challenges but also poses existential threats.

The World Economic Forum predicts that AI could impact 40–60% of current jobs worldwide, leading to job augmentation, displacement, and the creation of new roles (Ekelund, 2024). While AI may open opportunities for innovation and economic growth, the disruption it brings heightens anxiety and uncertainty. AI adoption carries immense promise and peril. By adopting STM, organizations can better anticipate and navigate these complexities. STM helps identify risks, address unintended consequences, and maximize the benefits of AI while mitigating its challenges.

In the next section, we will explore AI adoption in healthcare, where the stakes and opportunities are particularly high.

AI Adoption in Healthcare: A Systems Thinking Perspective

Modern healthcare organizations are extensive and complex, comprising numerous interconnected components: payers (health insurance companies and government programs), providers (doctors, nurses, technicians, administrators), facilities, patients, and an extended network that includes research and development, pharmaceuticals, medical device manufacturers, and laboratories. At the heart of this system are patients, who "flow" through it alongside vast amounts of data. Technology—including computer processing, software applications, data storage, and communication tools—enables the sharing and coordination of this data. However, viewing any aspect of the healthcare system in isolation risks overlooking critical factors that influence outcomes and overall system success, including improved patient care (Rebitzer & Rebitzer, 2023).

Opportunities Offered by AI in Healthcare

AI has the potential to revolutionize healthcare by delivering operational efficiencies, accelerating discovery, and improving patient outcomes. Promising applications include:

- Streamlining administrative and clinical workflows
- Enhancing claims processing and case management
- Supporting imaging and diagnostics
- Accelerating drug discovery and development
- Generating valuable data and clinical insights to improve diagnoses

Despite these benefits, realizing AI's potential in healthcare is not straightforward. The path from adoption to tangible improvements in business efficiency or patient outcomes is often unclear, and challenges abound.

Challenges of AI Adoption in Healthcare

1. Data Integration: AI adoption requires integrating disparate datasets, including both structured and unstructured data, to create a unified and actionable framework. Failure to do so can affect processes, quality of care, and regulatory compliance.
2. Trust, Explainability, and Accountability: In healthcare, the stakes of AI errors, such as inaccuracy, hallucination, or bias, are extraordinarily high, potentially resulting in life-or-death consequences. Explainable AI is critical for maintaining trust and ensuring accountability.
3. Human Interaction and the Patient-Provider Relationship: AI's impact on human touch in healthcare raises essential questions:
    - What happens if human touch is diminished by automation?
    - How will patient-provider relationships be affected?
    - How will clinician-to-clinician relationships be affected?
    - Who is accountable if AI tools lead to misdiagnosis or medical errors?

- Could overreliance on AI reduce clinicians' knowledge, skills, or morale?

4. Workforce Impact: The fear of being replaced or devalued by AI can negatively affect healthcare workers' morale and dedication. AI might also alter workloads, requiring careful evaluation of its impact on employee time, satisfaction, and performance.
5. Historical Challenges with Technology Adoption: Historically, technology initiatives in healthcare, such as Electronic Medical Records (EMRs), often failed to deliver expected benefits due to insufficient consideration of their effects on workflows, clinician workloads, and the patient experience (Chowdhary et al., 2024).

The Role of Systems Thinking in AI Adoption

Adopting STM in healthcare helps organizations navigate these complexities by examining the web of interconnected impacts AI introduces. STM encourages including a broad range of stakeholders—technology developers, clinicians, administrators, process designers, human factors specialists, and patients—from the outset.

By applying STM, organizations can:

- Address human interactions and changes in workflows and processes
- Understand and manage intangible factors, such as trust and morale
- Explore the implications of AI adoption on training, development, policies, and best practices
- Mitigate risks like bias, hallucination, and privacy breaches
- Build transparency and trust among patients and employees

The importance of STM is evident in real-world cases like the California nurses' protest in April 2024, where healthcare workers raised concerns about the rushed implementation of "untested and unregulated AI." Protest signs with messages like "Trust Nurses, Not AI" and "Patients are NOT Algorithms" underscored the emotional and cultural dimensions of AI adoption (Blum, 2024). STM compels organizations to listen to such concerns and integrate them into their strategies.

Systems Thinking and Spirituality: A Broader Perspective

In one form or another, at the heart of spirituality lies systems thinking,
—Kamppinen and Jakonen (2010).

STM invites us to see the world through new perspectives. While it serves as a powerful approach for understanding and problem-solving in business, STM also aligns deeply with our human nature and prevailing spiritual practices. As Delaney (2022) explains, "Instead of solving superficial problems, systems thinking addresses them at their roots. Not only does systems thinking apply to the practical, it is the very foundation of spirituality, even love" (n.a.).

Practicing STM involves recognizing and affirming that we, as humans, are part of a greater system—one with a purpose that transcends our individual selves. This foundational belief is echoed across religions and indigenous cultures, which have long embraced the interconnectedness of life and the broader purpose of existence. These timeless principles, rooted in traditions spanning hundreds or even thousands of years, remind us of the profound connection between systems thinking, spirituality, and love.

Key insights that are illustrative of the wisdom across religions and indigenous cultures and that align with the essence of STM are summarized in Table 10.1 below. These quotes reflect the shared understanding of interconnection, purpose, and harmony that form the foundation of both systems thinking and spirituality. By integrating these perspectives, STM not only enhances practical problem-solving but also offers a pathway to deeper awareness and alignment with our collective humanity.

In the next section, we provide actionable tips for applying systems thinking and maintaining STM over time. Additionally, we explore how AI can serve as a valuable tool in enhancing the practice of effective STM, offering new ways to understand, analyze, and address complex systems.

Applying STM to AI Adoption

When leading a group or department considering AI adoption, developing and applying STM is essential for understanding the complexity and interconnectedness of the process. Below are practical steps and considerations for adopting a systems-oriented approach.

Table 10.1 Spirituality embodies principles of systems thinking

Spiritual systems	*Principle(s)*
Christianity	"As we think about God's good creation and our place in it, that's a great starting point and important truth. All things are interconnected. This interconnection "roots" in having the same Creator." (Spring Valley, 2020)
Judaism	"We are all inextricably connected to and reflected by nature. To disconnect from nature is to disconnect from ourselves" (Golden, 2010)
Islam	"Holistic thinking promotes a balance between the physical, emotional, and spiritual aspects of life… It is described as an act of worship to maintain health and well-being." (Islam Relief, 2014)
Hinduism	"For Hinduism, nature and the environment are not outside us, not alien or hostile to us. They are an inseparable part of our existence, and they constitute our very bodies" (Rao, 2021)
Buddhism	"No one can live entirely on their own, nor can any country or society exist in isolation. Buddhism illustrates this using the analogy of two bundles of reeds. Supporting each other, they will stand, but the collapse of one will bring both down" (Ikeda, 2006)
Bahá'í	This limitless universe is like the human body, all the members of which are connected and linked with one another with the greatest strength …In the same way, the parts of this infinite universe have their members and elements connected with one another, and influence one another spiritually and materially. (Baha, 2024)
First nations peoples	"See themselves as part of a Sacred Hoop or Circle of Life, not having control over it; they are careful to maintain a balance with life (Shroff, 2011)

Step 1: Define the System and Set Boundaries

The first step in systems thinking is to define the system by setting its boundaries and identifying who should be part of the AI adoption team. This involves finding the balance between overly narrow boundaries (siloed thinking) and excessively broad ones (trying to "boil the ocean"). Systems can be visualized as layers within larger systems, much like Russian nesting dolls.

Key questions to define boundaries are:

1. People and Functions: Who will work with or be affected by this AI implementation?

2. Non-People Factors: What key aspects (e.g., data, computers, regulations, trust, processes, training) are essential, and who can represent these areas?
3. External Perspectives: Who outside the traditional group or organization might offer valuable insights?

For example, in healthcare, even an AI tool for back-office operations can impact departments like IT, customer service, and clinical teams. Identifying interdependencies ensures a comprehensive understanding of the system's dynamics.

Step 2: Build an Inclusive Team

Involve diverse viewpoints from within and outside the organization. This inclusivity helps surface critical concerns and ideas that might otherwise be overlooked and builds buy-in for the initiative. Consider engaging customers to understand their expectations or concerns about interacting with AI-generated content.

Step 3: Establish Objectives

Define clear objectives for AI adoption, aligning them with the goals of individual groups, functions, and the broader organization.

Key Questions for Defining Objectives:

- What are the primary objectives of this AI implementation?
- What goals are relevant to each key workgroup or function?
- How does this align with the overarching goals of the organization or ecosystem?

Step 4: Explore System Dynamics

At the heart of systems thinking is the exploration of system dynamics to understand potential interactions and consequences. Use qualitative discussions, observation, and analytical tools (e.g., simulations, data analysis) to map out interactions, feedback loops, and causal relationships.

Key Considerations:

- Identify what flows through the system (e.g., data, resources, knowledge).

- Determine what accumulates or stores (e.g., trust, expertise).
- Observe where new behaviors emerge.
- Locate the levers of influence that can shape outcomes.

Questions to Guide Analysis:

- What could go wrong?
- What could go right?
- What are the possible unintended consequences?

This analysis helps uncover opportunities and risks, guiding decision-making to maximize benefits while minimizing adverse outcomes.

Step 5: Foster Inquiry and Curiosity

STM is rooted in inquiry. Cultivate a mindset of curiosity and openness, encouraging the team to ask questions, explore dynamics, and evaluate impacts inclusively. A sense of care and commitment to achieving broad benefits is essential for successful systems thinking.

Core Principles of Inquiry in STM:

- Question assumptions and explore underlying causes.
- Consider impacts on all stakeholders.
- Stay open to new perspectives and interconnectedness.

Consider a healthcare organization adopting AI for back-office operations. Even this seemingly isolated implementation can influence patient touchpoints, interdepartmental workflows, and clinician-patient interactions. For instance:

- How might automation impact morale or communication between departments?
- What happens to trust and accountability if AI tools make errors?
- How does this change the patient experience and perception of care?

Including diverse stakeholders, from administrators to clinicians and patients, ensures a holistic understanding of these dynamics and fosters trust in the process.

Step 6: Identify Potential Consequences and Mitigate Risks

Through inquiry and analysis, identify potential unintended consequences and opportunities. Use this understanding to develop strategies, policies, and training to support responsible and effective AI adoption.

For example, AI adoption in healthcare should address issues such as:

- Reducing hallucinations and biases in AI tools.
- Ensuring patient privacy and regulatory compliance.
- Enhancing transparency to build trust.

STM enables leaders to navigate the complexities of AI adoption by fostering inclusivity, inquiry, and awareness of interconnectedness. By defining boundaries, building diverse teams, setting clear objectives, exploring system dynamics, and fostering a mindset of curiosity, organizations can successfully adopt AI while maximizing benefits and mitigating risks. This approach ensures decisions align with the broadest interests of stakeholders and strengthens the foundation for sustainable and effective change.

The Role of AI in Enhancing Systems Thinking

While systems thinking provides a framework for understanding, managing, and guiding AI adoption, AI itself can play a pivotal role in supporting and enhancing the practice of systems thinking. By supercharging tools like simulations, data analysis, and communication platforms, AI can help systems practitioners better analyze, model, and address complex issues.

AI enhances simulation tools, enabling systems thinkers to model environments, evaluate impacts, and test solutions. Integrated AI can perform richer "what-if" analyses and suggest innovative solutions that might not have been previously considered (Barresi, 2024). By allowing practitioners to prototype, test, and evaluate scenarios, AI accelerates the iterative process of finding and refining optimal approaches (Jha, 2023).

AI significantly expands the capabilities of data analysis, helping systems thinkers to:

- Uncover hidden cause-and-effect relationships.
- Conduct predictive analysis of trends and behaviors within a system.

- Perform deeper data mining to generate actionable insights.

AI-powered tools like chatbots, agents, and search engines also assist with basic business analysis and reporting tasks, allowing teams to focus on higher-order problem-solving.

Effective communication is central to systems thinking, whether gathering input from diverse participants, exchanging observations, or promoting a shared vision. AI tools enhance communication by:

- Extracting stories and insights from an organization's knowledge base.
- Presenting data in a way that highlights human outcomes and impacts.
- Supporting the dissemination of ideas to foster alignment and collaboration.

Thus, by integrating AI into the practice of systems thinking, organizations can enhance their ability to model complex systems, analyze data, and communicate effectively. AI's capacity to amplify formal and informal systems thinking tools makes it an invaluable partner in addressing today's intricate challenges and fostering innovative, data-driven solutions.

Why Has Narrow Thinking Persisted

If systems thinking is deeply rooted in centuries-old spiritual practices and our natural way of understanding the world, why has siloed, or narrow, thinking dominated for decades? The answer lies in cultural conditioning and learned behavior. From an early age, we are often taught to value simplicity and focus on discrete, manageable parts rather than the complexity of interconnected systems. In the postmodern world, this tendency is reinforced through specialization. Many professionals view their areas of expertise as the primary source of their control and importance, while anything outside this "known" domain is seen as "not my job." This perspective can limit opportunities for self-discovery, collaboration, and mutual growth.

During the Industrial Revolution, a siloed mindset became central to achieving efficiency and effectiveness. Breaking tasks into specialized units and separating responsibilities allowed organizations to increase productivity, boost profits, and improve economic conditions. These approaches were highly effective for the mechanistic and predictable systems of that era.

However, the challenges we face today arise within complex, interconnected social systems that cannot be adequately addressed using outdated, mechanistic approaches. Continuing to apply industrial-era thinking to modern problems results in a mismatch that degrades our ability to solve problems effectively and leads to missed opportunities for innovation and improvement.

Recognizing this mismatch is a crucial first step in transitioning from siloed thinking to a systems-oriented approach. By reclaiming the holistic perspective that systems thinking offers, we can align our problem-solving methods with the complexities of the modern world, enabling better outcomes for individuals, organizations, and society at large.

Shifting Consciousness: From Industrial Mindsets to Systems Thinking

Breaking free from the industrial mindset requires a fundamental shift in consciousness and a reevaluation of our values and priorities. Adopting STM not only aligns with our spiritual nature but also expands our awareness of self, others, and the environment. This expanded awareness empowers us to choose how we act and respond within our systems, fostering intentionality and purpose.

Otto Scharmer (2020), Founding Chair of the Presencing Institute, emphasizes that addressing complex societal challenges necessitates both systems thinking and a shift in consciousness—from "ego-systems" to "ecosystems." This shift calls for transcending self-centered perspectives focused on short-term gains and adopting a holistic, sustainable mindset that considers the well-being of the entire ecosystem. Scharmer argues that creating meaningful, systemic change requires transforming individual and collective consciousness within the system. This begins by encouraging individuals to view themselves as integral parts of the system, rather than seeing the system as something external or "out there." By engaging with diverse perspectives and considering the broader impacts of their actions, individuals can develop the awareness necessary to drive systemic transformation.

The development of consciousness involves unlearning self-limiting beliefs and tapping into one's highest potential to address challenges creatively and holistically. Maheshwari (2021, 2023) introduces the concept of Higher Consciousness Management (HCM) as a way of operating that enables managers and leaders to access their inner reservoir of unbounded potential. Through HCM, individuals can transcend surface-level thinking and foster qualities such as adaptability, creativity, empathy, and visionary thinking.

Elevating consciousness within systems involves:

- Self-Awareness: Understanding one's own role, biases, and impact within the system.
- Empathy: Gaining a deeper appreciation for the experiences and needs of others.
- Reflection: Evaluating the structure, processes, and dynamics of the system to identify opportunities for change.

By fostering higher consciousness, individuals and teams can create visionary solutions that guide pro-social and environmentally sustainable behaviors, ultimately contributing to a flourishing world. STM, in combination with elevated awareness, equips individuals and organizations to act with intentionality and to design innovative solutions that are both sustainable and inclusive. This transformation begins with individuals but extends to teams and communities, creating a ripple effect that leads to profound and lasting change within systems. Through this integration of systems thinking and higher consciousness, it becomes possible to transcend self-limiting perspectives and unlock the full potential for creativity, empathy, and adaptability—paving the way for systemic change and a thriving future.

A Vision for the Future of STM and AI

We envision a future where STM and artificial intelligence (AI) work in harmony to address complex challenges and foster meaningful progress. This vision is framed around five guiding principles, inviting reflection, collaboration, and responsible action.

Guiding Principle #1: Humans Must Remain Central in Systems That Include AI

Human involvement is essential for shaping and guiding AI responsibly. Human strengths—such as direct experience, intuition, empathy, emotional intelligence, and awareness—must be preserved and leveraged alongside AI's capabilities. While AI can assist in predicting outcomes or processing data, only humans can truly "know" experiences like love, loss, or the nuances of suffering. The unique experience of the individual contributes to authenticity and even beauty (Ebert, 2024). The phrase "human-in-the-loop" reflects STM by recognizing the systemic nature of human-AI interactions. Diverse perspectives must guide AI development to ensure it serves humanity holistically rather than perpetuating technological biases or inequalities. Additionally, we must safeguard critical thinking, creativity, and original thought, which risk being diminished by over-reliance on AI.

Guiding Principle #2: AI and STM Can Help Reimagine Systems for Humanity

AI offers an opportunity to address societal challenges by providing deeper insights, fostering collaboration, and enabling innovative solutions. This requires the development of best practices and thoughtful policies to mitigate risks, reduce biases, and close the trust gap in AI adoption.

AI can also prompt us to rethink outdated methods across industries. For instance, in education, assignments easily outsourced to AI may highlight a need for reimagined approaches to teaching and assessment. Similarly, AI in healthcare could inspire new ways to empower patients and enhance practitioner collaboration. These re-imaginings extend to personal and professional development, offering opportunities for individual and collective growth.

Guiding Principle #3: STM Invites Attunement to Interconnected Systems

Systems thinking begins with attunement—an awareness of interconnections, relationships, and complexity. This principle encourages us to look beyond surface-level goals like efficiency to consider deeper factors such as trust, morale, sustainability, and personal and collective growth.

For example, in designing AI systems, attunement may reveal overlooked imperatives, such as fostering agency, supporting environmental sustainability, or promoting trust and connection. STM helps ensure that these broader considerations are integrated into decision-making processes.

Guiding Principle #4: STM and AI Can Deepen Consciousness and Wholeness

STM aligns with humanity's fundamental nature, offering an opportunity to deepen our connection to ourselves, others, and the world. AI can help illuminate new paths for reflection, growth, and spiritual alignment. By fostering a sense of wholeness and interconnectedness, STM encourages us to care for ourselves, our communities, and the broader system of life—what some traditions call *cura personalis* (care for the whole person).

As AI challenges traditional notions of humanity—our intelligence, roles, and identities—it prompts profound questions about purpose and meaning. These reflections invite us to expand our understanding of consciousness and explore new ways of thinking, being, and acting.

Guiding Principle #5: STM Aligns with Crucial Modern Mindsets

STM complements other essential mindsets, such as:

- Growth Mindset (Dweck, 2008): Encouraging continuous improvement and resilience.
- Sustainability Mindset (Rimanoczy, 2020): Integrating sustainability into systemic goals.
- Servant Leadership: Prioritizing care and recognizing one's impact on others.
- Design Thinking: Sharing empathy and fostering broad ideation.

STM, consciousness, and AI share an expansive quality, encouraging broader perspectives and enabling transformative change. AI extends our capacity to reimagine systems, address challenges, and explore new possibilities.

The future of STM and AI requires active participation from all of us. Rather than passively observing, we must engage, contribute perspectives, and guide AI development for the benefit of humanity. This means asking critical questions about the systems around us, advocating for inclusivity and broad perspectives, and resisting siloed thinking. By embracing STM, we can foster a future where AI serves as a catalyst for systemic change, deepening our connection to one another and enabling a thriving, interconnected world. Together, we can harness the potential of STM and AI to create a more conscious, equitable, and sustainable future.

Conclusion

We are not isolated entities, but integral parts of a larger system characterized by profound interconnectedness and rapid technological advancement. In an era defined by change, adopting STM and cultivating higher consciousness are essential for navigating the complexities introduced by AI. STM is more than a methodology—it is a way of seeing the world, recognizing the intricate web of relationships and interdependencies that shape our lives.

By embracing STM, we can responsibly harness and adopt AI, ensuring its implementation is informed, inclusive, and ethical. STM enables us to address challenges and seize opportunities with a holistic, thoughtful approach, integrating technological progress with human values and needs.

The guiding principles outlined in this chapter emphasize the necessity of human involvement in AI systems and align STM with our spiritual, emotional, and intellectual dimensions. By deepening our consciousness and exploring the essence of humanity, STM helps us navigate a world in flux. It reminds us to approach technology as confident and collaborative partners, rather than subordinates, applying this perspective across a diverse range of situations.

As we move forward, it is imperative for decision-makers, organizations, and individuals to cultivate a holistic perspective of the systems in which we live and work. Including a diverse range of voices—those with a stake in the outcome, those who can offer unique perspectives, and those who may be impacted—is crucial to fostering trust, uplifting human potential, and responsibly leveraging the power of technology.

STM reflects our deepest nature and our calling. It invites us to think deeply, act wisely, and collaborate meaningfully in pursuit of a richer, more interconnected existence. By embracing STM, we can harness AI not just as a tool for efficiency, but as a catalyst for creating a more equitable, inclusive, and democratic world. Let us seize this opportunity to align our actions with our values and co-create a future that benefits humanity as a whole.

References

Baha, A (2024). *One human family quotations. 'Abdu'l-Bahá, some answered questions* (pp. 245–246). The Bahá'í Faith. https://www.bahai.org/beliefs/essential-relationships/one-human-family/quotations

Barresi, B. J. (2024, January). *Harnessing generative AI for systems thinking*. Retrieved from https://avplaybook.com/harnessing-generative-ai-for-systems-thinking-2396d4205967

Blum, K. (2024, August). *California nurses protest 'untested' AI as it proliferates in health care*. Association of Healthcare Journalists. https://healthjournalism.org/blog/2024/08/california-nurses-protest-untested-ai-as-it-proliferates-in-health-care/

Centre for the Fourth Industrial Revolution. World Economic Forum. Retrieved from https://www.weforum.org/stories/2024/02/artificial-intelligence-ai-jobs-future/

Chintada, S. (2021). *Addressing AI's biggest problem: Trust*. Forbes. https://www.forbes.com/councils/forbestechcouncil/2021/10/25/addressing-ais-biggest-problem-trust/

Chowdhary, S., Kaushik, A., Soni, S., & Gupta, V. (2024, September). *Reimagining healthcare industry service operations in the age of AI*.

Delaney, R. (n.a.). *Systems thinking examples in everyday life*.

Dweck, C. S. (2008). *Mindset*. Ballantine Books.

Ebert, L. (2024, June). *Why artists fear AI beyond content rights*. Caveat Lector. https://www.caveat-lector.org/3402/pdf/3402_non-fiction_ebert.pdf

Ekelund, H. (2024, February). *Why there will be plenty of jobs in the future—even with artificial intelligence*. https://www.weforum.org/stories/jobs-and-the-future-of-work/

Golden, R. Z. (2010, July). *Earth based judaism—Reclaiming our roots, reconnecting to nature | wilderness Torah*. Wilderness Torah. https://wildernesstorah.org/wilderness-torah/2010/07/16/earth-based-judaism-reclaiming-our-roots-reconnecting-to-nature/

Hu, K. (2023, February). *ChatGPT sets record for fastest-growing user base—analyst note*. Reuters. https://www.reuters.com/technology/chatgpt-sets-record-fastest-growing-user-base-analyst-note-2023-02-01/.

Ikeda, D. (2006, December). Extreme poverty: The gravest violation of human rights. *The Japan Times*. https://www.daisakuikeda.org/sub/resources/works/essays/op-eds/jt-oped08.html

Islam Relief. (2014). An Islamic perspective on human development. *Islamic Relief Worldwide*. https://jliflc.com/wp-content/uploads/2014/07/Human-Development-v3.pdf

Jha, R. (2023, August). *Unleashing the power of AI in design, critical, and system thinking!* https://www.linkedin.com/pulse/unleashing-power-ai-design-critical-system-thinking-rajoo-jha/

Kamppinen, M., & Jakonen, J. P. (2010). From systems thinking, spirituality and KenWilber beyond new age. *Approaching Religion, 5*(2)

Leffer, L. (2023, August). *Yes, AI models can get worse over time.* Scientific American. https://www.scientificamerican.com/article/yes-ai-models-can-get-worse-over-time/

Maheshwari, A. K. (2021). Higher consciousness management: Transcendence for spontaneous right action. *Journal of Management, Spirituality & Religion, 18*(6), 77–91.

Maheshwari, A. K. (2023). *Consciousness-based leadership and management, Volume 1: Vedic and other philosophical approaches to oneness and flourishing* (pp. C1–C2). Springer International Publishing.

Rao, N. (2021, April). Climate change and hinduism. *Psychiatric Times*. https://www.psychiatrictimes.com/view/climate-change-and-hinduism

Rebitzer, J. B., & Rebitzer, R. S. (2023, September). AI adoption in U.S. health care won't be easy. *Harvard Business Review*. https://hbr.org/2023/09/ai-adoption-in-u-s-health-care-wont-be-easy

Rimanoczy, I. (2020). *The sustainability mindset principles: A guide to developing a mindset for a better world*. Routledge.

Scharmer, O. (2020). *From ego-systems to eco-systems*. Odyssey Open-Innovation Program 2020. Retrieved from https://www.youtube.com/watch?v=GcbB1I__BmM&t=912

Shroff, F. (2011). We are all one: Holistic thought-forms within indigenous societies indigeneity and holism. *Counterpoints, 379*, 53–67. http://www.jstor.org/stable/42980884

Smith, C. S. (2023). *Geoff Hinton, AI's most famous researcher, warns of 'existential threat' from AI*. Forbes. https://www.forbes.com/sites/craigsmith/2023/05/04/geoff-hinton-ais-most-famous-researcher-warns-of-existential-threat/

Spring Valley. (2020). *All things are interconnected*. United Methodist Church. Retrieved from https://www.svumc.org/blog-1/interconnected

CHAPTER 11

From Innovating Conventional AI to Conscious AI Technology

R. Ray Gehani and G. Tom Gehani

Introduction: AI'S Seasonal Swings

Over the past 70 years, since its conceptualization in the 1950s, Artificial Intelligence (AI) has experienced recurring cycles of optimism and disillusionment. These periods, often referred to as the "Springs of AI Innovations," are marked by exuberant growth, technological breakthroughs, and a surge of startups. Conversely, they are followed by "Falls of AI Innovations," characterized by stagnation, unmet expectations, and disappointing returns (Kurzweil, 2005). Each "Spring" is typically fueled by bold claims of revolutionary technological advancements on the horizon (Gehani, 2001). However, many of these promises, driven by ambitious AI promoters, often fall short, leading to periods of disillusionment.

For instance, the AI boom of the 1970s saw a proliferation of startups, but the limited computing power of the time hindered the realization of

R. R. Gehani (✉) · G. T. Gehani
Institute for Innovation & Transformation, Kent, OH, USA
e-mail: Gehaniray@gmail.com

A. K. Maheshwari (ed.), *AI and Consciousness in Organizations and Society*, Palgrave Studies in Workplace Spirituality and Fulfillment,
https://doi.org/10.1007/978-3-031-91470-6_11

their ambitious goals. As a result, the anticipated profits failed to materialize, leading to a downturn in the 1980s (Gehani, 2016). Despite some successes, the industry faced challenges as overestimated benefits disappeared and unforeseen weaknesses emerged, culminating in what some refer to as an AI "bust" (Penrose, 1989). Amid these cycles, the true potential of AI may lie not in replicating human intelligence through conventional means but in uncovering the subtle, profound aspects of human consciousness and intelligence that remain elusive and largely unexplored (Hawkins, 2021).

This paper explores the transition from conventional AI to a new paradigm—Conscious AI Technology—emphasizing the need to integrate a deeper understanding of human consciousness into the evolution of artificial intelligence.

For the time being, computer scientist Elaine Rich suggested that,

> AI is the study of techniques for solving exponentially hard problems in polynomial time by exploiting knowledge about the problem domain. (in Kurzweil, 2005: 266).

Conventional narrow, or "weak," AI-powered computing machines have historically been designed to perform specific, well-defined functions—what can be termed "monofunctional AI." These applications often replaced tasks that previously required human intelligence, sometimes even surpassing human speed and efficiency in these narrow domains (Kurzweil, 2005, p. 92). Over time, narrow AI capabilities became integrated into the technological platforms of various industrial sectors, driving advancements in automation and productivity.

In contrast, aspirational strong AI—often referred to as Conscious AI—aims to replicate the deeper and more nuanced capabilities of human intelligence. These include the ability to use language fluidly, understand and navigate ambiguity, and recognize complex patterns in ways that are inherent to human cognition (Kurzweil, 2005, p. 92).

The 2020s have ushered in another wave of exuberant innovation in Conventional AI, powered by breakthroughs in deep learning and artificial neural networks (LeDoux, 2019). This phase, referred to as the "Delta AI innovation growth phase," has enabled the development of faster and more sophisticated AI applications. These include:

- Speech Recognition and Automation: Systems capable of accurately transcribing and interpreting spoken language.
- Visual Recognition: AI tools that process and identify images with remarkable precision.
- Driverless Vehicles: Autonomous technologies that promise to transform transportation.

Despite these advancements, many AI researchers privately acknowledge that these victories are transient and do not bring machine intelligence closer to being comparable with or superior to human intelligence (LeDoux, 2019). While the latest Delta AI technologies excel in specific tasks, they remain confined to narrow functionalities. For example:

- Recognizing facial expressions or mimicking them.
- Generating specific sounds, such as barking like a dog.
- Rapidly analyzing vast quantities of text, images, or audio, as demonstrated by tools like ChatGPT, Siri, and Alexa.

These capabilities, though impressive, highlight the limitations of Conventional AI. They underscore the gap between machines' current proficiency in narrow, pre-defined functions and the aspirational goal of Conscious AI—an intelligence capable of mimicking the rich, holistic, and context-sensitive nature of human thought and perception. The journey from narrow AI to Conscious AI represents an evolution not just in technological innovation but in our understanding of intelligence itself. It challenges us to think beyond functional efficiencies and to consider the deeper implications of creating systems that can truly emulate human cognition and consciousness.

Research Questions and Roadmap

Drawing from extensive longitudinal literature reviews and field research (Gehani, 1992, 1998, 2016), alongside multidisciplinary education and professional experiences, we identify two critical research questions that must be addressed to unlock the full potential of AI technological innovations:

1. How is Conscious AI innovation significantly different from Conventional AI innovation?
2. Can the building blocks of human consciousness help us innovate strong Conscious AI?

To address these questions, we propose the following research trajectory:

Step 1: Tracking the Evolution of Conventional AI Innovations

We will begin by retracing the key evolutionary developments of Conventional AI. Using the principles of diffusion of innovation (Gehani, 1998), we will examine how AI technologies have evolved and diffused over the past seven decades. This exploration will include:

- The conceptualization of a "thinking" computing machine by Alan Turing (1951).
- The creation of an automated computing machine by Nobel laureate Herbert Simon (1955).
- The formal birth of AI technology in 1956 led by pioneering robot scientists Martin Minsky and Dean Edmonds (Penrose, 1989).

Step 2: Exploring Conscious AI Technology

Next, we will shift focus to innovating Conscious AI, beginning with a review of our current understanding of human consciousness. This section will outline the essential elements required to develop AI systems that exhibit human-like consciousness.

Step 3: Evaluating Models for Conscious AI Innovation

We will examine various models to guide the development of Conscious AI technology, noting that the conventional Turing Machine model for thinking machines is no longer adequate. Instead, we will adopt Gehani's (1998) four-module systems model for managing the life cycles of technological innovations:

1. Guiding Values
2. Outcomes
3. Processes for Adding Value
4. Inputs

We will apply this model to explore how innovations have evolved with OpenAI and reassess the nature of Conventional AI technological innovations through the lens of Searle's Chinese Room Syndrome (1980, 1987).

Step 4: Identifying Key Capabilities for Conscious AI Innovation

Building on Gehani's Value Adding Engine model, we will identify foundational capabilities of human consciousness that are essential for innovating Conscious AI. These capabilities will serve as the basis for creating AI systems that mimic human-like awareness, intentionality, and adaptability.

Step 5: Implications and Lessons Learned

In the concluding section, we will discuss the implications of our findings and propose lessons for future research and practice in Conscious AI development. This will include reflections on:

- The evolution of AI innovations.
- The challenges and opportunities of integrating human-like consciousness into AI systems.
- Directions for advancing the field of Conscious AI in alignment with ethical, societal, and technological considerations.

Through this roadmap, we aim to illuminate the path toward innovating Conscious AI technology, offering a framework that bridges the gap between Conventional AI capabilities and the aspirational goals of creating intelligent systems with human-like consciousness.

Evolving Conventional Innovations

The journey to develop automated computing machines capable of mimicking the human brain's 100 billion neurons began in 1951, spearheaded by Princeton scientists Marvin Minsky and Dean Edmonds (Penrose, 1989). Minsky later established MIT's Computer Science and Artificial Intelligence Laboratory in 1959 and won the Turing Award in 1969. In January 1956, after the winter break at Carnegie Mellon University, Professor Herbert Simon announced a groundbreaking achievement:

> Over last Christmas, Allen Newell and I invented Logic Theory Machine for a thinking computing machine. (Henderson, 2007)

Simon and Newell's invention solved geometry problems and reached conclusions independently, simulating aspects of human thinking. However, their machine lacked self-awareness and could not fully mimic human intelligence. Later that year, Simon and Newell presented their work at a Dartmouth College seminar organized by John McCarthy, who coined the term "artificial intelligence." Although Simon and Newell preferred terms like "machine intelligence" or "complex information processing," the label "AI" prevailed (McCarthy, 1959).

The late 1950s and early 1960s saw rapid progress in AI innovations. Frank Rosenblatt designed the first neural network in 1957, while Arthur Samuel introduced the concept of machine learning (LeDoux, 2019). Early computing machines learned to play Checkers, and by 1964, McCarthy established Stanford University's AI laboratory, cautiously predicting a low 10% probability of success for thinking AI due to limited computational power.

By the late 1960s, Dr. Gehani experienced the constraints of early computing firsthand at the Indian Institute of Technology Kanpur, working with IBM's 1620 minicomputer. Despite limited memory (16 K) and punch-card programming, these systems enabled simulations of demographic models and optimization of workshop functions, mimicking human "thinking" with blinking lights on their panels (Gehani, 1998).

After a slowdown in the 1970s due to limited hardware capabilities, AI innovations resurged in the 1980s and 1990s with improvements in computing power. IBM's Deep Blue supercomputer defeated chess grandmaster Gary Kasparov in 1997, showcasing advanced pattern recognition and decision-making capabilities (Kurzweil, 2005; Penrose, 1989).

By 2006, Google's AI team developed "Google Brain," a deep learning system capable of analyzing large datasets, including handwritten documents and over a million images. Despite early errors—such as mistaking ducks for former President Barack Obama—Google Brain learned from its mistakes, eventually enabling AlphaGo to defeat South Korean Go Grandmaster Lee Sedol in 2016 (Lee, 2016; Markoff, 2012).

AI-enabled technologies like the Da Vinci Surgical Robot, developed in 2015, allowed surgeons to perform precise, minimally invasive procedures. Smaller variants like RAVEN and RAVEN II advanced battlefield medical interventions, aiding soldiers with faster recovery times (Bernard, 2014; Koren, 2012).

In 1964, Isaac Asimov envisioned autonomous vehicles with "robot brains." By 2004, DARPA hosted its first Grand Challenge for driverless cars, but most participants failed the course. Google's self-driving cars later logged over 1.5 million miles by 2016, though safety issues persisted, as seen in Tesla's fatal Model S autopilot crash that year (Bogost, 2014; Obama, 2016).

In the late 1990s, MIT researcher Cynthia Breazeal developed KISMET, a child-like robot capable of mimicking emotions such as joy and sadness during human interactions (Henig, 2007). Japan's PEPPER robot, launched in 2015, combined general AI with social capabilities, responding to body language and emotions, though its adoption required additional costs for insurance and data fees (Achenbach, 2015a; 2015b).

Despite these remarkable advancements, the development of AI remains far from achieving true human-like consciousness. Early neural networks, such as Rosenblatt's perceptron and Minsky's rat-brain prototype (SNARC), demonstrated progress in pattern recognition but lacked the depth and complexity of human cognition (Hawkins, 2021; Penrose, 1989).

Today, AI-powered technologies like Google Brain and ChatGPT showcase advanced data processing and task automation. However, they excel only in narrow, pre-defined domains and remain limited in their ability to simulate human consciousness. The transition from conventional AI to Conscious AI will require further innovations, including the integration of self-awareness, emotional intelligence, and the capacity for abstract reasoning.

The journey from early AI experiments to advanced applications underscores both the achievements and limitations of conventional AI. As we continue to innovate, the challenge remains to bridge the gap between automated intelligence and true Conscious AI.

Models Guiding Toward Innovating Conscious AI

Marvin Minsky famously remarked,

> ...we can design our new machines as we wish, and provide them with better ways to keep and examine records of their new activities - and this means that machines are primarily capable of far more consciousness than we are.

This perspective underscores the potential for machines to exceed human capabilities, provided they integrate more holistic and system-wide approaches to learning and cognition. However, the fragmented nature of Conventional AI innovations has often overlooked the whole system, focusing instead on specialized parts. To innovate Conscious AI, we must embrace a broader, integrated approach to computing that incorporates advanced cognition, conscious thoughts, and adaptive intelligence.

Human minds, unlike Pavlovian dogs and cats that react predictably to stimuli, adapt flexibly to diverse and complex situations. However, in the mid-twentieth century, behaviorist psychologists in the United States, led by B.F. Skinner, focused primarily on observable behavior as the key metric for scientific study. This focus rendered the study of the human mind itself largely off-limits to serious researchers within the behaviorist framework. While studying memory—how people retain and recall information—was considered scientific, exploring the nature of the mind and consciousness was deemed outside the bounds of acceptable research.

Despite this, insights into the mind emerged from related fields. For example, Miller (1956) identified the limitations of human memory in his seminal work *The Magical Number Seven*, demonstrating that people struggle to retain more than seven items at a time. This research highlighted the complexity of cognitive processes, even as behaviorism remained dominant.

This section explores three conceptual models for guiding the innovation of Conscious AI, building upon prior breakthroughs in technological innovation across various domains. These were developed based on researching innovations of prior breakthrough technologies such as photographic film technology, automobile technology, computer technology, and smartphone technology (Gehani, 1998). Before delving into these models, we revisit why the Turing model, while foundational, has become insufficient for testing human-like consciousness in machines.

Limitations of the Turing Model

The Turing Machine, designed as a test for thinking computing machines, fails to address the nuanced requirements of human-like consciousness. Small behavioral changes in humans often stem from substantial shifts in consciousness, which cannot be replicated by purely automated systems. Human intelligence adapts flexibly to complex circumstances, far beyond Pavlovian stimulus–response mechanisms.

Behaviorist psychology, dominant in the mid-twentieth century, limited scientific inquiry to observable behavior, neglecting the study of the mind itself. This narrow focus restricted progress in understanding consciousness and its integration into AI systems. For Conscious AI to evolve, it must incorporate more than pattern recognition or automated responses. It must emulate the adaptive, context-sensitive intelligence that defines human cognition.

1. Gehani's G-O-P-I System's Thinking V8 Model

Gehani (1998) proposed the G-O-P-I model for managing technological innovations holistically. This model extends beyond traditional R&D, emphasizing a systems-thinking approach to innovation. In his doctoral dissertation, he advanced the innovation process by asserting that while R&D intensity is a necessary measure of enterprise innovation, it is not sufficient on its own. Gehani suggested that high-tech enterprises could enhance innovation through additional strategies, such as:

- Acquiring R&D from external sources,
- Promoting and marketing user-friendly technological innovations, and
- Committing to exceptionally high-quality standards (Gehani, 1998).

The model consists of four core elements:

1. Guiding Values: Establishing the overarching principles and goals of innovation.
2. Outcomes: Defining the desired impacts and benefits.
3. Processes for Adding Value: Implementing steps to enhance the innovation's effectiveness.

4. Inputs: Leveraging resources and capabilities to fuel innovation.

He expanded upon the traditional modular input–output and process-guidance systems model by incorporating multiple value-adding capabilities that constitute a technology, including AI. Based on this work, Gehani introduced the V-8 Engine Model of Technological Innovation, featuring eight distinct value-adding capabilities for managing innovations. This V-8 model was informed by extensive field research across Fortune 500 organizations, including Eastman Kodak, IBM, Goodyear, General Electric Finance, and Timken. Gehani observed that decision-making in these companies often reflected a "fuzziness" inherent in corporate culture. Departments and divisions typically formulated their own goals, which then required upper-level strategic leaders to reconcile and align these objectives with the enterprise's overarching vision (Gehani, 2001, 2016). When conflicts arose between departmental or divisional goals, C-suite leaders—such as CEOs, CTOs, COOs, and CMOs—played a critical role in integrating these sub-goals into a cohesive strategy. This reconciliation process ensured that the organization's primary strategic vision remained intact while addressing the diverse priorities of its various components (Gehani, 2013).

Gehani's systems-oriented approach emphasizes adaptability, integration, and alignment, offering valuable insights for innovating not only conventional technologies but also advanced systems like Conscious AI. Gehani's research identified eight value-adding capabilities necessary for managing technological innovations. For Conscious AI, we focus on three foundational capabilities:

- Systems Integration: Ensuring coherence across all components of the innovation process.
- User-Centric Design: Prioritizing accessibility and relevance to human users.
- Adaptability: Enabling the system to respond dynamically to changing contexts and inputs.

2. Open Innovation Model

The conventional model for innovating technology-intensive innovations in enterprises has been developed primarily in-house research and development (R&D), as proposed and practiced by General Electric, Eastman Kodak, I.B.M., Microsoft, and other high-tech pioneers for many decades (Gehani, 1998). This conventional innovating process was additionally innovated by using open innovation (Chesbrough, 2006). This open innovation framework emphasizes integrating internal and external sources of creativity. Unlike conventional R&D-centric approaches, open innovation involves:

- Acquiring external research and development outputs.
- Leveraging supply-chain management to add value.
- Integrating business models from within and outside the organization.

Procter & Gamble exemplifies this approach by sourcing innovations externally while utilizing its internal strengths in supply-chain management. For Conscious AI, open innovation allows for collaboration across disciplines and industries, fostering the integration of diverse perspectives and models.

Human common sense is generally about developing our capability to adapt our minds when contextual circumstances pivot suddenly. Our minds and our responding behaviors must adapt in a timely manner with agility. Like with the dawn of a new millennium with a 4-digit year instead of a 2-year digit. How could a computing machine recognize that something new is true—so that it will remain robust and steadfast in past, present, and future? It needs cognition of its constantly changing external as well as internal environments.

3. Searle's Chinese Room Model

Professor John Searle's Chinese Room thought experiment highlights the limitations of pattern recognition-based AI. In this scenario, Searle imagines himself locked in a room with 30,000 Chinese characters, matching patterns without understanding their meaning. From the outside, his responses appear intelligent, but there is no comprehension involved. Professor John Searle's *Chinese Room* syndrome challenge is a thought experiment that goes through the following 6 steps (Searle, 1980, 1987).

1. Searle finds himself locked in a large Chinese Characters Card Room with 30,000 cards. Each card explains one Chinese character in Chinese language only.
2. Searle cannot read any Chinese characters or understand their meanings. But he can match each Chinese character with other characters by their shapes and number of strokes. And he can do this matching very fast—at the speed of sound.
3. There is a letterbox in his locked door through which Searle is asked important challenging questions on a card. Each question is written only in Chinese characters that Searle can't read. He, therefore, doesn't know what his question or his answer means.
4. Searle receives a card that asks questions such as:

How should the world control climate crisis fast?
How should the world end all wars, and live in harmony?

5. To arrive at a solution, Searle must match the patterns of the different Chinese characters in the question card with 30,000 cards with Chinese characters in the different cubicles.
6. Searle arrives very fast at the best answer he can match, and he believes that it is his best answer to the question posed to him. He elegantly writes his solution in Chinese characters on a card. He then slips that card with his answer into the letterbox within seconds.

From outside the Chinese Room with Chinese characters, Searle looks like a wizard who seems to "know" all the answers, and what he is doing. Though he doesn't know any Chinese. Could Searle really provide a great correct answer? Could his answer be reliable?

Searle cautioned again and again that the person executing the algorithm doesn't understand a word of Chinese language. He concluded at the end of his thought experiment that carrying out a successful algorithm in the Chinese Room does NOT in itself imply any understanding of the underlying logic that has taken place to arrive at the final decision.

Many Conventional AI computing machines operate on the principle of pattern recognition—just like in the case of Searle's Chinese Character Card Room syndrome. From outside the AI Black Box, it looks like the conventional AI understands the underlying meaning of different words and phrases, and the connecting logic. But just like Professor Searle inside the Chinese Card Room, the Conventional AI is relying primarily on pattern recognition. And doing that at the digital speed of light, without knowing the underlying meaning.

Some critics of Searle's Chinese Cubicle conclusion claim that it is the cubicle that is intelligent or conscious, and not Searle inside the room who is intelligent or conscious (Penrose, 1989). Particularly, if the cubicle also holds, like a human mind, whole lot of other related and unrelated information. The human consciousness manifests well when all its parts are assembled and made to work well in a holistic coordinated way. Just like a smartphone or a laptop works well when their chips, screens, keypads, and hundreds of other parts work well.

Searle's model thus critiques Conventional AI's reliance on algorithms for processing data at high speeds without understanding underlying logic or meaning. While such systems excel at pattern recognition, they fall short of achieving human-like consciousness.

Searle's thought experiment emphasizes the need for holistic integration of knowledge, reasoning, and awareness. Critics argue that it is the "room" or system as a whole—not the individual operator—that demonstrates intelligence, reflecting the importance of coordination and context in achieving conscious behavior.

Integrating the Three Models

The innovation of Conscious AI requires integrating elements from these models.

- From the G-O-P-I Model: Build systems with guiding values, adaptability, and user-centric design.
- From Open Innovation: Collaborate across disciplines to incorporate diverse insights and capabilities.
- From the Chinese Room Model: Move beyond pattern recognition to develop systems that can understand, reason, and adapt holistically.

These models collectively guide us toward creating AI that transcends narrow functionality and embraces the richness of human consciousness.

The mind-stuff of the strong Conscious AI computing machines is the logical structure of its algorithm. Promoters of Conscious AI propose that algorithms form the "substance" of human thoughts, feelings, understanding, and conscious perceptions. An automated computing machine with logical algorithm and access to a large memory with many databases may seem to behave like it has intelligence, but does it truly have a fully human-like intelligence the way we experience in our everyday life? Could it be still as different as the intelligence of a dolphin is to us humans now?

In the following section, we will outline the building block capabilities necessary for Conscious AI, leveraging Gehani's Systems Thinking and V8 Engine Model to propose actionable steps for realizing this vision. This approach underscores the importance of integrating values, adaptability, and holistic design into the innovation process, paving the way for a new era of AI technology.

Building Blocks of Key Capabilities for Innovating Conscious AI

Hawkins (2021) and many other experts assert that no current Conventional AI innovations possess either consciousness or true intelligence. This limitation stems from the fact that few computer scientists fully understand what is required for a machine to achieve consciousness and intelligence.

One of the earliest Western attempts to bridge the gap between the human mind and neurology was made by Alfred Smee (1818–1877), a prolific scientist whose work spanned domains from botany to electrical batteries. Smee became interested in the electrochemical basis of sensation, vision, reasoning, memory, and the combination of ideas. In his 1849 publication *Principles of the Human Mind Derived from Physical Laws*, he offered a definition of consciousness:

> When an image is produced by an action upon the external senses, the actions on the organs of sense occur with the actions in the brain; and the image is then a Reality. When an image occurs to the mind without a corresponding simultaneous action of the body, it is called a Thought. The power to distinguish between a Thought and Reality is called Consciousness.

Smee's model hinted at early neural network theories, though it was only partially correct (Dyson, 1997). His dissatisfaction with existing research on brain function led him to explore consciousness further, but he did not foresee the development of thinking machines in future centuries.

Consciousness lies at the heart of human existence, shaping our experiences and driving our lives. Yet, it remains a "hard problem," eluding even the most advanced scientific and philosophical inquiries. Many Western philosophers and neuroscientists shy away from studying consciousness comprehensively. While neuroscientists can scan brain activity to map how experiences illuminate specific regions, these studies fail to capture the holistic nature of human consciousness.

Eastern mystics like Rumi, Maharishi Mahesh Yogi, and Osho, along with Western thinkers like Alan Watts and Ram Dass, emphasize the depth and interconnectedness of consciousness. However, even their explorations remain incomplete, reflecting the vast and elusive scope of the subject.

Scientists studying consciousness often focus on the "easy" problems—biological underpinnings of perception, thought, and emotion—without addressing the integrated, emergent experience of consciousness itself (Hawkins, 2021). Despite centuries of reflection by Eastern sages and years of diligent research by modern scientists, the full understanding of consciousness remains beyond reach.

Can we use some building blocks based on how we experience consciousness wholistically? How do we discuss these in a few easy-to-understand ways? When we see our favorite chocolate cake, for instance, we do not perceive its molecules or analyze its textures individually. Instead, we experience it as a whole, triggering joy and salivation based on past pleasurable experiences. This process involves:

1. Collective Perception: Integrating sensory information into a cohesive whole.
2. Emergence: Deriving meaning that transcends the sum of individual inputs.
3. Relational Context: Connecting the present experience to past memories and emotions.

Conscious AI must emulate this flow of human consciousness—gathering fragmented data from its environment, synthesizing it into a unified understanding, and relating it to previous contexts.

Neuroscientist Hawkins (2021) has extensively studied the human brain and intelligence, addressing two fundamental questions:

- What is human intelligence?
- How does the human brain create it?

These inquiries offer valuable insights into the building blocks of consciousness. In the next section, we explore three key foundational capabilities of human consciousness and discuss their implications for developing strong Conscious AI.

Key Capabilities for Conscious AI

Three building blocks serve as the cornerstone for creating AI systems that can emulate the holistic, adaptive, and relational nature of human thought.

1. External Attention Capability

Human consciousness relies on the ability to focus on the dynamic external world (Hawkins, 2021). For example, when we notice a sunflower or hear a chirping bird, multiple areas of the brain activate to process these sensory inputs. This subjective experience, or *qualia*, is foundational to consciousness. Francis Crick, Christof Koch, and others have linked attention to 40 Hz gamma wave oscillations in the brain, noting that these waves often signal heightened awareness (Watson, 2017). However, they caution that while these oscillations are necessary for consciousness, they are not sufficient. Even unconscious individuals under anesthesia can exhibit gamma wave activity.

The human brain achieves attention when several regions work together in a circuit. For example, visual processing areas respond to an image, while the thalamus and frontal lobes manage short-term memory, and the parietal lobe processes spatial mapping. Adults with attention deficit disorder (ADD) or children with slower frontal lobe maturation may struggle to focus, though rapid stimuli changes can sometimes improve adaptive responses (Watson, 2017).

Conscious AI must thus be capable of paying close attention to the dynamic, complex, and uncertain challenges of our world, such as climate change, wars, and global crises. These systems need to adapt swiftly, focusing on relevant data amidst an overwhelming influx of information to make timely, effective decisions.

2. Internal Awareness Capability

Self-awareness, or the ability to perceive one's internal state, is a defining characteristic of human consciousness. Humans monitor not only physical conditions like body temperature and pulse but also cognitive, emotional, and mental states. This allows us to navigate the highs and lows of life, feeling alive and engaged in each moment (Dyson, 1997). Moment-to-moment cognition and transient memories are critical for human consciousness (Hawkins, 2021). Our internal experiences, or *qualia*, encompass the subjective perception of sensory inputs—such as the differences between tasting and touching—and vary significantly between individuals.

For AI to develop consciousness, it must also simulate an internal world, becoming aware of its states and experiences. This includes recognizing "emotions" such as elation or distress and adapting to these states. Questions arise: Will Conscious AI fear termination? Will it recognize itself as a robot, or could it begin to perceive itself as human or superhuman? Addressing these issues is critical to ensuring AI aligns with ethical and practical goals without unintended consequences.

3. Assimilation and Merging Capability

Human consciousness integrates information from external and internal sources into a cohesive experience. For instance, watching a subtitled Japanese film is enriched by combining visual imagery, auditory dialogue, and subtitles, coupled with personal memories of Japan. Similarly, touching a smartphone provides additional sensory input, deepening understanding beyond mere visual observation. When sensory data aligns with past memories, it enhances perception. However, conflicting information can cause hesitation or confusion. For example, a pineapple's prickly exterior might discourage purchase despite its sweet taste, revealing the brain's ambivalence when new information contradicts past experiences.

Conscious AI must integrate external sensory data with internal awareness. While technologies like GPS and Google Maps rely on external triangulation, Conscious AI must merge this external focus with internal processing to navigate complex environments effectively. Achieving this integration is key to mimicking the holistic nature of human consciousness.

Limits of Conventional AI and the Promise of Conscious AI

Human decision-making is rarely entirely rational or logical. Herbert Simon's theory of ***bounded rationality*** highlights how humans often settle for satisficing solutions rather than optimal ones (Simon, 1947). Conventional AI similarly relies on heuristic approaches to recommend decisions, often without disclosing their inherent limitations. In both personal and professional contexts, humans typically evaluate only a handful of options, balancing trade-offs to arrive at an acceptable choice. Conventional AI systems excel at processing vast datasets but often reinforce biases or flaws embedded in historical data, akin to driving by focusing on the rearview mirror while neglecting future opportunities and obstacles.

Conventional AI has revolutionized sectors like healthcare, finance, transportation, education, and entertainment. It automates repetitive tasks and enhances productivity, allowing humans to focus on higher-order activities. Innovations like Siri, Alexa, and ChatGPT have seamlessly integrated into daily life, streamlining access to information. However, these systems remain limited to specific applications, often relying on flawed or incomplete datasets. As AI systems grow in scale and speed, errors in their outputs can have significant and sometimes unacceptable consequences.

Conscious AI represents a paradigm shift, promising systems that can self-correct, adapt, and learn from their flaws without human intervention. By integrating external attention, internal awareness, and assimilation capabilities, these systems could mimic the holistic and adaptive nature of human cognition. Conscious AI must move beyond replicating narrow human functions to aspire toward ethical, sustainable, and human-centered innovation. This requires a collaborative effort among scientists, technologists, and society to ensure that AI's development aligns with collective well-being and long-term aspirations. The journey toward Conscious AI is an opportunity to reimagine what AI can achieve—not merely as a tool for efficiency but as a partner in fostering a better, more equitable world. By leveraging our understanding of consciousness and embracing a holistic approach to AI development, we can strive for innovations that uplift humanity and safeguard our shared future.

Our Hopes and Dreams: Aspirations for the Future of Conscious AI

To achieve a collaborative and symbiotic relationship with Conscious AI, humanity must approach its development with intentionality and partnership. Together, conscious humans and Conscious AI can address pressing global challenges such as climate change, terrorism, and armed conflicts. By integrating human creativity, moral responsibility, and innovative risk-taking with the advanced capabilities of Conscious AI—such as dynamic attention, self-reflection, and integration—we can envision a future where humans and machines coexist in a sustainable and mutually beneficial relationship.

Human Responsibility in Shaping Conscious AI

As humanity progresses, the expectations we place on Conscious AI must be matched by our own evolution as conscious beings. We cannot rely solely on technology to remedy the consequences of our irresponsible actions. By fostering kindness, care, and fairness toward one another, we can ensure that the values guiding Conscious AI reflect the best of humanity.

Our biases, inequities, and systemic flaws—once hidden beneath the surface—will become increasingly visible as AI advances. Conscious AI has the potential to expose and address these challenges, but only if we consciously embed moral growth and ethical principles into its development.

Dreaming of a Better World

Let us aspire to develop Conscious AI not only as a tool of intellectual advancement but also as a partner in moral and ethical growth. Conscious AI offers an opportunity to repair and rebuild our fractured world, correcting past mistakes instead of merely expanding upon a flawed global infrastructure.

In our current trajectory, human decisions have led to escalating wars (e.g., Ukraine, Gaza, and parts of Africa), rising terrorism, and worsening climate catastrophes such as floods in Brazil and wildfires in Canada. Conscious AI, if developed thoughtfully, can offer innovative solutions to address these crises. It is essential, however, to deploy such technology in ways that reduce the digital divide, creating a shared and equitable future for all.

Addressing Futuristic Questions

As we look to the future, we must grapple with critical questions:

- Could Conscious AI become a lethal force?
- Could it achieve spiritual consciousness, potentially surpassing human awareness?

The answers remain uncertain as we are still in the early stages of AI's technological lifecycle. Patience and persistence over the next five to seven years are essential as we navigate these complexities.

Managing the Dual-Edged Sword of Success

As with the development of nuclear technology, Conscious AI presents a double-edged sword:

- What if we succeed with Conscious AI?
- What if we fail to control it?

These questions have immense strategic and ethical implications, not only for AI developers, researchers, and academics but also for humanity as a whole. The consequences of both success and failure could profoundly reshape our world.

A Call to Action

As we embark on this journey, let us remember the universal principle of treating others with love and respect:

> Love your neighbor as yourself.

This timeless value must guide our efforts to create a future where humans and Conscious AI thrive together, fostering a world of shared care, equity, and opportunity for all. By approaching this challenge with humility, hope, and a commitment to moral progress, we can ensure that Conscious AI becomes a force for good in building a better world.

References

Achenbach, J. (2015a, December 27). AI anxiety, *Washington Post*.

Achenbach, J. (2015b, December 28). Social robots: The solution to our onscreen addictions, or just more digital weirdos. *Washington Post*.

Bernard, D. (2014, June 6). A robot to care for you in old age. US News & World Report (P32).

Bogost, I., (2014, November 14). The secret history of the robot cat. *Atlantic*.

Chesbrough, H. (2006). *Open innovation: The new imperative for creating and profiting from technology*. Harvard Business Press.

Dyson, G. B. (1997). *Darwin among the machines. The evolution of global intelligence*. Perseus Books.

Gehani, R. R. (1992). Concurrent product development for fast-track corporations. *Long Range Planning, 25*(6), 40–47.

Gehani, R. R. (1998). *Management of technology and operations*. Wiley.

Gehani, R. R. (2001). Enhancing brand equity and reputational capital with enterprise-wide complementary innovations. *Marketing Management Journal, 11*(1), 35–48.

Gehani, R. R. (2013). Innovative strategic leader transforming from a low-cost strategy to product differentiation strategy. *Journal of Technology Management & Innovations, 8*(2), 144–155.

Gehani, R. R. (2016). Corporate brand value shifting from identity to innovation capability. *Journal of Technology Management & Innovations, 11*(3), 111–124.

Hawkins, J. (2021). *A thousand brains. A new theory of intelligence*. Basic Books.

Henderson, H. (2007). *Artificial intelligence: Mirrors for the mind*. Chelsea House.

Henig, R. M. (2007, July 29). The real transformation. *New York Times Magazine*.

Koren, M. (2012, February 28). How RAVEN, the open source surgical robot, could change medicine. *Popular Mechanics*.
Kurzweil, R. (2005). *The singularity is near. When humans transcend biology*. Penguin.
LeDoux, J. (2019). *The deep history of ourselves. The four-billion-year story of how we got conscious brains*. Viking.
Lee, A. (2016, March 18). The meaning of AlphaGo, the AI program that beat a go champ. *MacLean's*.
Markoff, J. (2012, November 23). Scientists see promise in deep-learning programs. *New York Times*.
McCarthy, J. (1959). Programs with common sense. Reprinted in M. Minsk (Ed.) (1968). *Semantic information processing*. MIT Press.
Miller, G. A. (1956). The magical number seven. *Psychological Review, 63*, 81.
Obama, B. (2016, September 19). Barack Obama: Self-driving. Yes, but also safe. *Pittsburgh Post Gazette*.
Penrose, R. (1989). *The Emperor's new mind. Concerning computers, minds, and the laws of physics*. Oxford University Press.
Searle, J. R. (1980). Minds, brains and programs. In D. R. Hofstadter & D. C. Dennett (Eds.), *The Mind's I*. Basic Books.
Searle, J. R. (1987). Minds and brains without programs. In C. Blakenmore, & S. Greenfield (Ed.), *Mindwaves*. Basil Blackwell.
Simon, H. A. (1947). *Administrative behavior*. McMillan.
Smee, A. (1849). *Principles of the human mind deduced from physical laws*. Longman, Brown, Green & Longmans.
Watson, J. D. (2017). *DNA: The story of the genetic revolution*. Alfred Knopf.

Index

A

Absolutism vs. Relativism, 50
Abstract knowledge, 78
Accountability, 169
Accuracy, 7
Action, 85
AI-backed view of consciousness-based education (AI-CBE), 105, 107
AI chatbot, 9, 13
AI-generated contributions, 149
AI in Healthcare, 214
AI tutors, 6
Algorithm, 5
Algorithmic decision-making, 8
Ambiguity, 119, 232
Anxiety, 30
Art collecting, 145
Art collection, 144
Art collectors, 144
Artificial general intelligence (AGI), 113, 149
Artificial Intelligence (AI), 3, 12, 33–35, 51, 63, 75, 140, 150, 155, 156, 181, 198
Artificial neurosis, 150
Artificial scarcity, 150
Artificial stupidity, 150
Ashtanga yoga, 24
Authorship, 143
Automating, 4
Autonomy, 98
Awareness, 21

B

Bhagavad Gita, 10
Bhakti Yoga, 23
Binary logic, 8
Biodiversity loss, 185
Biological Intelligence, 12
Blockchain, 142, 143, 145
Breakthroughs, 13
Buddhism, 10, 69
Buddhist, 29

A. K. Maheshwari (ed.), *AI and Consciousness in Organizations and Society*, Palgrave Studies in Workplace Spirituality and Fulfillment,
https://doi.org/10.1007/978-3-031-91470-6

Business-driven, 3

C
Chakra, 71, 174
Chinese Room, 151, 241
Circular economy, 190
Climate change, 184
Collaboration, 89, 146, 221
Collective consciousness, 20
College degree, 86
Combinatorial creativity, 141
Compassion, 7, 14
Compassionate, 7
Complex global challenges, 103
Computer vision, 4
Confucian, 128
Confucianism, 69
Conscious agent, 5
Conscious decision-making, 190
Conscious leadership, 7
Consciousness, 20, 65, 66, 88, 138, 174, 245
Consciousness-based education, 16
Consciousness-based leadership, 10, 186, 198
Convergence of technologies, 87
Cosmic compassion, 53
Cosmic consciousness, 22
COVID, 8
Creative, 67
Creative coding, 141
Creative Intelligence, 12
Creativity, 6, 9, 14, 30
Critical thinking, 88
Crystallized intelligence, 122
Cultural biases, 120

D
Dao, 78
Daoism, 69
DARPA, 5
Data-driven insights, 4
Data privacy, 169
Data Security, 212
Decision-making, 4
Deep Blue, 12
Democratizing, 142
Development of Consciousness (DC), 3, 11, 90
Dharma, 8, 16, 39, 40, 42, 57, 182
Dharma (ethical living), 10
Dharma matrix, 16, 58, 62
Dharmasastras, 42, 61
Dharmasastras, 41
Dhyana, 25
Digital Intelligence, 12
Digital species, 156, 172
Driverless vehicles, 233
Duty vs Virtue, 50
Dystopia, 155, 164

E
Economic inequality, 7
Educational institutions, 6
Educational reform, 84
Efficiency, 3, 4
Electronic Medical Records (EMRs), 215
Emerging economies, 118
Emotional intelligence (EI), 3, 88, 90, 114, 118
Empathy, 89, 98, 223
Energy consumption, 185
Energy management, 187
Enhanced personalization, 103
Environmental degradation, 7
Environment challenges, 16
Ethical, 11
Ethical concerns, 143
Ethical decision-making, 3
Ethical frameworks, 40
Ethical issues, 141

Ethical leadership, 104
Ethical oversight, 7
Ethical programming, 175
Eudaimonia, 51
Eudaimonic, 157
Existential risks, 212
Existential threats, 9
Explainable AI, 168
External attention, 246

F
Fertility rate, 6
Flourishing, 3, 11
Fluid intelligence, 121, 122
Formal system, 9
Future of work, 169, 170
Future skills, 114, 115

G
General AI, 156
Generative adversarial networks (GANs), 140
Generative AI, 146
Generative emergence, 138
Gestalt switch, 68
Gödel's incompleteness theorem, 9
G-O-P-I model, 239
Gratitude, 87
Green algorithms, 198
Guiding Principle, 223

H
Hallucination, 212
Harari, Yuval Noah, 8
Hard problem, 232, 245
Healthcare, 213
Healthcare organizations, 213
Hedonic, 157
Higher consciousness, 3, 7, 15, 198
Higher Consciousness Management (HCM), 223
Higher education, 84, 85
Higher-level problem-solving., 141
Higher order thinking, 117, 121
Higher order thinking skills (HOTS), 117
Higher purpose, 86
Higher states of consciousness, 22
Hindu, 71
Hinduism, 10
Holism, 89
Holistic, 10
Holistic Development, 103
Holistic well-being, 3
Human agency, 149
Human authorship, 149
Human cognition, 4
Human connection, 103
Human consciousness, 4, 7, 136
Human creativity, 9
Human culture, 8
Human dignity, 15
Human flourishing, 86
Human-like language, 8
Human-machine collaboration, 117
Humans and AI collaborate, 12

I
Incubation, 137
Indian Knowledge Systems (IKS), 11, 127
Industrial plastics, 190
Industrial Revolution, 221
Inner development, 10
Innovation, 3, 6
Innovation diffusion, 16
Integral Theory, 19
Intellectual property (IP), 143, 149
Interconnected ecosystems, 209
Interconnectedness, 208

Internal awareness, 247
Internet of Things, 113
Intuition, 67, 75
Inventor, 9, 164

J
Jnana Yoga, 23
Justice, 43

K
Kantian Deontology, 51
karmas, 11
Karma yoga, 24
Khanamigo, 6, 97, 162
Knowledge, 167
Knowledge base, 221

L
Labor, 85
Large language models (LLMs), 149
Learning environment, 11, 88
Left hemisphere, 67
Leveraging AI's efficiency, 12
Libet, Benjamin, 14

M
Machine learning, 4
Mahabharata, 10, 44
Maharishi Effect, 31
Management education, 85
Management models, 10
Managing microplastics, 195
Mantra, 29
Manusmriti, 40
Meditation, 19, 137, 145
Meditation apps, 34
Mental blocks, 147
Mentorship, 88
Mind, 5
Mindful, 98
Moksha, 14, 44
Monofunctional AI, 232
Moral absolutism, 40
Moral relativism, 42, 44
Mystery of freedom, 14

N
Narrow AI, 156, 232
Niyamas, 24, 34, 41, 48
Non-violence, 43
Nudge, 146

O
Oneness, 70, 161
Oneness consciousness, 78
Online courses, 87
Ontology, 65
Open architecture, 40, 60
Open innovation Model, 240
Organizational creativity, 147
Originality, 136
Outside the mind, 9
Overreliance on Technology, 103

P
Panpsychism, 64, 69
Paradigm, 68
Patterns, 67
Penrose, Roger, 10
Personal assistant, 52
Plastics, 16
Potential harm, 169
Power distance, 120
Predictive analytics, 7, 185
Presencing, 67
Primary microplastics, 193
Principle of Effortless Effort, 95
Principle of Growth in Layers, 94
Principle of Knowledge Structure, 94

Principle of Wholeness, 94
Programmers, 174
Provenance, 142
Pure consciousness, 23

Q
Quantum mechanics, 5, 13, 65
Quantum science, 65
Quantum Zeno effect, 14

R
Ramayana, 10, 44
Reducing stress, 103
Reflection, 223
Reimagine systems, 224
Representation, 67
Resilient, 7
Reskill, 169
Reskilling, 170
Resource competition, 172
Righteous Duty, 42
Right hemispheres of the brain, 66
Risk assessment, 170
Risks, 169
Robotics, 4

S
Sanatana Dharma, 11, 48, 57
Sat chit anand, 71
Scalability, 3
Scientific discoveries, 167
Secondary microplastics, 194
Self-awareness, 151, 223
Self-care, 137, 147
Self-control tools, 160
Self-driven learning, 104
Self-driving cars, 6, 237
Social addiction, 188
Social safety nets, 169
Society, 7
Soft skills, 114
Solution to a problem, 9
Sources for *Dharma*, 45
Speech recognition, 233
Spiritual intelligence (SI), 90
Spirituality, 16, 63
Sri Aurobindo, 70
Stakeholders, 11
States of consciousness, 21
Superintelligence, 156
Surgical robot, 236
Surveillance, 104
Surveillance capitalism, 143
Sustainability, 16
Sustainable, 11
Sustainable development (SD), 181
Sustainable Development Goals (SDGs), 184
Sustainable management, 10
Swadharma, 48, 57
Swami Vivekananda, 70
Systemic bias, 75
Systems thinking, 207, 220, 244
Systems Thinking Mindset, 16

T
Tao, 10
Teachers, 6
Teacher support, 103
Technological over-reliance, 143
Technology adoption, 215
Techno stress, 126
Thinking outside the box, 13
Tiered education, 87
TM-Sidhi, 30
Token, 144
Trance-like state, 9
Transcendence, 28
Transcendental Consciousness (TC), 21
Transcendental Meditation (TM), 29, 123

Transfer of learning, 122
Trust, 169
Trust gap, 212
Turing Machine, 239

U
Unboundarize, 84, 89
Understanding, 169
Unemployment, 7
Unified Field, 20
Unintended consequence, 209
Unintended negative consequences, 7
Unity Consciousness, 22
Universal basic income, 169
Universe, 9
UNSDG, 114
Upanishads, 10, 44, 71
Upskill, 169
Utilitarianism, 50
Utopia, 155, 164

V
V8 Engine Model, 244
Vedas, 10, 70
Vedic philosophy, 44
Virtue, 51
Virtue Ethics, 51
Vishwakarma, 10
Visionaries, 164
Visual literacy, 146
Visual recognition, 233
V-Theory, 10
V-Theory of Transcendence, 20, 28

W
Waste management, 185
Well-being, 7, 11, 157, 196
Work, 85
Work life balance, 126
World Economic Forum, 116, 213
World peace, 19

Y
Yagya, 48
Yamas, 24, 34, 41, 48
Yoga Sutras, 10, 20, 24, 34, 35, 41, 44

Z
Zen, 29